I0011226

ESP32 For IoT With Arduino

Maxwell Vector

Contents

14

Chapter 1

IoT Fundamentals for ESP32

Conceptual Foundations of the Internet of Things

1 Definition and Scope

The Internet of Things (*IoT*) is understood as an extensive network comprising heterogeneous devices that are endowed with sensing, actuation, and computation capabilities. These devices, often termed "things," are uniquely identified and can interact autonomously via standardized communication protocols. This conceptualization is predicated on the notion that physical objects are imbued with digital capabilities, allowing them to collect, process, and exchange data. The synergy between these devices and the underlying network infrastructure fosters an environment wherein operations are executed in a distributed manner, ensuring a highly responsive and adaptable ecosystem.

2 Architectural Layers in IoT

Modern *IoT* systems are characterized by a multilayered architecture that encapsulates distinct functional groups. The lowest layer, the physical layer, consists of a myriad of sensors and actuators that acquire real-world data and perform tangible actions. Overlying this is the network or transport layer, which orchestrates the transmission of data through protocols such as TCP/IP and UDP, ensuring that information flows seamlessly between nodes. The uppermost application layer is responsible for high-level data processing, decision making, and interfacing with user-centric or cloud-based services. This stratified design not only enhances modularity but also underpins the scalability and interoperability of IoT deployments.

Connectivity Paradigms in IoT

1   Communication Protocols and Standards

Connectivity within the IoT milieu is achieved through a diverse set of communication protocols and standards that govern both the physical and logical exchange of data. Lower-level protocols, often defined by organisations such as the $IEEE$, manage signal transmission and error correction over various media. Meanwhile, higher-level protocols like $MQTT$, $HTTP$, and the Constrained Application Protocol ($CoAP$) define the rules and conventions for message formatting, data encoding, and session management. These protocols collectively establish a robust framework that ensures data integrity, minimizes latency, and accommodates the requirements of both low-power and high-throughput applications.

2   Wireless Technologies and Modes of Operation

Wireless communication is a pivotal aspect of IoT, with technologies such as $WiFi$, $Bluetooth$, and $ZigBee$ facilitating the establishment of dynamic and often ad-hoc networks. Each technology exhibits distinct trade-offs in terms of range, power consumption, and data rate. In many instances, modes of operation such as infrastructure mode, ad-hoc mode, and mesh networking are deployed to maximize reliability and resiliency. These modes enable devices to dynamically adjust their connectivity strategies in response to environmental factors such as interference, mobility, and energy availability, thereby ensuring continuous and effective communication within the network.

ESP32: Integration within the IoT Ecosystem

1 Architectural and Technical Features of the ESP32

The ESP32 microcontroller consolidates a multitude of advanced features that are integral to its prominence in the *IoT* landscape. Architecturally, it integrates dual-mode wireless communication capabilities, specifically *WiFi* and *Bluetooth*, within a compact, energy-efficient package. The device is engineered with multiple digital and analog interfaces, rendering it capable of interfacing with a wide array of sensors and actuators. Its embedded processing units and sophisticated power management mechanisms further bolster its utility in environments where resource constraints dictate stringent operational requirements. These characteristics jointly engender an optimal platform for tasks that demand real-time processing and localized decision making.

2 Positioning of the ESP32 in IoT Deployments

Within the broader context of *IoT* deployments, the ESP32 occupies a critical role as an edge-computing device. Its inherent ability to process and locally manage data reduces the dependency on centralized cloud services and mitigates the latency associated with remote data processing. The ESP32's compact form factor and versatile interfacing options make it particularly well-suited for distributed sensor networks and actuator control systems. In applications that require rapid response and autonomous operation, this microcontroller serves as a nexus, facilitating immediate interactions with both peripheral devices and wider network infrastructures.

Common Applications Utilizing ESP32 in the IoT Realm

1 Consumer and Home Automation Systems

In consumer applications, the ESP32 is frequently deployed as the nucleus of home automation systems where interconnected devices manage ambient conditions, security mechanisms, and energy consumption. Its integration of wireless communication protocols enables appliances, lighting systems, and security devices to operate in unison, thereby creating intelligent living environments that adapt to the preferences and requirements of their inhabitants. The ESP32's versatility and cost-effectiveness contribute to its widespread adoption in household applications where decentralized control and real-time monitoring are paramount.

2 Industrial Monitoring and Control Applications

Industrial settings leverage the ESP32's robust feature set to implement sophisticated monitoring and control systems. The microcontroller's ability to interface with a multitude of sensors enables continuous data acquisition from diverse operational parameters, such as temperature, pressure, and mechanical stress. Data collected by these sensors is processed locally, allowing for prompt control decisions and the efficient management of critical industrial processes. Furthermore, the incorporation of standardized communication protocols ensures that data is relayed accurately and swiftly to central monitoring systems, thereby facilitating a high degree of automation and process optimization in complex industrial environments.

ESP32 For IoT With Arduino Code Snippet

```
#include <WiFi.h>

// WiFi credentials
const char* ssid = "YOUR_SSID";
const char* password = "YOUR_PASSWORD";

// Analog sensor configuration
const int sensorPin = 34;            // ESP32 ADC pin for sensor input
const float Vref = 3.3;              // Reference voltage for ADC
↪ conversion (in Volts)
const int adcResolution = 4095;      // 12-bit ADC resolution for ESP32

// Temperature conversion constants (example for a TMP36-like
↪ sensor)
// Equation: Temperature (°C) = (Voltage - 0.5) * 100
const float offsetVoltage = 0.5;   // Voltage offset (in Volts)
const float scaleFactor = 100.0;   // Scale factor (in °C per Volt)
```

```
// Moving Average Filter Parameters for noise reduction
const int numSamples = 10;  // Number of samples for the moving
↪    average
float sensorBuffer[numSamples];
int sampleIndex = 0;
float sensorSum = 0.0;
bool bufferFilled = false;

// Timing variables for non-blocking periodic tasks
unsigned long previousMillis = 0;
const unsigned long sampleInterval = 2000; // Sampling interval in
↪    milliseconds

// Function to initialize and maintain WiFi connection
void connectWiFi() {
  Serial.print("Connecting to WiFi");
  WiFi.mode(WIFI_STA);
  WiFi.begin(ssid, password);

  // Wait until connection is established
  while (WiFi.status() != WL_CONNECTED) {
    Serial.print(".");
    delay(500);
  }

  Serial.println();
  Serial.println("WiFi connected!");
  Serial.print("IP Address: ");
  Serial.println(WiFi.localIP());
}

// Function that updates the moving average filter with a new sensor
↪    reading
float updateMovingAverage(float newReading) {
  // If the buffer is not yet filled, accumulate initial readings
  if (!bufferFilled) {
    sensorBuffer[sampleIndex] = newReading;
    sensorSum += newReading;
    sampleIndex++;
    if (sampleIndex >= numSamples) {
      sampleIndex = 0;
      bufferFilled = true;
    }
    return sensorSum / sampleIndex;  // Return average of available
    ↪    samples
  } else {
    // Once the buffer is full, subtract the oldest value and add
    ↪    the new reading
    sensorSum = sensorSum - sensorBuffer[sampleIndex] + newReading;
    sensorBuffer[sampleIndex] = newReading;
    sampleIndex = (sampleIndex + 1) % numSamples;
    return sensorSum / numSamples;
```

```
  }
}

// Function to read the analog sensor and compute temperature from
↪  raw ADC value
float readTemperature() {
  int rawValue = analogRead(sensorPin);

  // Convert the raw ADC value to voltage
  float voltage = (rawValue * Vref) / adcResolution;

  // Convert voltage to temperature in Celsius using the calibration
  ↪  formula
  // Temperature = (Voltage - offsetVoltage) * scaleFactor
  float temperature = (voltage - offsetVoltage) * scaleFactor;
  return temperature;
}

void setup() {
  Serial.begin(115200);

  // Preliminary sensor buffer initialization to stabilize the
  ↪  moving average filter
  for (int i = 0; i < numSamples; i++) {
    int raw = analogRead(sensorPin);
    float reading = (raw * Vref) / adcResolution;
    sensorBuffer[i] = reading;
    sensorSum += reading;
    delay(50); // Short delay to allow ADC stabilization between
    ↪  readings
  }
  bufferFilled = true;
  sampleIndex = 0;

  // Establish WiFi connection
  connectWiFi();
}

void loop() {
  unsigned long currentMillis = millis();

  // Check WiFi connection periodically; reconnect if connection is
  ↪  lost
  if (WiFi.status() != WL_CONNECTED) {
    connectWiFi();
  }

  // Execute sensor reading and processing at fixed time intervals
  if (currentMillis - previousMillis >= sampleInterval) {
    previousMillis = currentMillis;

    // Read temperature value from the sensor
    float temperature = readTemperature();
```

```
  // Update moving average filter with the latest temperature
  ↪  reading
  float filteredTemperature = updateMovingAverage(temperature);

  // Optionally, recover filtered voltage value from filtered
  ↪  temperature for verification:
  // filteredVoltage = (filteredTemperature / scaleFactor) +
  ↪  offsetVoltage
  float filteredVoltage = (filteredTemperature / scaleFactor) +
  ↪  offsetVoltage;

  // Output computed values to the Serial Monitor for debugging
  Serial.println("===================================");
  Serial.print("Raw Temperature (°C): ");
  Serial.println(temperature);
  Serial.print("Filtered Temperature (°C): ");
  Serial.println(filteredTemperature);
  Serial.print("Estimated Voltage (V): ");
  Serial.println(filteredVoltage);
  Serial.println("===================================");
}

// Additional non-blocking tasks (e.g., network requests, MQTT
↪  messaging) can be integrated here
}
```

Chapter 2

Arduino Programming Fundamentals

Basic Language Constructs

1 Primitive Data Types and Variable Declarations

The Arduino programming language is inherently derived from established C/C++ conventions, and its treatment of primitive data types reflects this lineage. Fundamental types such as *int*, *float*, *double*, and *char* serve as the elemental building blocks for data representation. Each variable declaration embeds semantic intent regarding the allocation of memory and the precision of the stored numerical or textual information. In the context of programming for the ESP32, careful attention to type selection is paramount due to hardware constraints and the necessity for optimized performance within a resource-restricted environment. The explicit declaration of these variables not only facilitates improved compiler diagnostics but also aids in the clarity of program logic when interfacing with low-level hardware registers.

2 Operators, Expressions, and Control Structures

Arithmetic, relational, and logical operators in the Arduino language adhere to well-established precedence rules, ensuring that expressions evaluate in a deterministic manner. Such operations perform the dual role of manipulating data values and enforcing conditional logic in program execution. The structure and evaluation of expressions follow formal rules akin to those found in theoretical models of computation, where operator associativity informs the ordering of computation.

Control structures—including conditional statements and iterative loops—constitute the backbone of program execution flow. The use of structured constructs, such as various forms of the *if* statement or loop constructs like *for*, *while*, and *do-while*, introduces a level of abstraction that aids in the delineation of decision-making processes. Their integration allows for the deterministic progression of program state, facilitating not only predictable outcomes but also controlled interaction with the ESP32's peripheral hardware.

Program Structure of Arduino Sketches for ESP32

1 Core Functions and Execution Paradigm

The canonical structure of an Arduino sketch is epitomized by its bifurcation into two primary functions: *setup*() and *loop*(). The *setup*() function is envisioned to execute once upon power-up or reset, thereby initializing hardware components, configuring communication interfaces, and establishing the necessary preconditions for subsequent operations. In contrast, the *loop*() function embodies the perpetual execution cycle characteristic of embedded systems, repeatedly invoking code segments that interrogate sensor inputs, control actuators, or update system states. This dual-function paradigm encapsulates the principles of event-driven programming, where system initialization is decoupled from continuous reactive processes.

2 Modularity and Code Organization

The architectural design of an Arduino sketch promotes modularity and code segmentation as indispensable elements in crafting comprehensible and maintainable applications. While the core functions provide a framework for sequential execution, the practice of encapsulating discrete operations within auxiliary functions and libraries enhances the clarity and reusability of code. In this paradigm, each function is designed to perform a well-defined task, interfacing with shared resources in a manner that mitigates redundancy. This methodical decomposition of program logic is analogous to the principles observed in classical software engineering, wherein abstraction and modularization serve as instruments for managing complexity, particularly when interfacing with the multifaceted hardware capabilities of the ESP32.

3 Abstraction and Underlying Hardware Interactions

At the intersection of high-level abstraction and low-level hardware interaction lies the essence of Arduino programming for the ESP32. While the language abstracts many of the idiosyncrasies associated with direct hardware manipulation, it nevertheless permits fine-grained control through explicit function calls embedded within the pre-established sketch framework. The design philosophy maintains an equilibrium between ease of use and the precision required for efficient hardware utilization. The abstraction layers permit the encapsulation of intricate hardware control mechanisms while preserving the ability to inspect and modify fundamental operations as dictated by the demands of diverse IoT applications.

4 Compilation and Resource Management Considerations

The process of compiling an Arduino sketch translates human-readable source code into an intermediary binary format, meticulously optimized to meet the constraints of the ESP32's architecture. During this transformation, the compiler enforces strict typing, evaluates constant expressions, and optimizes memory usage. In light of the limited computational and memory resources available on microcontrollers, the deliberate use of variable scoping, dynamic versus static memory allocation, and the judicious inclusion of libraries are indispensable practices. Such considerations ensure that the resulting firmware embodies both efficiency and reliability while interfacing seamlessly with the ESP32's hardware resources.

ESP32 For IoT With Arduino Code Snippet

```cpp
// Comprehensive ESP32 for IoT with Arduino code snippet
↪   demonstrating core language constructs,
// important equations, formulas, and algorithms as discussed in the
↪   chapter "Arduino Programming Fundamentals."

#include <Arduino.h>

// Global Constants and Primitive Data Type Declarations
const int sensorPin = 34;          // ADC sensor pin on ESP32 (GPIO
↪   34 supports analog input)
const int ledPin = 2;              // LED digital output pin
↪   (commonly available on ESP32 boards)
const float VREF = 3.3;            // Reference voltage for ADC
↪   conversion (in volts)
const int ADC_RESOLUTION = 4095;   // 12-bit ADC resolution (0 to
↪   4095 for ESP32)

// Function Prototypes (demonstrating modularity)
float readSensorAverage(int samples);
float calculateVoltage(float adcValue);
float calculateTemperature(float voltage);
void updateStatusLED(float temperature);

void setup() {
  // Begin Serial communication for debugging and monitoring outputs
  Serial.begin(115200);

  // Configure the LED pin as output
  pinMode(ledPin, OUTPUT);

  // Set ADC resolution to 12 bits (specific to ESP32)
  analogReadResolution(12);

  // Initialization message
  Serial.println("ESP32 For IoT With Arduino Program Started...");
}

void loop() {
  // Demonstration of iterative sampling: Compute the average ADC
  ↪   value over multiple samples
  const int numSamples = 10;
  float avgAdcValue = readSensorAverage(numSamples);

  // Equation: Voltage = (Average ADC Value / ADC Resolution) *
  ↪   Reference Voltage
  float voltage = calculateVoltage(avgAdcValue);
```

```cpp
  // Convert the measured voltage into temperature using a
  ↪ sensor-specific conversion factor.
  // Formula assumed: Temperature (°C) = Voltage (V) * 100.
  float temperature = calculateTemperature(voltage);

  // Output the calculated sensor data to the Serial Monitor
  Serial.print("Average ADC Value: ");
  Serial.print(avgAdcValue);
  Serial.print(" | Voltage: ");
  Serial.print(voltage, 3);
  Serial.print(" V | Temperature: ");
  Serial.print(temperature, 2);
  Serial.println(" °C");

  // Update LED blinking behavior based on the temperature threshold
  updateStatusLED(temperature);

  // Delay to control the sensor read cycle and processing frequency
  delay(2000);
}


// Function to compute the average sensor reading from multiple ADC
↪ samples
// Implements a simple algorithm using a 'for' loop and arithmetic
↪ operators.
float readSensorAverage(int samples) {
  long sum = 0;
  for (int i = 0; i < samples; i++) {
    int reading = analogRead(sensorPin); // Read a single ADC value
    sum += reading;    // Accumulate the ADC values
    delay(10);         // Brief delay for ADC stabilization between
    ↪ readings
  }
  // Equation: average = total sum of readings / number of samples
  return ((float)sum) / samples;
}


// Function to convert the averaged ADC value to the corresponding
↪ voltage.
// Equation: Voltage = (Average ADC Value / ADC Resolution) * VREF
float calculateVoltage(float adcValue) {
  return (adcValue * VREF) / ADC_RESOLUTION;
}


// Function to calculate temperature from the measured voltage.
// Sensor conversion formula: Temperature (°C) = Voltage (V) * 100
float calculateTemperature(float voltage) {
  return voltage * 100.0;
}


// Function to update the on-board LED blink rate based on the
↪ measured temperature.
// Demonstrates control structures using an if-else statement.
```

```
void updateStatusLED(float temperature) {
  if (temperature > 30.0) {
    // For temperatures above 30°C, blink the LED rapidly (fast
    ↪    response)
    digitalWrite(ledPin, HIGH);
    delay(100);
    digitalWrite(ledPin, LOW);
    delay(100);
  } else {
    // For temperatures at or below 30°C, blink the LED slowly
    ↪    (normal response)
    digitalWrite(ledPin, HIGH);
    delay(500);
    digitalWrite(ledPin, LOW);
    delay(500);
  }
}
```

Chapter 3

C++ Essentials for ESP32 Programming

Variables in C++: Declaration, Initialization, and Scope

A variable in C++ constitutes an abstraction that embodies a designated area of memory, associated with an identifier and constrained by a specific data type. The act of declaring a variable necessitates an explicit specification of type, which in turn dictates the permissible operations and the extent of the value domain. Such declarations enforce a static contract on memory allocation, ensuring that storage is reserved and that operations conform to the language's semantic rules. In the environment of ESP32 programming, where resource limitations are a primary concern, the meticulous attention to variable initialization and scope is imperative. The compiler enforces strict typing rules, affording a degree of robustness that precludes inadvertent memory corruption. The static analysis performed during compilation serves as an early indicator of potential inconsistencies between declared intentions and operational implementations, thereby fostering reliability in embedded systems.

Data Types in C++: Primitive Constructs and Their Implications

Data types in C++ represent the foundational building blocks upon which computational expressions are constructed. The primitive types, including *int*, *float*, *double*, *bool*, and *char*, are defined by specific attributes such as range, precision, and memory utilization. The selection of an appropriate data type is not a mere syntactic formality but a critical decision impacting both the precision of arithmetic operations and the efficiency of code execution. For instance, the choice between *float* and *double* can significantly affect the fidelity of numerical computations, particularly in applications that involve analog sensor readings or the processing of transient signals. Additionally, the dichotomy between signed and unsigned integers imposes further constraints that ensure values remain within predictable bounds—a consideration of utmost importance in embedded programming where every byte of memory incurs a cost. The theoretical underpinnings of these primitive data types echo formal type systems in mathematical logic, thereby providing a rigorous framework for ensuring correctness and predictability in program execution.

Operators and Expressions: Structural Composition and Evaluation Order

Operators in C++ serve as the principal mechanism for constructing expressions that encapsulate both computation and logical decision-making. The language's repertoire of operators—including arithmetic operators such as $+$, $-$, $*$, and $/$; relational operators like $==$ and $! =$; and logical operators such as $\&\&$ and $||$—is underpinned by well-defined rules of precedence and associativity. These rules prescribe a definitive order of evaluation, ensuring that even deeply nested or compound expressions yield consistent and deterministic outcomes. Each operator performs a specific transformation on its operands, yielding results that are subsequently incorporated into larger computations. The structural composition of expressions, when viewed through the lens of abstract syntax and operational semantics, aligns with formal specifications found in algebraic structures. In situations where operator overloading is employed, these conventional operators are extended to user-defined types, thereby enhancing the expressiveness of the language without compromising the inherent logic of expression evaluation. Such rigor in the formulation and execution of expressions is vital for the precise control required in Arduino sketches on the ESP32, where each computational step can have significant hardware-level ramifications.

ESP32 For IoT With Arduino Code Snippet

```
#include <Arduino.h>

// Define the analog sensor pin for ESP32 ADC (range 0-4095)
const int SENSOR_PIN = 34;

// Number of samples to calculate the moving average (for noise
↪   reduction)
const int NUM_SAMPLES = 10;

// Array to store recent sensor readings for filtering
float samples[NUM_SAMPLES];

// Index of the current sample in the circular buffer
int sampleIndex = 0;

// Sum of the current samples (used to calculate the moving average)
float sampleSum = 0.0;

//-----------------------------------------------------------------
// Function: initSamples()
// Description:
//    Initializes the sample array and resets the index and sum.
//-----------------------------------------------------------------
void initSamples() {
  for (int i = 0; i < NUM_SAMPLES; i++) {
    samples[i] = 0.0;
  }
  sampleIndex = 0;
  sampleSum = 0.0;
}

//-----------------------------------------------------------------
// Function: computeMovingAverage()
// Description:
//    Updates the circular buffer with a new sensor reading,
//    calculates, and returns the moving average of the samples.
//    This algorithm serves as a noise reduction strategy.
// Parameters:
```

31

```
//   newValue - The latest sensor reading (voltage value).
// Returns:
//   The current moving average of the sensor readings.
//----------------------------------------------------------------
float computeMovingAverage(float newValue) {
  // Remove the oldest sample from the sum
  sampleSum -= samples[sampleIndex];
  // Store the new sensor reading in the samples array
  samples[sampleIndex] = newValue;
  // Add the new reading to sampleSum
  sampleSum += newValue;
  // Update the circular index for the samples array
  sampleIndex = (sampleIndex + 1) % NUM_SAMPLES;
  // Return the average of the samples
  return sampleSum / NUM_SAMPLES;
}


//----------------------------------------------------------------
// Function: adcToVoltage()
// Description:
//   Converts the raw ADC reading (0 - 4095) to a voltage value,
//   based on the ADC resolution and reference voltage.
//   Equation: voltage = (adcValue / 4095.0) * 3.3
// Parameters:
//   adcValue - The raw analog reading from the sensor.
// Returns:
//   The corresponding voltage reading in volts.
//----------------------------------------------------------------
float adcToVoltage(int adcValue) {
  return (adcValue / 4095.0) * 3.3;
}


//----------------------------------------------------------------
// Function: voltageToTemperature()
// Description:
//   Converts the sensor voltage to a temperature value in Celsius.
//   For demonstration, the TMP36 sensor equation is used:
//   temperature (°C) = (voltage - 0.5) * 100
//   This formula assumes that the sensor outputs 750mV at 25°C.
// Parameters:
//   voltage - The (filtered) voltage reading from the sensor.
// Returns:
//   The calculated temperature in Celsius.
//----------------------------------------------------------------
float voltageToTemperature(float voltage) {
  return (voltage - 0.5) * 100.0;
}

void setup() {
  // Initialize serial communication at 115200 baud rate for
  ↪   debugging
  Serial.begin(115200);
```

```
  // Configure the SENSOR_PIN as an input
  pinMode(SENSOR_PIN, INPUT);

  // Initialize the samples array for the moving average filter
  initSamples();

  Serial.println("ESP32 For IoT With Arduino: Sensor Reading and
  ↪  Processing");
  Serial.println("--------------------------------");
}

void loop() {
  // Read the raw ADC value from the sensor pin (range 0-4095)
  int adcValue = analogRead(SENSOR_PIN);

  // Convert the raw ADC value to voltage using the formula:
  // voltage = (adcValue / 4095.0) * 3.3
  float voltage = adcToVoltage(adcValue);

  // Apply a moving average filter to smooth out voltage
  ↪  fluctuations
  float filteredVoltage = computeMovingAverage(voltage);

  // Calculate temperature (°C) from the filtered voltage reading
  // using the conversion formula:
  // temperature (°C) = (voltage - 0.5) * 100
  float temperature = voltageToTemperature(filteredVoltage);

  // Output the raw ADC value, filtered voltage, and computed
  ↪  temperature to Serial Monitor
  Serial.print("ADC Value: ");
  Serial.print(adcValue);
  Serial.print(" | Voltage: ");
  Serial.print(filteredVoltage, 3);
  Serial.print(" V | Temperature: ");
  Serial.print(temperature, 2);
  Serial.println(" °C");

  // Delay for 500 milliseconds before next sensor reading
  delay(500);
}
```

Chapter 4

Control Structures in Arduino

Conditional Statements

The conditional branch mechanism constitutes a fundamental aspect of program control in the Arduino environment. Within this paradigm, decision-making is orchestrated by evaluating Boolean expressions that determine the execution of designated code blocks. The canonical form—the if statement—ensures that when a Boolean predicate E evaluates to true, the subsequent block of instructions is executed; in instances where an alternative execution pathway is defined, an else clause may follow to capture the false evaluation of E. Complementing the if construct, the switch statement offers a framework for multi-way branching by matching the value of an integral expression against a series of constant labels. The rigorous semantics of these conditional structures are predicated on the evaluation of relational operators ($<$, $>$, $==$) and logical operators ($\land$, $\lor$, $\neg$), whose operations adhere to a strictly defined precedence and associativity. Such well-defined characteristics are indispensable in the context of resource-constrained embedded systems, where each comparative evaluation carries implications for both execution timing and memory usage.

Iterative Constructs

Iteration introduces the capacity for repeated execution of specified code segments, and is instrumental in managing repetitive tasks such as sensor data acquisition and actuator control on the ESP32. The iteration constructs in Arduino are typified by the for, while, and do-while loops. The for loop encapsulates an initialization phase, a Boolean termination condition, and a post-iteration update expression, collectively establishing a predetermined number of iterations denoted by a variable such as n. In contrast, the while loop inspects a Boolean predicate prior to each iteration, thereby ensuring that the code segment is executed only while the condition remains true. The do-while loop guarantees an initial execution of its code block prior to evaluating the controlling predicate, a characteristic that distinguishes it from its pre-test counterparts. The formal execution of these loops is governed by deterministic conditions that protect against errant iterations, a feature critical for achieving the real-time response required in embedded system applications.

Other Control Flow Mechanisms

Supplemental to the primary constructs of conditional branching and iterative looping, auxiliary control flow directives serve to further refine program execution. The break directive, for instance, enacts an immediate termination of the nearest enclosing loop or switch construct, facilitating an abrupt cessation of iterative processing when certain conditions are met. In parallel, the continue statement enables the suspension of the remaining instructions in a loop iteration, prompting an immediate transition to the subsequent evaluation cycle. Additionally, the return directive, utilized within function bodies, provides a mechanism for exogenous termination of a procedural context, thereby allowing for early exit based on dynamic criteria. Although these mechanisms operate at a granular level within the control flow architecture, their judicious application is essential for preserving the deterministic sequence of operations inherent in the ESP32's execution model.

Nested and Composite Control Structures

The strategic nesting of conditional and iterative constructs enables the formulation of complex logical architectures that exhibit multi-tiered decision-making capabilities. In such nested frameworks, the synthesis of an outer conditional statement with an embedded loop, or vice versa, produces an intricate control scheme wherein the operational flow is partitioned into successive evaluative layers. This composite structuring mandates a meticulous treatment of scope, evaluation order, and potential side effects; each nested level introduces additional considerations for resource management and execution latency. The formal analysis of such constructs often entails the application of complexity metrics, where the cumulative operational cost can be characterized by an expression such as $O(n^k)$, with the exponent k reflecting the depth of nesting. The capacity to construct and analyze these composite structures is central to the development of robust applications in a constrained processing environment.

Formal Semantics and Evaluation Order

The operational correctness of control structures in the Arduino paradigm is underpinned by a rigorous formal semantics that delineates the order of evaluation for both conditional and iterative constructs. The Boolean expressions employed in conditional statements are evaluated in strict accordance with the rules of operator precedence and associativity defined in the C++ standard. In particular, the phenomenon of short-circuit evaluation—wherein logical operators such as $\land$ and $\lor$ may suspend further evaluation once the outcome is determined—serves to enhance both efficiency and predictability of execution. In iterative constructs, the delineation between pre-test and post-test loops is critical, as it determines the guaranteed execution frequency of the loop body relative to the evaluation of its controlling predicate. These formal rules ensure that the progression of execution conforms to a deterministic sequence, thereby facilitating the analytical verification of program behavior in contexts where timing and resource constraints are paramount.

ESP32 For IoT With Arduino Code Snippet

```
#include <Arduino.h>

// Define sensor analog pin for ESP32 (example: GPIO34)
#define SENSOR_PIN 34

// Global threshold value for sensor readings
const int thresholdValue = 512;

//
↪    -------------------------------------------------------------------
// Function: computeSensorAverage
// Purpose:  Computes the average reading from the sensor over a
↪    number of samples
// Algorithm: Uses a for-loop to sum up 'samples' readings and
↪    returns their average
// Equation: avg = ( (reading_i)) / samples
// Complexity: O(samples)
//
↪    -------------------------------------------------------------------
int computeSensorAverage(int sensorPin, int samples) {
  long sum = 0;
  for (int i = 0; i < samples; i++) {
    int val = analogRead(sensorPin);
    sum += val;
    delay(10); // Wait for sensor stabilization between readings
  }
  return sum / samples;
}


//
↪    -------------------------------------------------------------------
// Function: processValue
// Purpose:  Demonstrates conditional branching using if/else and
↪    switch statements.
//           It evaluates sensor data and categorizes it into
↪    different levels.
//
↪    -------------------------------------------------------------------
void processValue(int value) {
  // Conditional Statement: using if...else
  if (value >= thresholdValue) {
    Serial.println("High sensor value detected.");
  } else {
    Serial.println("Sensor value is within normal range.");
  }

  // Multi-way branching: using switch-case statement
```

```
    int caseValue = value / 200; // Dividing the sensor range into
    ↪   categories
    switch (caseValue) {
      case 0:
        Serial.println("Category: Very Low");
        break;
      case 1:
        Serial.println("Category: Low");
        break;
      case 2:
        Serial.println("Category: Medium");
        break;
      case 3:
        Serial.println("Category: High");
        break;
      default:
        Serial.println("Category: Very High");
        break;
    }
}


//
↪   -----------------------------------------------------------------
// Function: loopIterations
// Purpose:  Illustrates iterative constructs using for, while, and
↪   do-while loops.
//           It also demonstrates the usage of break, continue
↪   directives.
//
↪   -----------------------------------------------------------------
void loopIterations() {
  // For-loop: Calculate a running total from 1 to 10
  int total = 0;
  for (int i = 1; i <= 10; i++) {
    total += i;
    // If iteration reaches 5, skip the detailed print by using
    ↪   continue.
    if (i == 5) {
      continue;
    }
    Serial.print("Iteration ");
    Serial.print(i);
    Serial.print(": Total so far = ");
    Serial.println(total);
  }

  // While-loop: Count down from 5 to 0
  int counter = 5;
  while (counter >= 0) {
    Serial.print("While loop counter: ");
    Serial.println(counter);
    counter--;
  }
```

```
  // Do-while loop: Ensure at least one execution of the loop block
  int doCounter = 0;
  do {
    Serial.print("Do-while loop iteration: ");
    Serial.println(doCounter);
    doCounter++;
  } while (doCounter < 3);
}

//
↪  ----------------------------------------------------------------------
// Function: nestedControlStructure
// Purpose:  Shows an example of nested loops combined with
↪  conditional statements
//           to illustrate complex control flows and multi-tiered
↪  decision-making.
//
↪  ----------------------------------------------------------------------
void nestedControlStructure() {
  Serial.println("Nested Control Structures:");

  // Outer loop using for-loop
  for (int i = 0; i < 3; i++) {
    Serial.print("Outer loop i = ");
    Serial.println(i);

    // Inner loop using while-loop
    int j = 0;
    while (j < 3) {
      // Conditional check inside nested loops
      if ((i + j) % 2 == 0) {
        Serial.print("  i+j is even: ");
      } else {
        Serial.print("  i+j is odd: ");
      }
      Serial.print(i);
      Serial.print(" + ");
      Serial.print(j);
      Serial.print(" = ");
      Serial.println(i + j);
      j++;
    }
  }
}

//
↪  ----------------------------------------------------------------------
// setup: Initializes serial communication and prints startup
↪  message.
//
↪  ----------------------------------------------------------------------
void setup() {
```

39

```cpp
  Serial.begin(115200);
  delay(1000); // Wait for serial monitor to initialize
  Serial.println("Starting ESP32 IoT Control Structures Demo...");
}

//
↪  -----------------------------------------------------------------------
// loop: Main loop executing sensor readings, processing, and
↪  demonstrations
//      of various control structures.
//
↪  -----------------------------------------------------------------------
void loop() {
  // Compute average sensor value from SAMPLE readings (using
  ↪  for-loop)
  int sensorAvg = computeSensorAverage(SENSOR_PIN, 5);
  Serial.print("Average sensor value: ");
  Serial.println(sensorAvg);

  // Process sensor value using conditional and switch-case
  ↪  constructs
  processValue(sensorAvg);

  // Demonstrate iterative constructs: for, while, do-while loops
  loopIterations();

  // Demonstrate nested and composite control structures
  nestedControlStructure();

  // Use a simple early exit strategy:
  // If the sensor value exceeds a critical threshold, log a message
  ↪  and exit loop early.
  if (sensorAvg > 900) {
    Serial.println("Critical sensor value detected. Restarting
    ↪  process safely.");
    // Here we could incorporate a watchdog timer or system reset
    ↪  logic.
    return;
  }

  // Delay before running the loop again
  delay(2000);
}

/*
 * ------------------------------------------------------------
 * Formal Semantics and Complexity Analysis:
 * ------------------------------------------------------------
 * 1. Time Complexity of Nested Loops:
 *    The nested for and while loops in nestedControlStructure()
 ↪  yield:
 *        T(n) = O(n_outer * n_inner) = O(3 * 3) = O(9)
```

40

```
*     For general cases, if the outer loop runs 'n' times and the
↪    inner loop 'm' times,
*     the complexity is O(n * m). In scenarios where n = m, this can
↪    be represented as O(n^2).
*
* 2. Conditional Evaluation Pseudocode:
*        if (E) {
*            // Execute true branch
*        } else {
*            // Execute false branch
*        }
*
*     Note: In C++/Arduino, Boolean expressions are evaluated with
↪    short-circuit rules:
*            - For 'E1 && E2', if E1 is false, E2 is not evaluated.
*            - For 'E1 || E2', if E1 is true, E2 is not evaluated.
*
* 3. Iteration Constructs:
*     - For-loop: Executes a code block a predetermined number of
↪    times.
*     - While-loop: Evaluates the condition before executing the
↪    loop body.
*     - Do-while loop: Ensures the loop body executes at least once
↪    before condition check.
*
* These control structures form the backbone of deterministic
↪    execution required for
* real-time operations in resource-constrained systems such as the
↪    ESP32.
*  ----------------------------------------------------------
*/
```

Chapter 5

Functions and Modular Programming

Designing Reusable Functions

In embedded systems programming, particularly within the constraints imposed by the ESP32 architecture, the formulation of reusable functions occupies a central role in achieving both efficiency and clarity. A reusable function is conceived as a discrete, self-contained unit of operation that encapsulates a specific task or computation, thereby enabling isolation of functionality from the broader program context. This discrete encapsulation not only fosters ease of maintenance but also permits the independent verification of complex operations. In essence, the definition of a function establishes a formal contract: a well-specified interface with clearly delineated input parameters and output values, permitting the systematic reuse of algorithmic logic across various operational scenarios.

The design of such functions necessitates rigorous attention to the principles of abstraction and minimal coupling. By limiting interaction with external state and by ensuring that all requisite data is passed through parameters, the function is rendered both predictable and devoid of side effects that might compromise other modules. The resultant formalism in function design adheres to a paradigm wherein the function's internal logic is shielded from inadvertent perturbations in the global state, thereby contributing to enhanced reliability and testability in accordance with theoretical models of program modularity.

Scope and Variable Binding

An in-depth understanding of scope and variable binding is paramount to achieving correct and robust modularization in ESP32 projects. Scope refers to the region within a program where a given identifier is valid and accessible, while variable binding is the association between a variable and its storage location in memory. In structured programming, proper delineation of scope—typically through the usage of local and global variables—ensures that a function's internal computation remains isolated from unintended interactions with external data. This isolation adheres to the principle that variables declared within a function or a block possess a limited lifetime and are managed according to a well-defined allocation and deallocation scheme.

When considering the theoretical underpinnings of scope, one may invoke concepts of lexical scoping, wherein the binding of variables is determined statically by the syntactic structure of the program. Consequently, each function defines a new environment in which variable bindings are localized, thereby safeguarding against erroneous data manipulation that could arise from ambiguous or overlapping names. From a complexity standpoint, these scoping rules are instrumental in maintaining predictable execution behavior, as they obviate the need for runtime checks that may otherwise impede performance in a resource-constrained embedded system.

Organizing Code into Logical Modules

The systematic organization of code into logical modules represents a critical methodology for managing the inherent complexity of sophisticated ESP32 applications. Modular programming is an architectural approach that decomposes a program into discrete, functional units—each module encapsulates a cohesive set of responsibilities and interacts with other modules through explicitly defined interfaces. This partitioning is not only a reflection of sound software engineering practices but also an operational necessity in environments where resource management, such as memory allocation and real-time responsiveness, is of paramount concern.

In the context of modularity, each module is designed to exhibit high internal cohesion and low external coupling. Such an arrangement ensures that modifications within one module do not propagate unintended side effects in disparate regions of the codebase. Moreover, logical modules are often aligned with the separation of concerns principle, wherein different functional layers—ranging from sensor data processing to communication protocols—are isolated into independent units. This segregation facilitates rigorous unit testing and enables parallel development streams, as modifications within one module can be validated independently of the system as a whole.

The formalization of modular design may be analogized to the mathematical construct of a function mapping elements from one set to another, where the interface represents the domain and codomain of the mapping. Just as the integrity of such mappings is preserved by the strict adherence to function definitions, so too is the integrity of a software system safeguarded by the judicious delineation of module boundaries. This architecture enables the seamless integration of reusable components, which can be recombined or repurposed with minimal friction, thereby streamlining the development process and enhancing the scalability of the final application.

ESP32 For IoT With Arduino Code Snippet

```
#include <Arduino.h>

// Global definition of sensor pin for analog input (ESP32 ADC
↪    channel)
const int sensorPin = 34;   // Change based on your wiring

// ------------------------------------------------------------
// Reusable Function: Calculate Voltage from ADC Reading
// Equation: voltage = (adcValue * referenceVoltage) / adcResolution
// For a 12-bit ADC on the ESP32 (0-4095) and a reference voltage of
↪    3.3V.
float calculateVoltageFromADC(int adcValue) {
  const float referenceVoltage = 3.3;   // Voltage reference of
↪    ESP32
  const int adcResolution = 4095;        // 12-bit ADC resolution
  float voltage = (adcValue * referenceVoltage) / adcResolution;
  return voltage;
}

// ------------------------------------------------------------
// Reusable Function: Apply Calibration Formula to Voltage Reading
```

```
// Here we use a simple linear transformation as: calibratedValue =
↪   a * voltage + b
float applyCalibration(float voltage) {
  const float a = 1.05;  // Scale factor for calibration
  const float b = -0.1;  // Offset correction
  float calibratedValue = a * voltage + b;
  return calibratedValue;
}


// ------------------------------------------------------------
// Reusable Function: Compute Moving Average of Sensor Readings
// This algorithm incrementally updates the average to filter out
↪   noise.
// newSample: Latest ADC reading
// prevAverage: Previously computed average
// sampleCount: Number of samples processed so far (must be >= 1)
float computeMovingAverage(int newSample, float prevAverage, int
↪   sampleCount) {
  return ((prevAverage * (sampleCount - 1)) + newSample) /
  ↪   sampleCount;
}


// ------------------------------------------------------------
// Modular Function: Process Sensor Data
// This function encapsulates the complete workflow:
// 1. Read raw ADC value from the sensor.
// 2. Convert the ADC reading to a voltage using a mathematical
↪   equation.
// 3. Apply a calibration formula to adjust the voltage.
// 4. Compute a moving average to smooth out sensor noise.
// This encapsulation demonstrates abstraction, minimal coupling,
↪   and clear scope.
void processSensorData() {
  // Read the raw ADC value from the sensor
  int rawValue = analogRead(sensorPin);

  // Convert raw reading into a voltage
  float voltage = calculateVoltageFromADC(rawValue);

  // Apply a calibration formula to the voltage
  float calibratedVoltage = applyCalibration(voltage);

  // Compute moving average to reduce noise.
  // Using static variables to preserve state between function
  ↪   calls.
  static int sampleCount = 0;
  static float movingAverage = 0.0;
  sampleCount++;
  movingAverage = computeMovingAverage(rawValue, movingAverage,
  ↪   sampleCount);

  // Output the results to the Serial Monitor
  Serial.print("Raw ADC: ");
```

```
  Serial.print(rawValue);
  Serial.print(" | Voltage: ");
  Serial.print(voltage, 3);
  Serial.print(" V");
  Serial.print(" | Calibrated Voltage: ");
  Serial.print(calibratedVoltage, 3);
  Serial.print(" V");
  Serial.print(" | Moving Average: ");
  Serial.println(movingAverage, 3);
}

// ------------------------------------------------------------
// Arduino Setup Function: Initialize Serial Communication and Pin
↪   Modes
void setup() {
  Serial.begin(115200);        // Start serial communication at
  ↪   115200 baud
  pinMode(sensorPin, INPUT);  // Set sensor pin as input
}

// ------------------------------------------------------------
// Arduino Loop Function: Continuously process sensor data every
↪   second
void loop() {
  processSensorData();  // Process sensor reading and calibrate
  ↪   result
  delay(1000);          // Delay for 1 second between readings
}
```

Chapter 6

Arrays and Strings Manipulation

Fundamental Concepts of Arrays

Arrays constitute a fundamental data structure within the domain of embedded systems, characterized by their ability to store a fixed-size sequence of homogeneous elements in contiguous memory. In formal terms, an array may be represented as a mapping from a finite, ordered index set, typically $0, 1, ldots, n - 1$, to a set of elements, where n denotes the length of the array. This structure enables constant time, $O(1)$, access to any element via its index. In the context of Arduino programming on the ESP32, such arrays are often allocated either statically or dynamically, with the former ensuring that memory is assigned at compile time and the latter introducing a level of flexibility at the expense of potential runtime overhead. The mathematical model underlying arrays forms the basis for more elaborate constructs that facilitate systematic data manipulation and storage efficiency within resource-constrained environments.

Memory Layout and Indexing Properties

The physical arrangement of array elements in continuous memory is dictated by the principles of linear data organization, where each successive element is stored at a fixed offset from the preceding one.

This predictable memory layout not only simplifies index computations, expressed succinctly as the address of an element being the sum of the base address and the product of the index with the size of an individual element, but also bolsters data locality. Such locality plays a crucial role in optimizing system performance, particularly in microcontroller architectures such as the ESP32 where efficient memory usage directly impacts real-time processing capabilities. The inherent characteristics of arrays necessitate rigorous bounds checking to avoid undefined behavior due to out-of-range access, a challenge that is accentuated in embedded applications by the often limited memory availability and stringent real-time requirements.

C-Style String Representation and Null-Termination

Within the realm of Arduino programming, strings are frequently manipulated as arrays of characters following the conventions of the C programming language. These C-style strings are delineated by a terminating null character, conventionally denoted as ' backslash0', which signifies the end of the string. The null-terminator ensures that string manipulation functions, such as those for copying, concatenation, and length determination, can operate without prior knowledge of the string's allocated size. The reliance on null-termination introduces both operational simplicity and potential sources of error, as inadvertent omissions or misplacements of the null character can precipitate buffer overflows or memory corruption. Consequently, the proper understanding of low-level, pointer-based string handling techniques and the meticulous management of the null character are indispensable for the successful manipulation of textual data in ESP32 applications.

The Arduino String Class and Dynamic Memory Management

In contrast to traditional C-style strings, the Arduino String class abstracts several of the complexities intrinsic to manual memory management. This class encapsulates a dynamically allocated array of characters, thereby enabling operations such as concatenation, substring extraction, and case conversion through a rich set of member functions. The dynamic allocation inherent in the String class permits variable-length string manipulation, but it concurrently necessitates vigilance regarding memory fragmentation and heap integrity in environments with finite resources. This abstraction facilitates a higher level of programming simplicity while still imposing the need for developers to consider underlying constraints, such as the costs associated with dynamic resizing and the implications of garbage collection or memory leaks. Methods provided by this class articulate well-defined interfaces for manipulation, thereby promoting modularity and code reuse within the architectural design of IoT applications on the ESP32.

Applications and Manipulation Techniques in Resource-Constrained Environments

The effective manipulation of arrays and strings within ESP32-based applications is paramount for handling data derived from sensor inputs, user interfaces, and network communications. Arrays act as the primary repositories for bulk numerical or categorical data, where each element may represent discrete sensor readings or other quantifiable parameters. Their utilization is optimized through techniques such as pre-allocation, iterative traversal, and in-place modification, which minimize processing overhead and reduce memory fragmentation. Strings, on the other hand, are employed to manage textual information, command sequences, and configuration data. Their manipulation requires a careful balance between flexibility and efficiency; operations on strings must account for computational complexity and the inherent cost of memory reallocations. Advanced manipulation techniques often involve tokenization, pattern matching, and efficient concatenation methods that maintain data integrity while adhering to strict performance constraints. The judicious design of algorithms that perform these operations directly influences the responsiveness and reliability of embedded systems, rendering a deep understanding of both array structures and string handling mechanisms essential for robust ESP32 application development.

ESP32 For IoT With Arduino Code Snippet

```
#include <Arduino.h>
#include <string.h>

// Memory Address Calculation Formula:
// For an array 'arr', the address of element arr[i] is computed as:
//      address = base_address + (i * sizeof(arr[0]))
// This equation exemplifies the contiguous memory layout in
↪    embedded systems.

#define ARRAY_SIZE 5

// Function: Print each array element along with its computed memory
↪    address.
void printArrayMemoryLayout(int *arr, int size) {
  Serial.println("Array Memory Layout:");
  for (int i = 0; i < size; i++) {
    // Pointer arithmetic: (arr + i) gives the address of arr[i].
    uintptr_t addr = (uintptr_t)(arr + i);
    Serial.print("Index ");
    Serial.print(i);
    Serial.print(" -> Value: ");
    Serial.print(arr[i]);
    Serial.print(" at Address: 0x");
    Serial.println(addr, HEX);
  }
}

// Function: Demonstrate C-Style string manipulation including
↪    null-termination,
// concatenation, and tokenization.
void manipulateCStrings() {
  // Initialize a base C-style string with proper null-termination.
  char baseString[50] = "ESP32";
  char appendString[] = " IoT with Arduino";

  // Combining the strings: use strcpy to copy and strcat to append.
  char fullString[100];
  strcpy(fullString, baseString);    // fullString now contains
↪    "ESP32"
  strcat(fullString, appendString);   // fullString becomes "ESP32
↪    IoT with Arduino"

  Serial.println("C-Style String Manipulation:");
  Serial.print("Combined String: ");
  Serial.println(fullString);

  // Tokenization: split the combined string using a space as
↪    delimiter.
```

```
  Serial.println("Tokenized Words:");
  char *token = strtok(fullString, " ");
  while (token != NULL) {
    Serial.println(token);
    token = strtok(NULL, " ");
  }
}

// Function: Demonstrate usage of the Arduino String class for
↪   dynamic string manipulation.
void manipulateArduinoString() {
  // Using the String class to simplify operations such as
↪   concatenation.
  String greeting = "Hello";
  greeting += ", ESP32 IoT!";  // Append text dynamically.

  Serial.println("Arduino String Class Manipulation:");
  Serial.println(greeting);

  // Extract a substring and convert the entire string to lower
↪   case.
  String extracted = greeting.substring(7, 12); // Expected to
↪   extract "ESP32"
  Serial.print("Extracted Substring: ");
  Serial.println(extracted);

  String lowerGreeting = greeting;
  lowerGreeting.toLowerCase();
  Serial.print("Lowercase String: ");
  Serial.println(lowerGreeting);

  // Note: Although the String class abstracts dynamic memory
↪   management,
  // caution is advised to avoid heap fragmentation in
↪   resource-constrained environments.
}

// Function: Calculate the sum of an integer array (algorithm
↪   demonstration).
int sumArrayElements(const int *arr, int size) {
  int sum = 0;
  for (int i = 0; i < size; i++) {
    sum += arr[i];
  }
  return sum;
}

void setup() {
  // Initialize serial communication.
  Serial.begin(115200);
  while (!Serial) {
    ; // Wait for serial port to connect (only needed for native USB
↪   devices).
```

```
  }

  Serial.println("ESP32 IoT with Arduino Code Demo - Arrays and
  ↳  Strings Manipulation");

  // Array manipulation demo: static allocation of sensor readings.
  int sensorReadings[ARRAY_SIZE] = { 100, 200, 300, 400, 500 };
  printArrayMemoryLayout(sensorReadings, ARRAY_SIZE);

  // Execute and display the result of the sum algorithm.
  int total = sumArrayElements(sensorReadings, ARRAY_SIZE);
  Serial.print("Sum of array elements: ");
  Serial.println(total);

  // Demonstrate C-style string operations.
  manipulateCStrings();

  // Demonstrate Arduino String class operations.
  manipulateArduinoString();
}

void loop() {
  // Empty loop: All functionality demonstrated during setup().
}
```

Chapter 7

Pointers and Memory References in Arduino

Fundamental Concepts of Pointers

Pointers constitute a fundamental abstraction in low-level programming by representing variables whose values are memory addresses. For a given data type T, a pointer is declared as type $T*$, indicating that it stores the address of a memory location containing an object of type T. This concept facilitates direct memory access, thereby affording efficient manipulation of stored data. The abstraction provided by pointers circumvents the overhead of higher-level data access mechanisms and is indispensable in managing the fixed and dynamic memory regions inherent to embedded systems such as the ESP32. The theoretical underpinnings of pointers are entrenched in the notion of indirection, which allows the dissociation of an object's identity from the physical location where its value resides.

Pointer Arithmetic and Memory Addressing

Pointer arithmetic is integral to the utilization of pointers in systems where memory is organized linearly. When a pointer p is associated with a memory address, the expression $p + i$ computes a new pointer positioned at an offset of $i \times \text{sizeof}(T)$ bytes from the original memory location, where T denotes the data type to which

p points. This arithmetic property derives from the contiguous allocation of array elements and other sequential data structures in memory. Consequently, operations involving pointers can traverse arrays, linked lists, or other data structures efficiently by leveraging the predictable nature of memory offsets. The precision offered by pointer arithmetic ensures that every increment or decrement corresponds exactly to the size of the underlying elements, thereby maintaining alignment and facilitating constant time, $O(1)$, access to any element within a contiguous block of memory.

Reference Variables and Alias Semantics

In contrast to pointers, reference variables serve as implicit aliases for existing objects, effectively binding a new name to an already established variable. The declaration of a reference follows the syntactic form $T\&r = x$, where x is an object of type T. Once initialized, a reference cannot be made to refer to a different object, and it inherently provides direct access to the original memory location without the necessity for explicit dereferencing. This property simplifies the manipulation of complex data structures while preserving the integrity of the original data. The semantics of references enforce strict aliasing, ensuring that any modification made through the reference is immediately reflected in the associated object. This deterministic behavior enhances the clarity of memory interactions and circumvents the pitfalls often associated with erroneous pointer manipulation, such as dangling pointers or unintended memory modifications.

Memory Management in ESP32 Applications

Embedded systems, notably those built around the ESP32, operate under stringent memory constraints, necessitating an exacting approach to resource management. The judicious use of pointers and references is central to achieving memory efficiency in such environments. Pointers enable the explicit control over dynamic memory allocation, allowing practitioners to manage buffers, handle variable-length data streams, and interface with hardware registers with minimal overhead. In scenarios where dynamic allocation is involved, pointers facilitate precise control over memory layouts and the rapid traversal of contiguous memory regions. Conversely, references offer a mechanism for static memory management by ensuring that access to pre-allocated variables is both efficient and safe. The interplay between pointers and references thus allows for an optimized memory model, where dynamic and static memory regions are managed with minimal fragmentation and overhead. This model is particularly critical in real-time computing environments, where deterministic memory access and low latency are imperative for maintaining system responsiveness.

ESP32 For IoT With Arduino Code Snippet

```
#include <Arduino.h>

// Function to print an array's elements using pointer arithmetic
void printArray(int* arr, int size) {
  Serial.print("Array Elements: ");
  for (int i = 0; i < size; i++) {
    // Pointer arithmetic: *(arr + i) computes address offset i *
    ↪   sizeof(int)
    Serial.print(*(arr + i));
    Serial.print(" ");
  }
  Serial.println();
}

void setup() {
  // Initialize serial communication
  Serial.begin(115200);
  while (!Serial) {
    ; // Wait for serial port to connect; needed for some ESP32
    ↪   boards
  }

  // --- Fundamental Pointer Concepts ---
  int value = 42;          // A simple integer variable
  int* ptr = &value;       // Pointer storing the address of 'value'
  Serial.println("Pointer Fundamentals:");
  Serial.print("Value accessed through pointer: ");
  Serial.println(*ptr);

  // --- Pointer Arithmetic and Memory Addressing ---
  int numbers[5] = {10, 20, 30, 40, 50};
  int* pNumbers = numbers; // Pointer to the first element of the
  ↪   array
  // Using pointer arithmetic to calculate the sum of array
  ↪   elements.
```

```cpp
  // Equation demonstrated: p + i points to the memory address
  ↳  offset by i*sizeof(int)
  int sum = 0;
  for (int i = 0; i < 5; i++) {
    sum += *(pNumbers + i);  // Equivalent to numbers[i]
  }
  Serial.println("Pointer Arithmetic:");
  Serial.print("Sum of array elements: ");
  Serial.println(sum);

  // --- Reference Variables and Alias Semantics ---
  int originalVar = 100;
  int &aliasVar = originalVar; // 'aliasVar' now serves as an alias
  ↳  for 'originalVar'
  Serial.println("Reference Variable Demo:");
  Serial.print("Original variable: ");
  Serial.println(originalVar);
  // Modifying aliasVar automatically changes originalVar
  aliasVar += 50;
  Serial.print("Modified variable via reference: ");
  Serial.println(originalVar);

  // --- Memory Management in ESP32 Applications ---
  Serial.println("Dynamic Memory Allocation:");
  int n = 5;
  // Allocate memory dynamically for an array of n integers
  int* dynamicArray = (int*) malloc(n * sizeof(int));
  if (dynamicArray != NULL) {
    // Initialize the dynamic array using pointer arithmetic
    for (int i = 0; i < n; i++) {
      *(dynamicArray + i) = (i + 1) * 10; // Stores: 10, 20, 30, 40,
      ↳  50
    }
    // Print the dynamically allocated array
    printArray(dynamicArray, n);
    // Free the allocated memory to optimize limited resources
    free(dynamicArray);
  } else {
    Serial.println("Memory allocation failed.");
  }
}

void loop() {
  // Empty loop: In a real IoT application, tasks would be scheduled
  ↳  here.
}
```

Chapter 8

Object-Oriented Programming Concepts

Classes and Objects in Arduino

A class in the context of Arduino sketches for the ESP32 constitutes a user-defined data type that encapsulates both state and behavior. This encapsulation is achieved through the definition of member variables that represent the internal state, and member functions that prescribe the behavior of the objects. The formal declaration of a class establishes a blueprint, delineating the attributes and operations common to all instances. Each object, as an instantiation of this class, occupies its own region of memory, thereby maintaining a distinct state that is manipulated by member functions. The design of classes adheres to principles of modularity and abstraction, allowing complex behaviors to be represented in a compact and logically coherent form. The process of object instantiation involves allocating memory and, if defined, executing a constructor routine that initializes the object's state to a predetermined set of values.

Inheritance in Arduino Sketches

Inheritance serves as a foundational mechanism for achieving hierarchical classification within Arduino sketches. In this paradigm, a base class encapsulates general attributes and behaviors, which can subsequently be extended by one or more derived classes. Through public inheritance, a derived class inherits the interface and data members of the base class, enabling code reuse and the systematic augmentation of functionality. The architectural implications of inheritance are particularly significant when addressing the constrained resource environment of the ESP32, as careful design is required to mitigate the overhead associated with extended class hierarchies. The interplay between access specifiers—public, protected, and private—ensures that the encapsulated data maintains its intended integrity while supporting selective exposure of functionality. This mechanism enables the derivation of specialized classes that cater to specific application domains without compromising the logical structure imposed by the general base class.

Polymorphism and Dynamic Binding

Polymorphism embodies the capability of a system to seamlessly manipulate objects of different classes through a common interface, thereby facilitating a design that is both flexible and extensible. In the C++ framework that underpins Arduino programming, polymorphism is primarily realized through the use of virtual functions. Such functions, declared in a base class, allow derived classes to override the behavior with implementations that are specific to the derived type. The mechanism of dynamic binding ensures that, during runtime, the correct function implementation is invoked based on the actual object type rather than the declared type. This resolution process typically involves the use of a virtual table, whose lookup operations incur an overhead that is designed to remain constant in time, i.e., $O(1)$, ensuring efficient execution across diverse IoT applications. The design of polymorphic structures in embedded environments must carefully balance the benefits of dynamic dispatch with the limitations imposed by constrained memory and computational resources. Their successful employment results in code architectures that maintain a high degree of abstraction, promoting both reusability and maintainability while respecting the performance parameters crucial to the ESP32 platform.

ESP32 For IoT With Arduino Code Snippet

```
#include <Arduino.h>

//---------------------------------------------------------------------
// Base Class: Sensor
//---------------------------------------------------------------------
class Sensor {
  protected:
    int sensorPin;   // ADC pin associated with the sensor

  public:
    // Constructor: initialize sensorPin
    Sensor(int pin) : sensorPin(pin) { }

    // Pure virtual function to ensure derived classes implement
    ↪  sensor reading
    virtual float readValue() = 0;
};

//---------------------------------------------------------------------
// Derived Class: TemperatureSensor
//---------------------------------------------------------------------
class TemperatureSensor : public Sensor {
  private:
    float calibrationOffset; // Calibration offset to adjust sensor
    ↪  reading

  public:
    // Constructor: initializes base Sensor and sets calibration
    ↪  offset
    TemperatureSensor(int pin, float offset) : Sensor(pin),
    ↪  calibrationOffset(offset) { }

    // Override readValue to return temperature in Celsius
    virtual float readValue() {
      // Simulate an analog reading on the ESP32 (12-bit ADC: values
      ↪  between 0 and 4095)
      int adcValue = analogRead(sensorPin);

      // Convert ADC value to voltage.
      // Formula: voltage = (adcValue / 4095.0) * referenceVoltage
      // For ESP32, referenceVoltage is typically 3.3V.
      float voltage = (adcValue / 4095.0) * 3.3;

      // Convert voltage to temperature using the sensor's specific
      ↪  transfer function.
      // Example formula: Temperature (°C) = (Voltage - 0.5) * 100 +
      ↪  calibrationOffset
      // Explanation:
```

59

```cpp
        //   - 0.5V is considered the baseline corresponding to 0°C.
        //   - Each 10mV (0.01V) represents an increment of 1°C.
        float temperature = (voltage - 0.5) * 100.0 +
        ↪  calibrationOffset;

        return temperature;
    }
};

//-------------------------------------------------------------------------
// Derived Class: HumiditySensor
//-------------------------------------------------------------------------
class HumiditySensor : public Sensor {
  public:
    // Constructor: initialize base Sensor with the given ADC pin
    HumiditySensor(int pin) : Sensor(pin) { }

    // Override readValue to return humidity as a percentage
    virtual float readValue() {
      int adcValue = analogRead(sensorPin);

      // Convert ADC value to humidity percentage.
      // Formula: Humidity (%) = (adcValue / 4095.0) * 100
      float humidity = (adcValue / 4095.0) * 100.0;

      return humidity;
    }
};

//-------------------------------------------------------------------------
// Global Setup for Demonstrating Polymorphism
//-------------------------------------------------------------------------
// Create an array of pointers to Sensor (base class) objects.
// This demonstrates dynamic binding: the correct readValue() is
// ↪  called depending on the object type.
Sensor* sensorArray[2];

void setup() {
  Serial.begin(115200);

  // Initialize sensors on example ADC channels:
  // Temperature sensor on ADC pin 34 with no calibration offset.
  sensorArray[0] = new TemperatureSensor(34, 0.0);
  // Humidity sensor on ADC pin 35.
  sensorArray[1] = new HumiditySensor(35);

  // Allow time for the serial connection to establish.
  delay(1000);
}

void loop() {
  Serial.println("=== Sensor Readings ===");
```

```
// Iterate over sensors and use polymorphism (dynamic binding) to
↪   call the appropriate readValue() method.
for (int i = 0; i < 2; i++) {
  float value = sensorArray[i]->readValue();
  if (i == 0) {
    Serial.print("Temperature: ");
    Serial.print(value);
    Serial.println(" °C");
  } else {
    Serial.print("Humidity: ");
    Serial.print(value);
    Serial.println(" %");
  }
}

// Pause before the next reading cycle.
delay(2000);
}
```

Chapter 9

Utilizing Arduino Libraries Effectively

The Role of Libraries in ESP32 Development

Libraries constitute a cornerstone within the ecosystem of embedded system development, particularly for the ESP32 platform. They encapsulate collections of well-engineered functions, classes, and data structures that abstract away low-level hardware operations and protocol intricacies. Such encapsulation permits the reuse of robust and optimized code, thereby mitigating the need to reinvent fundamental functionalities. The utilization of libraries fosters a modular programming paradigm in which discrete components may be assembled systematically, ensuring that complex projects maintain a high degree of clarity and coherence. This modularity not only streamlines the integration of peripheral functionalities but also enables the isolation of domain-specific operations from the core logic of an application.

The architectural significance of libraries lies in their ability to standardize and encapsulate recurring operations, ranging from input/output management to advanced networking protocols. The adoption of these prepackaged modules permits a focused allocation of intellectual resources toward innovation rather than routine implementation details. In the context of the ESP32, with its constrained computational resources and emphasis on energy efficiency, the judicious use of libraries becomes indispensable. A conscientious integration of libraries often results in more reliable and predictable system behavior, a factor that is crucial when managing the convergence of real-time processing and network interfacing.

Integration and Incorporation of External Libraries

The process of augmenting ESP32 projects with external libraries encompasses several technical considerations. At the heart of this integration lies the mechanism by which the development environment locates and compiles external code modules. This often involves the configuration of include paths and project settings to ensure that the compiler recognizes the repository of available library functions and classes. A methodical incorporation of libraries requires an acute awareness of their initialization patterns, dependency hierarchies, and initialization routines, which may each have implications on program startup sequences and performance.

In complex projects the initial inclusion of multiple libraries necessitates a carefully orchestrated build system. The modular structure of libraries enables a separation of concerns wherein the functional responsibilities are distributed among various code modules. This distribution permits the development and subsequent debugging of discrete system components in isolation. Furthermore, the abstraction afforded by libraries facilitates a clear demarcation between hardware-oriented operations and high-level algorithmic logic, thereby improving the maintainability and scalability of the codebase. The integration process, when performed with precision, yields a seamless interface between user-developed modules and precompiled functions of external libraries.

Managing Library Dependencies and Version Control

The interdependence of multiple libraries within an ESP32 project introduces challenges related to compatibility and version control. Library dependencies, if not managed meticulously, can result in conflicting definitions, redundant functionality, or inefficient resource usage. Establishing an explicit dependency graph is instrumental in delineating the relationships among various libraries.

This graph provides clarity on which modules are core to the functionality and which serve as auxiliary enablers. Furthermore, semantic versioning plays a crucial role in determining compatibility; adherence to this convention ensures that incremental updates do not inadvertently disrupt the established interface contracts between interdependent libraries.

An effective strategy for dependency management involves the systematic documentation of library versions and the configuration of build systems to enforce version constraints. Through automated dependency checkers and build script validations, inconsistencies may be detected early in the development cycle. Such proactive measures reduce integration risks and mitigate the impact of potential incompatibility issues. By rigorously applying these practices, developers can ensure a stable software foundation that gracefully adapts to evolving library landscapes without sacrificing core project integrity.

Balancing Memory and Performance Constraints in Library Usage

The ESP32 platform, by virtue of its embedded nature, imposes stringent constraints on both memory allocation and processing power. The inclusion of external libraries introduces additional overhead that must be balanced against the system's resource limitations. Detailed analysis of the memory footprint and computational complexity is imperative when selecting libraries for critical tasks. Each library represents not only a repository of functions and classes but also an allocation of fixed and dynamic memory resources, which may vary depending on the library's internal implementation details.

A comprehensive evaluation of library performance necessitates an understanding of algorithm complexities and memory allocation patterns. In particular, libraries that employ dynamic memory management or rely on iterative algorithms must be scrutinized for their worst-case scenarios. The careful selection and analysis of libraries, in this context, ensure that the extended functionality does not compromise the overall performance metrics of the ESP32 project. Adopting evaluation strategies that include profiling and benchmarking provides empirical data which can guide the refinement of library selection and integration practices.

Customization and Extension of Library Modules

While libraries are designed to encapsulate general-purpose functionalities, advanced application scenarios often demand modifications that tailor these modules to specific requirements. The inherent modularity of well-architected libraries permits extensions and customizations without undermining the foundational codebase. Such modifications may involve the addition of new functions, the refinement of existing algorithms, or the integration of supplementary data structures to accommodate unique operational contexts. The open-source nature of many Arduino libraries further facilitates this form of customization, promoting collaborative innovation and iterative improvement.

Custom extensions must be undertaken with rigorous attention to compatibility and architectural integrity. Modifications are most effective when they adhere to the established patterns and interfaces originally defined by the library authors, thereby ensuring that extension modules remain interoperable with other components. The design principles underpinning object-oriented programming and modular software architectures support the implementation of such modifications in a controlled and predictable manner. When executed with precision, these enhancements extend the utility of libraries beyond their original scope while maintaining system coherence.

Documentation and Community-Sourced Resources in Library Management

High-quality documentation is a critical asset in the effective utilization of external libraries. Comprehensive documentation provides detailed exegeses of library functions, data structures, and operational paradigms, thereby serving as an indispensable resource for both novice and experienced developers. The clarity and depth of documentation directly influence the ease with which integration challenges can be resolved. Meticulous records of function signatures, behavioral descriptions, and internal algorithms empower developers to anticipate the interactions between library components and their own code modules.

The communal resources surrounding Arduino libraries often include online forums, academic articles, and community-maintained repositories. These resources enrich the foundational documentation by incorporating empirical insights and experiential knowledge. Engagement with these community-driven channels provides access to a continuum of support that extends beyond static documentation. Such collective efforts foster an environment in which iterative improvements and collaborative refinements continually elevate the quality and adaptability of the available libraries.

Troubleshooting and Debugging Library Integration

The complexity inherent in the integration of external libraries necessitates robust methodologies for troubleshooting and debugging. Library-related issues may manifest as runtime anomalies, build-time conflicts, or subtle deviations from expected behavior. A systematic approach to diagnosing these issues involves the isolation of interfacing components and the incremental verification of library functionalities. Diagnostic tools, including logging frameworks and memory profilers, are instrumental in localizing the source of anomalies, particularly in systems where multiple libraries coalesce to form a unified application.

A methodical debugging process often begins with the validation of library installation and configuration parameters. By confirming that each component adheres to its documented interface, it becomes feasible to pinpoint discrepancies arising from misconfigurations or version mismatches. Rigorous error-reporting mechanisms and diagnostic protocols not only streamline the resolution of integration issues but also contribute to a deeper understanding of the underlying operational frameworks of the libraries. This comprehensive diagnostic approach is essential for maintaining a resilient and efficient development environment on the ESP32 platform.

ESP32 For IoT With Arduino Code Snippet

```
// Comprehensive ESP32 For IoT With Arduino Code Example
// This sketch demonstrates the integration of multiple Arduino
↪    libraries,
```

```
// implementation of dependency management, periodic task scheduling
↪   using Ticker,
// sensor calibration using a fundamental linear equation (y = slope
↪   * x + intercept),
// JSON packaging of data, EEPROM storage, and debugging of memory
↪   usage.

// Include required libraries
#include <WiFi.h>
#include <ArduinoJson.h>
#include <EEPROM.h>
#include <Ticker.h>

// Dependency Check: Ensure that ArduinoJson version 6 or above is
↪   used.
#if ARDUINOJSON_VERSION_MAJOR < 6
  #error "ArduinoJson version 6 or above is required."
#endif

// WiFi configuration parameters
const char* ssid = "Your_SSID";
const char* password = "Your_Password";

// EEPROM configuration
const int EEPROM_SIZE = 512;

// Sensor calibration parameters
// Calibration equation: calibrated_value = raw_value * slope +
↪   intercept
const float slope = 1.05;
const float intercept = -0.5;

// Global variables for sensor data
int sensorRawValue = 0;
float sensorCalibratedValue = 0.0;

// Create a Ticker object for scheduling periodic tasks
Ticker periodicTask;

// Function Declarations
void connectToWiFi();
void readSensorData();
void calibrateSensor();
void logData();
void checkMemory();
void periodicCallback();

void setup() {
  // Initialize Serial communication for debugging
  Serial.begin(115200);
  delay(1000); // Allow time for serial monitor to initialize

  // Connect to WiFi and output status
```

67

```
  connectToWiFi();

  // Initialize EEPROM with predefined size
  EEPROM.begin(EEPROM_SIZE);

  // Schedule the periodic task to execute every 5 seconds
  periodicTask.attach(5, periodicCallback);

  Serial.println("Setup complete. Beginning periodic tasks...");
}

void loop() {
  // The main loop remains empty since all tasks are handled by
  ↪   periodic callbacks.
}

// Function to establish WiFi connection
void connectToWiFi() {
  Serial.print("Connecting to WiFi network: ");
  Serial.println(ssid);
  WiFi.begin(ssid, password);

  int retryCount = 0;
  while(WiFi.status() != WL_CONNECTED && retryCount < 20) {
    delay(500);
    Serial.print(".");
    retryCount++;
  }

  if(WiFi.status() == WL_CONNECTED) {
    Serial.println("\nSuccessfully connected to WiFi.");
    Serial.print("Assigned IP Address: ");
    Serial.println(WiFi.localIP());
  } else {
    Serial.println("\nFailed to connect to WiFi. Check credentials
    ↪   and try again.");
  }
}


// Function to simulate sensor data reading
// In an actual application, replace analogRead() with a call to
↪   your sensor library.
void readSensorData() {
  sensorRawValue = analogRead(34); // Read from analog pin 34
  ↪   (ESP32)
  Serial.print("Raw sensor value: ");
  Serial.println(sensorRawValue);
}

// Function to calibrate sensor reading using the linear equation:
// calibrated_value = raw_value * slope + intercept
void calibrateSensor() {
  sensorCalibratedValue = sensorRawValue * slope + intercept;
```

```
    Serial.print("Calibrated sensor value: ");
    Serial.println(sensorCalibratedValue);
}

// Function to log sensor data in JSON format and store the raw
↪   value to EEPROM
void logData() {
  // Create a JSON document to encapsulate sensor readings and WiFi
  ↪   RSSI
  StaticJsonDocument<200> jsonDoc;
  jsonDoc["raw_value"] = sensorRawValue;
  jsonDoc["calibrated_value"] = sensorCalibratedValue;
  jsonDoc["wifi_rssi"] = WiFi.RSSI();

  // Serialize JSON document into a string
  String jsonString;
  serializeJson(jsonDoc, jsonString);
  Serial.println("Sensor Data (JSON): " + jsonString);

  // Write the raw sensor value to EEPROM at address 0 for
  ↪   persistence
  EEPROM.put(0, sensorRawValue);
  EEPROM.commit();

  // Output ArduinoJson library version as part of dependency
  ↪   verification
  #if defined(ARDUINOJSON_VERSION_MAJOR)
    Serial.print("ArduinoJson Version: ");
    Serial.println(ARDUINOJSON_VERSION_MAJOR);
  #endif
}

// Function to check and display free heap memory (resource
↪   management check)
void checkMemory() {
  Serial.print("Free Heap Memory: ");
  Serial.println(ESP.getFreeHeap());
}

// Periodic callback function executed by Ticker every 5 seconds
void periodicCallback() {
  Serial.println("\n--- Periodic Task Execution ---");
  readSensorData();
  calibrateSensor();
  logData();
  checkMemory();
}
```

Chapter 10

Digital Input/Output Programming

Digital Signal Fundamentals

Digital signals are characterized by binary states, conventionally denoted as 0 and 1, that encapsulate the fundamental elements of information processing in electronic systems. The discrete nature of these signals allows for a precise delineation between two distinct voltage levels, which is pivotal in establishing logical decision boundaries within digital circuits. This quantization process, whereby continuous physical phenomena are represented in a binary format, underlies the capacity for error-resistant communication and robust computational operations. The theoretical framework for digital signals is further reinforced by meticulous thresholding criteria, ensuring that marginal variations do not compromise the fidelity of binary state recognition.

Hardware Architecture of Digital I/O Interfaces

The physical realization of digital input/output interfaces is governed by stringent electrical and architectural paradigms that stem from semiconductor design principles. Microcontrollers typically provide an array of digital pins, each of which is integrated into a complex matrix of peripheral registers and control circuits. These pins are endowed with configurable operational modes—ranging from input and output to bidirectional functionalities—that are contingent upon the microcontroller's internal circuitry. Key parameters such as voltage thresholds, current drive capabilities, and temporal response characteristics are defined by the intrinsic hardware design and are critical for maintaining signal consistency. The interplay between these electrical specifications and the digital logic implemented through hardware abstraction layers establishes a reliable conduit for external device interfacing.

Programming Abstractions for Digital Input

Programming digital inputs necessitates a systematic approach to the acquisition and interpretation of external binary signals via dedicated microcontroller pins. Software-level abstractions map low-level hardware operations into higher-level constructs that facilitate the monitoring of pin states. The configuration of input pins often involves the integration of internal or external pull-up and pull-down resistors, which serve to stabilize the default logical state and mitigate the effects of floating inputs. The techniques employed to ascertain state transitions include both periodic polling mechanisms and interrupt-driven paradigms, each offering distinct advantages in terms of response latency and computational overhead. This abstraction layer is critical for translating the raw electrical phenomena into logically coherent data that can be processed by complex algorithms.

Programming Abstractions for Digital Output

Digital output programming involves the translation of computational commands into physical voltage levels, thereby enabling the actuation of external devices. The abstraction of digital output operations encapsulates the logic required to toggle a pin between high and low states, in accordance with application-specific timing and synchronization requirements. Such operations are constrained by the microcontroller's hardware limits, including propagation delays and voltage drive capabilities. The software constructs devised for output management facilitate the initiation of standardized control protocols, ensuring that the delivery of output signals is both temporally precise and electrically stable. The coordination between these high-level abstractions and the inherent properties of the digital output circuitry is essential for maintaining operational coherence in real-world applications.

Signal Integrity, Debouncing, and Timing Considerations

Ensuring the reliability of digital input signals is contingent upon the stringent maintenance of signal integrity, particularly in environments subject to electrical noise and mechanical disturbances. Transient variations and rapid state fluctuations—commonly encountered in mechanical switches or sensor interfaces—necessitate the deployment of debouncing algorithms that effectively filter out spurious transitions. These algorithms employ temporal thresholds to distinguish between genuine signal transitions and ephemeral perturbations, thereby stabilizing the digital input. Concurrently, digital output operations demand careful synchronization, where the timing of state transitions is critically aligned with system-level events and temporal constraints. The confluence of debouncing strategies and precise timing mechanisms underscores the complexity of interfacing digital signals within the domain of resource-constrained systems.

Digital I/O in Internet of Things Interactions

Digital input/output programming forms an indispensable substrate for Internet of Things implementations, where the capability to interact with a diverse array of sensors and actuators is paramount. The binary nature of digital signals facilitates robust information exchange, permitting swift transitions between logical states that are instrumental in reactive system designs. In the context of IoT, digital I/O channels serve as the interface through which physical variables are transduced into digital data and, conversely, control signals are dispatched to external hardware. The architectural strategies governing the abstraction of digital I/O operations compel a balanced integration of low-level hardware manipulation and high-level programmatic control, thereby ensuring that system resources are judiciously managed in environments characterized by strict performance and energy constraints.

ESP32 For IoT With Arduino Code Snippet

```
// ESP32 Digital Input/Output Programming with Debouncing
// This comprehensive example demonstrates key concepts from the
↪   chapter:
//   1. Digital Signal Fundamentals:
//      - Digital signals operate with binary states: LOW (0) and
↪   HIGH (1).
//      - The threshold voltage (V_threshold) for detecting these
↪   states can be approximated by:
//          V_threshold = (V_LOW + V_HIGH) / 2
//   2. Programming Abstractions for Digital Input:
//      - Reading a push button using digitalRead() with internal
↪   pull-up to ensure a stable default state.
//   3. Debouncing Algorithm for Signal Integrity:
//      - To counteract spurious transitions, the code implements a
↪   debouncing algorithm using a time delay.
//      - Formula used: if ((millis() - lastDebounceTime) >
↪   debounceDelay) then accept new reading.
//   4. Programming Abstractions for Digital Output:
//      - Toggling an LED based on the validated digital input
↪   event.
//
// Pin Configuration:
//   - buttonPin: Configured as INPUT_PULLUP; returns LOW when the
↪   button is pressed.
//   - ledPin: Configured as OUTPUT; toggled ON/OFF based on button
↪   press.
//

// Define pin assignments (ensure these match your hardware setup)
const int buttonPin = 15;    // Digital input pin for the push
↪   button (ESP32 compatible pin)
const int ledPin    = 2;     // Digital output pin for the LED
↪   (often the built-in LED on ESP32 boards)

// Variables for debouncing
int buttonState = HIGH;      // Current stable state of the button;
↪   initialized HIGH due to pull-up resistor
int lastButtonState = HIGH;  // Previous reading of the button for
↪   change detection
unsigned long lastDebounceTime = 0; // Timestamp of the last switch
↪   in button state
```

```
const unsigned long debounceDelay = 50; // Debounce delay duration
↪  in milliseconds

// Variable to manage the LED state (false = OFF, true = ON)
bool ledState = false;

void setup() {
  // Initialize serial communication for debugging purposes.
  Serial.begin(115200);

  // Configure the button pin with an internal pull-up resistor.
  pinMode(buttonPin, INPUT_PULLUP);

  // Configure the LED pin as an output.
  pinMode(ledPin, OUTPUT);

  // Set the LED to an initial OFF state.
  digitalWrite(ledPin, LOW);

  // Print initialization message.
  Serial.println("ESP32 Digital I/O with Debouncing Initialized");
}

void loop() {
  // Read the current state from the digital input pin.
  int reading = digitalRead(buttonPin);

  // Check for any change in the button reading.
  // If there's a change, reset the debounce timer.
  if (reading != lastButtonState) {
    lastDebounceTime = millis();
  }

  // If the reading has remained stable longer than the
  ↪  debounceDelay,
  // consider the new reading as the actual button state.
  if ((millis() - lastDebounceTime) > debounceDelay) {
    // Only act if the button state has indeed changed.
    if (reading != buttonState) {
      buttonState = reading;

      // Since the button uses an internal pull-up, a LOW state
      ↪  indicates a press.
      if (buttonState == LOW) {
        // Toggle the LED state.
        ledState = !ledState;
        digitalWrite(ledPin, ledState ? HIGH : LOW);

        // Print the LED status to the serial monitor.
        Serial.print("Button pressed. LED is now ");
        Serial.println(ledState ? "ON" : "OFF");
      }
    }
```

```
  }

  // Save the current reading for the next iteration.
  lastButtonState = reading;

  // Minimal delay to reduce CPU load.
  delay(10);
}
```

Chapter 11

Analog Readings and PWM Output

Analog Signal Acquisition and the ADC Subsystem

The conversion of continuous physical phenomena into discrete numerical representations constitutes a fundamental operation in microcontroller-based systems. At the heart of this process is the analog-to-digital converter (ADC), an integral hardware component that transduces an input voltage V_{in} into a digital value by partitioning the voltage range, typically defined by the reference voltage V_{ref}, into 2^N distinct quantization levels, where N denotes the resolution in bits. The relationship governing the quantization process is expressed as

$$D = \left\lfloor \frac{V_{in}}{V_{ref}} \times \left(2^N - 1\right) \right\rfloor,$$

where D represents the digital output. This mapping is inherently subject to quantization errors and finite resolution limitations, necessitating a careful selection of the reference voltage to maximize the dynamic range and minimize the discretization error.

1 ADC Architecture and Conversion Characteristics

The ADC architecture employed in contemporary microcontrollers is frequently based upon either successive approximation registers or delta-sigma modulation techniques. The successive approximation method iteratively converges upon the input voltage by comparing it against a generated reference, thereby attaining a digital approximation within a finite number of conversion cycles. The accuracy and linearity of this conversion process are dictated by factors such as the design of the sample-and-hold circuit, the stability of the clock signal driving the conversion, and the intrinsic noise characteristics of the circuit components. These aspects combine to set performance bounds on the measured precision, influencing both the signal-to-noise ratio and the effective number of bits available for digital representation.

2 Signal Conditioning and Error Considerations

Prior to digital conversion, the analog signal is subject to a variety of conditioning operations intended to preserve the integrity of the measurement. Typical signal conditioning techniques include amplification, filtering, and impedance matching, each of which plays a role in mitigating distortions arising from thermal noise, electromagnetic interference, and sensor nonlinearities. In particular, the implementation of low-pass filtering attenuates high-frequency noise components, thereby reducing the probability of erroneous ADC readings attributable to transient voltage spikes. Additionally, calibration procedures are often employed to compensate for systematic errors such as offset and gain mismatches, ensuring that the resultant digital value faithfully represents the underlying analog input.

Pulse Width Modulation Synthesis and Applications

Pulse width modulation (PWM) emerges as a critical method for generating effective analog outputs in digital systems lacking a dedicated digital-to-analog converter. Rather than attempting to produce a continuously variable voltage, PWM modulates the time duration during which a digital output is asserted at a high state, such that the average voltage over one period approximates a desired analog value.

1 PWM Generation Principles and Frequency Analysis

The fundamental principle underlying PWM is the manipulation of the duty cycle, defined mathematically as

$$D = \frac{t_{on}}{T},$$

where t_{on} is the duration for which the output remains high within a period T. The effective or perceived analog voltage is directly proportional to the duty cycle, rendering PWM a viable technique for controlling power delivery to actuators and other analog devices. The choice of PWM frequency is of paramount importance, as it must be sufficiently high to ensure that the output appears smooth to the driven components yet properly synchronized with the response characteristics of the load. This frequency selection involves a trade-off between temporal resolution, electromagnetic compatibility, and the inherent physical constraints of the circuit elements.

2 Duty Cycle Computation and Actuator Dynamics

An in-depth examination of the duty cycle computation reveals a linear mapping between the digital sensor readings and the corresponding PWM output parameter. The transformation is formulated such that the measured digital value, representing the sensor input, is scaled to a PWM value that adheres to a predetermined range defined by PWM_{min} and PWM_{max}. This relationship is captured by the equation

$$PWM\_value = \left\lfloor \frac{D_{sensor} \times (PWM_{max} - PWM_{min})}{D_{sensor}^{max}} \right\rfloor + PWM_{min},$$

where D_{sensor} denotes the digital signal obtained from the ADC and D_{sensor}^{max} represents its maximum possible value. The precise modulation of the PWM output is critical in ensuring that the dynamic behavior of actuators, such as motors or variable resistive elements, remains both predictable and stable. The responsiveness of these actuators is intrinsically linked to the temporal characteristics of the PWM signal, with the duty cycle determining not only the average voltage applied but also the rate at which power is intermittently delivered. Such considerations are indispensable when interfacing digital control systems with analog devices, as they ensure that the overall system operates with the requisite fidelity and efficiency within its specified performance envelope.

ESP32 For IoT With Arduino Code Snippet

```
#include <Arduino.h>

// ADC and PWM configuration for ESP32
const int analogPin = 34;              // ADC input pin (ensure the
↪   chosen pin supports ADC)
const int pwmPin = 16;                 // PWM output pin

// ADC Settings
const int ADC_RESOLUTION = 12;         // ESP32 ADC resolution
↪   (12-bit)
const int ADC_MAX = (1 << ADC_RESOLUTION) - 1;  // Maximum ADC
↪   value: 4095 for 12-bit
const float Vref = 3.3;                // Reference voltage for ADC
↪   measurements (in volts)

// PWM Settings using ESP32 LEDC module
const int pwmChannel = 0;              // LEDC channel (0 to 15
↪   available on ESP32)
const int pwmFreq = 5000;              // PWM frequency in Hertz
const int pwmResolution = 8;           // PWM resolution (8-bit →
↪   range 0 to 255)

// PWM output scaling parameters (as defined by the design
↪   requirements)
// These values define the minimum and maximum PWM duty cycle levels
↪   to be applied.
const int PWM_min = 50;                // Minimum PWM duty cycle
↪   value
const int PWM_max = 200;               // Maximum PWM duty cycle
↪   value

void setup() {
  Serial.begin(115200);                // Initialize serial
↪   communication for debugging

  // Setup ADC input pin (on ESP32, analogRead works directly on
↪   supported pins)
```

```
    pinMode(analogPin, INPUT);

    // Configure PWM output using the LEDC module
    // ledcSetup(channel, frequency, resolution) initializes the
    ↪   channel.
    ledcSetup(pwmChannel, pwmFreq, pwmResolution);
    // Attach the PWM channel to the chosen output pin.
    ledcAttachPin(pwmPin, pwmChannel);
}

void loop() {
    // Read the analog value from the sensor via ADC. The value ranges
    ↪   from 0 to ADC_MAX.
    int adcValue = analogRead(analogPin);

    // Optional: Convert ADC reading to actual voltage using the
    ↪   formula:
    // Voltage = (adcValue / ADC_MAX) * Vref
    float voltage = ((float)adcValue / ADC_MAX) * Vref;

    // Compute the PWM output value using the scaling formula:
    // PWM_value = floor( (adcValue * (PWM_max - PWM_min)) / ADC_MAX )
    ↪   + PWM_min
    // Note: Integer division in C/C++ naturally performs the floor
    ↪   operation.
    int pwmValue = ((adcValue * (PWM_max - PWM_min)) / ADC_MAX) +
    ↪   PWM_min;

    // Update the PWM output on the specified channel.
    ledcWrite(pwmChannel, pwmValue);

    // Debug output: Display ADC reading, calculated voltage, and
    ↪   resulting PWM value.
    Serial.print("ADC Value: ");
    Serial.print(adcValue);
    Serial.print(" | Voltage: ");
    Serial.print(voltage, 3);  // voltage with 3 decimals precision
    Serial.print(" V | PWM Value: ");
    Serial.println(pwmValue);

    // Delay to allow stable ADC readings and PWM updates.
    delay(100);
}
```

Chapter 12

Serial Communication Essentials

Fundamental Principles of Serial Communication

Serial communication is predicated on the sequential transmission of binary data over a single channel. This method contrasts with parallel transmission by reducing the number of required interconnections and simplifying the interface between devices. In typical implementations, voltage levels are modulated to represent discrete logical states, with the timing of these changes governed by a predetermined baud rate. The resulting bit stream is the foundation for data exchange across terminals and microcontrollers, such as the ESP32 in embedded environments.

1 Data Representation and Signal Encoding

At its core, serial communication encodes information as a series of voltage transitions that represent binary digits. A high voltage level is used to denote a logical one, while a low level signifies a logical zero. The clarity of these transitions is crucial, as the receiver must correctly interpret the incoming voltage levels despite the presence of electrical noise and other interferences. The duration assigned to each bit, commonly referred to as the bit period, is given by

$$T_{bit} = \frac{1}{\text{baud rate}},$$

which establishes the temporal window during which each bit is transmitted. The modulation of these signals follows strict encoding rules to maintain data integrity, with these parameters selected carefully to balance transmission efficiency and error susceptibility.

2 Communication Modes: Asynchronous and Synchronous

Serial communication is implemented primarily in two operational modes: asynchronous and synchronous. In asynchronous communication, data is transmitted without a shared clock signal; synchronization is achieved through the insertion of a start bit preceding each data frame. This frame typically comprises the start bit, several data bits, an optional parity bit for rudimentary error detection, and one or more stop bits to signal the end of the transmission. In contrast, synchronous communication utilizes a common clock between the transmitter and receiver, which permits continuous data flows and potentially higher transmission rates. The choice between these modes depends on the specific application requirements, particularly in contexts where simplicity for debugging and ease of implementation are valued.

Data Framing and Timing Analysis

The structural arrangement of serial data into frames facilitates both the delineation of information and the reliable recovery of the transmitted signal at the receiver. Each frame is composed of distinct fields that collectively enable precise timing recovery and error detection.

1 Frame Structure in Serial Protocols

A typical serial frame is constructed with a clear delineation of its constituent parts. The frame ordinarily begins with a start bit, which signals the commencement of valid data transmission. This is followed by a defined number of data bits that represent the payload. In many configurations, an optional parity bit is incorporated to provide a simple form of error detection by enforcing a predetermined parity rule, either even or odd. The frame concludes with one or more stop bits, which mark the end of transmission. This structure can be abstractly represented as follows:

Frame = {Start Bit, Data Bits, Parity Bit (optional), Stop Bit(s)},

ensuring that the receiver can accurately identify the beginning and end of each discrete packet of information.

2   Baud Rate and Timing Synchronization

The baud rate is a critical factor in serial communication, as it defines the number of signal changes or symbols transmitted per second. The corresponding time allocated for each bit is determined by

$$T_{bit} = \frac{1}{\text{baud rate}},$$

which plays a pivotal role in the synchronization process between the transmitting and receiving units. Precise timing is essential; any deviation in the clock or misalignment of the sampling period can lead to errors in data interpretation. Consequently, both hardware and software mechanisms are employed to align the receiver's sampling intervals with the transmitter's bit stream, thereby ensuring that the sampling of each bit occurs within the correct temporal window.

Error Detection and Flow Control Mechanisms

Accurate data transmission over serial interfaces necessitates robust mechanisms for detecting and correcting errors, as well as managing the flow of data to mitigate the risk of overflow and other transmission issues. These techniques are fundamental in preserving data integrity across noisy or asynchronous channels.

1   Parity, Checksums, and Data Integrity

One of the simplest forms of error detection in serial communication is the parity check. In this scheme, the number of logical ones in a transmitted data segment is counted, and a parity bit is set to ensure that the total number of ones conforms to either an even or odd criterion. Although parity checking can detect isolated errors, its effectiveness is limited in the presence of multiple bit errors.

In applications where higher integrity is required, more advanced error detection methods such as checksums or cyclic redundancy checks (CRC) are employed. These techniques compute a numerical signature based on the transmitted data, thereby enabling the detection of a broader range of errors upon reception.

2   Flow Control and Buffer Management

To maintain reliable data transfer, especially at high baud rates, mechanisms for flow control play a crucial role. Flow control strategies are designed to coordinate the pace of data transmission between the sender and receiver, thereby preventing buffer overruns and ensuring that neither side is overwhelmed by data. Hardware-based flow control employs dedicated signalling lines to indicate readiness or to halt transmission, while software-based methods use in-band control signals to manage data flow. In environments where the ESP32 is tasked with both high-frequency data exchange and real-time debugging, these flow control techniques ensure that the communication channel remains stable and that data integrity is maintained under varying load conditions.

Serial Communication in Embedded Diagnostics

Serial communication channels are indispensable for diagnostic and debugging operations in embedded systems. The clear and reliable transfer of diagnostic information enables detailed monitoring of system performance and facilitates the rapid isolation and correction of faults.

1   Real-Time Debugging Applications

The inherent capability of serial interfaces to transfer data with minimal latency renders them well suited for real-time diagnostics. Diagnostic messages and operational metrics transmitted via a serial link provide a continuous stream of information regarding system states, operational parameters, and timing events. This uninterrupted flow of data is critical for detecting transient anomalies and for performing detailed analysis of the temporal behavior of embedded systems. The high temporal resolution afforded by serial communication thus enables a granular understanding of system performance during active operation.

2 Implementation Challenges in ESP32 Systems

Integrating serial communication into ESP32 architectures introduces unique challenges stemming from the multicore nature of the device and its concurrent operation of multiple subsystems. The necessity to manage precise timing, ensure proper synchronization, and handle high throughput within limited buffer capacities requires careful consideration during system design. Additionally, the interplay between serial data transmission and other real-time tasks necessitates rigorous attention to resource allocation and priority scheduling. Addressing these challenges is essential to maximize the efficacy of serial interfaces, particularly when employed as conduits for critical debugging and diagnostic information in complex embedded applications.

ESP32 For IoT With Arduino Code Snippet

```
// This comprehensive ESP32 code snippet demonstrates several key
↪    concepts
// discussed in the chapter on Serial Communication Essentials for
↪    IoT:
//   1. Calculation of bit time using the equation T_bit = 1 / (baud
↪    rate)
//   2. Construction of a serial frame following the structure:
//       {Start Bit, Data Bits, Parity Bit (optional), Stop Bit}
//   3. Implementation of a simple parity calculation for error
↪    detection
//   4. Demonstration of asynchronous serial data transmission using
↪    the ESP32

// Define the baud rate for serial communication
#define BAUD_RATE 9600

// Function to calculate the bit time based on the baud rate.
// The bit time T_bit (in microseconds) is computed as:
//     T_bit = (1 / baud rate) * 1e6
unsigned long calculateBitTime(int baudRate) {
  return (1000000UL / baudRate);
}

// Function to compute even parity for an 8-bit data byte.
```

```
// This function returns 0 if even parity is achieved, or 1
↪   otherwise.
byte calculateParity(byte data) {
  byte parity = 0;
  for (int i = 0; i < 8; i++) {
    parity ^= ((data >> i) & 0x01);
  }
  return parity;
}


// Function to simulate sending a serial frame.
// The frame structure is as follows:
//    - Start Bit: A defined value indicating the beginning (here, we
↪   use 0x00)
//    - Data Bits: The payload data byte
//    - Parity Bit: Calculated even parity for the data byte
//    - Stop Bit: A defined value indicating the end (here, we use
↪   0xFF)
void sendSerialFrame(byte data) {
  // Send Start Bit (logic LOW representation)
  Serial.write(0x00);

  // Send Data Bits (the actual data payload)
  Serial.write(data);

  // Calculate and send the Parity Bit (even parity calculation)
  byte parity = calculateParity(data);
  Serial.write(parity);

  // Send Stop Bit (logic HIGH representation)
  Serial.write(0xFF);
}


// Optional function to simulate receiving and decoding a serial
↪   frame.
// Note: In a real-world scenario, proper timing and buffering would
↪   be required.
void processReceivedFrame() {
  if (Serial.available() >= 4) {
    // Read the four parts of the serial frame.
    byte startBit = Serial.read();
    byte data = Serial.read();
    byte receivedParity = Serial.read();
    byte stopBit = Serial.read();

    // Verify start and stop bits.
    if (startBit != 0x00 || stopBit != 0xFF) {
      Serial.println("Frame error: Incorrect start or stop bit.");
      return;
    }

    // Recalculate parity for the received data and compare.
    byte computedParity = calculateParity(data);
```

```
    if (computedParity != receivedParity) {
      Serial.println("Parity error detected.");
    } else {
      Serial.print("Received data: 0x");
      Serial.print(data, HEX);
      Serial.println(" (Parity OK)");
    }
  }
}

void setup() {
  // Initialize the Serial Port with specified baud rate.
  Serial.begin(BAUD_RATE);
  while (!Serial) {
    ; // Wait for the serial port to be ready.
  }

  // Calculate bit time from the baud rate.
  unsigned long bitTime = calculateBitTime(BAUD_RATE);
  Serial.print("Bit Time (calculated using T_bit = 1/baud rate): ");
  Serial.print(bitTime);
  Serial.println(" microseconds");

  // Demonstrate sending a constructed serial frame.
  byte exampleData = 0b10101010; // Example payload data
  Serial.println("Sending serial frame...");
  sendSerialFrame(exampleData);
}

void loop() {
  // For demonstration, send a new frame every second with random
  ↪   data.
  static unsigned long lastSendTime = 0;
  unsigned long currentTime = millis();

  if (currentTime - lastSendTime >= 1000) {
    byte randomData = random(0, 256); // Generate random 8-bit data.
    Serial.print("Sending frame with data: 0x");
    Serial.println(randomData, HEX);
    sendSerialFrame(randomData);
    lastSendTime = currentTime;
  }

  // Process any incoming serial frames (if connected in a loopback
  ↪   or receiver scenario).
  processReceivedFrame();
}
```

Chapter 13

Managing Timers and Delays

Built-in Timer Functions in ESP32

The ESP32 microcontroller integrates a suite of hardware-based timer functions that serve as fundamental building blocks for time-sensitive operations. These built-in timers operate by counting clock cycles, with each timer configured to trigger an interrupt when a defined count is reached. Given a system clock frequency of f_{clk}, the operation of a timer configured to trigger after N clock cycles can be mathematically expressed as

$$T = \frac{N}{f_{clk}},$$

where T represents the duration of the interval. The hardware timers support both one-shot and periodic modes. In one-shot mode, a single interrupt is produced after the configured interval, whereas in periodic mode the timer automatically reloads and continues to generate interrupts at regular intervals. The low latency and minimal jitter inherent in these mechanisms enable the precise scheduling of operations, which is pivotal in embedded applications where timing accuracy is of paramount importance.

Delay Mechanisms: Blocking and Non-blocking Techniques

Delay mechanisms within the ESP32 environment can be broadly categorized into blocking delays and non-blocking delays. Blocking delays typically involve stalling the central processing unit for a specified duration, often achieved using busy-wait loops or operating system delay functions. Such a delay can be represented by the equation

$$t_{delay} = n \times t_{cycle},$$

where n denotes the number of iterative cycles and t_{cycle} is the duration per cycle. While blocking delays afford a straightforward means of controlling timing, they inherently preclude the execution of concurrent tasks, thereby reducing the overall responsiveness of the system.

In contrast, non-blocking delay techniques leverage either hardware timer interrupts or real-time operating system primitives to implement waiting periods without suspending the main execution thread. In these cases, the scheduling of a future event is decoupled from the primary execution path, allowing the microcontroller to manage other operations concurrently. This form of delay is particularly advantageous in multitasking environments where sustaining high throughput and responsiveness is essential. The nuanced implementation of non-blocking delays necessitates careful configuration of timer interrupts and synchronization mechanisms to ensure that the system maintains robust operational performance.

Temporal Precision and Scheduling Strategies

The precise management of timers and delays is central to effective scheduling strategies in an ESP32 program. Temporal precision is achieved by calibrating the hardware timers to match the specific timing requirements of various system operations, such as sensor sampling, data acquisition, and communication synchronization. The minimum achievable scheduling interval is constrained by the resolution of the underlying timer modules, necessitating careful adjustment of prescale values and interrupt configurations to meet sub-millisecond accuracy demands.

In a scheduling context, periodic timers can be configured to synchronize recurring tasks with exact intervals, thereby ensuring that temporal events occur consistently. When multiple timed events must be managed concurrently, it becomes imperative to design a scheduling framework that mitigates potential conflicts between interrupt service routines (ISRs). This involves assigning appropriate priorities to ISRs and ensuring that their execution overhead is minimized. The trade-offs between precise temporal control and overall system efficiency are determined by analyzing the execution time of scheduled tasks relative to the available processing resources. Optimal scheduling strategies are derived from a rigorous examination of these performance metrics, thereby achieving a balance that maintains system stability under varying operational loads.

ESP32 For IoT With Arduino Code Snippet

```
#include <Arduino.h>

// --- Hardware Timer Setup --- //
hw_timer_t * timer = NULL;
portMUX_TYPE timerMux = portMUX_INITIALIZER_UNLOCKED;
volatile bool timerFlag = false;

const int LED_PIN = 2;   // Built-in LED pin (may vary per board)

// Timer configuration parameters:
// We want a timer interval T defined by the equation:
//    T = N / (f_clk / prescaler)
// For an ESP32 with a base clock f_clk = 80MHz and a prescaler of
↪  80,
// the effective timer clock is 1MHz (each tick is 1 microsecond).
// To achieve a 1-second interval, set N = 1,000,000.
const int timerNumber = 0;        // Timer index (0 to 3 available)
const int prescaler = 80;         // Divides the 80MHz clock ->
↪  effective 1MHz
const uint64_t TIMER_INTERVAL_TICKS = 1000000; // Timer count value
↪  for 1 second

// --- Non-blocking Delay Setup --- //
unsigned long previousMillis = 0;
const unsigned long nonBlockingInterval = 1000;   // 1 second
↪  interval for non-blocking tasks

// --- Blocking Delay Example --- //
```

```cpp
// The equation for blocking delay is:
//   t_delay = n * t_cycle
// For instance, if t_cycle = 10ms and n = 5, then t_delay = 50ms.

// --- Timer Interrupt Service Routine --- //
void IRAM_ATTR onTimer() {
  portENTER_CRITICAL_ISR(&timerMux);
  timerFlag = true;
  portEXIT_CRITICAL_ISR(&timerMux);
}

void setup() {
  // Start Serial Monitor for debugging output
  Serial.begin(115200);
  while (!Serial) {
    ; // Wait for Serial connection.
  }

  // Configure the LED pin as output
  pinMode(LED_PIN, OUTPUT);

  // Initialize hardware timer with:
  // timerBegin(timerNumber, prescaler, countUp)
  timer = timerBegin(timerNumber, prescaler, true);
  timerAttachInterrupt(timer, &onTimer, true);
  // Set timer to trigger after TIMER_INTERVAL_TICKS cycles, in
  //   auto-reload (periodic) mode
  timerAlarmWrite(timer, TIMER_INTERVAL_TICKS, true);
  timerAlarmEnable(timer);

  // Calculate and log the timer interval using the formula:
  // T = N / (f_clk / prescaler)
  const uint32_t F_CLK = 80000000;  // Base clock frequency: 80MHz
  double effectiveClock = double(F_CLK) / prescaler; // Effective
  //   timer clock (1MHz)
  double T = double(TIMER_INTERVAL_TICKS) / effectiveClock;
  Serial.print("Configured hardware timer interval T = ");
  Serial.print(T, 6);
  Serial.println(" seconds");

  Serial.println("Setup complete. Starting timer and delay
  demos...");
}

void loop() {
  // --- Handle Hardware Timer Events (Non-blocking via Interrupt)
  //   --- //
  if (timerFlag) {
    portENTER_CRITICAL(&timerMux);
    timerFlag = false;
    portEXIT_CRITICAL(&timerMux);

    // Toggle the LED as a demonstration of hardware timer action
```

91

```
    digitalWrite(LED_PIN, !digitalRead(LED_PIN));
    Serial.println("Hardware Timer Interrupt: LED toggled");
}

// --- Non-blocking Delay Example using millis() --- //
unsigned long currentMillis = millis();
if (currentMillis - previousMillis >= nonBlockingInterval) {
    previousMillis = currentMillis;
    Serial.println("Non-blocking delay: Executing periodic task");
    // Place additional non-blocking operations here.
}

// --- Blocking Delay Example --- //
// Warning: The following blocking delay will halt loop execution.
// It is provided as an example of the equation: t_delay = n *
↪ t_cycle.
// Uncomment the block below to observe a blocking delay.
/*
for (int i = 0; i < 5; i++) {
    Serial.print("Blocking delay iteration ");
    Serial.println(i + 1);
    delay(10); // Each delay is 10ms; Total delay = 5 * 10ms = 50ms.
}
*/
}
```

Chapter 14

Implementing Interrupts in Arduino

Interrupt Fundamentals in Embedded Systems

Interrupts constitute a critical mechanism within embedded system architectures, enabling the processor to respond expeditiously to asynchronous external stimuli and time-sensitive internal events. An interrupt is a signal generated by hardware components or by software conditions that temporarily disrupts the normal sequential execution flow. During the occurrence of an interrupt, the controller typically saves the current processor state, locates the corresponding interrupt vector, and transfers execution control to an interrupt service routine (ISR). Such mechanisms are essential for decreasing response latency, as the delay between event occurrence and program response, denoted by $T_{latency}$, is minimized through immediate context switching. The precise operation of interrupts further hinges on the microcontroller's ability to maintain determinism by controlling the order and priority of ISR execution, hence ensuring that critical tasks are serviced within a rigorously defined temporal envelope.

Configuring Interrupts in Arduino

Within the Arduino environment, interrupt configuration is achieved through a well-defined mapping between external event sources and the microcontroller's hardware interrupt channels. The configuration process typically involves the selection of specific digital input pins and the specification of triggering conditions, such as rising edge, falling edge, or level detection. This process necessitates a comprehensive understanding of the underlying hardware registers and the relationship between the microcontroller's clock frequency, f_{clk}, and the temporal resolution of peripheral events. By setting appropriate trigger conditions and establishing the corresponding interrupt masks, the system ensures that events are detected with minimal latency. Moreover, parameters such as debounce windows and signal stabilization periods are frequently incorporated into configuration settings to mitigate spurious activations and to guarantee robustness in the presence of electrical noise or signal interference.

Design and Structure of Interrupt Service Routines

The efficiency and reliability of interrupt handling are largely determined by the design principles governing the interrupt service routines. ISRs are required to execute with minimal overhead, hence their internal structure is deliberately streamlined to perform only time-critical operations. The implementation dictates that ISRs must eschew blocking functions, avoid complex conditional logic, and refrain from any form of dynamic memory allocation. In addition, shared variables accessed within both the ISR and the main execution thread must be declared with the volatile qualifier, ensuring that the compiler does not optimize away repeated accesses and that the most current values are always in use. The adherence to these practices minimizes execution time and preserves system stability, as prolonged ISR execution may lead to increased interrupt latency or even the loss of subsequent interrupt events. Furthermore, the employment of atomic operations and critical sections provides a safeguard against race conditions, thereby ensuring the integrity of shared data across concurrent execution contexts.

Management of Concurrency and Synchronization in Interrupt Handling

Concurrent interrupt events necessitate a refined approach to synchronization so as to avoid erratic system behavior and resource contention. The asynchronous nature of interrupts requires that the system's design incorporates mechanisms for prioritization and inter-ISR communication. When multiple interrupt sources are active, the microcontroller must manage potential race conditions by enforcing strict ordering rules and, when necessary, temporarily disabling lower priority interrupts during critical operations. The use of hardware-supported atomic instructions facilitates the creation of critical sections in which data consistency is maintained without resorting to software-intensive locking techniques. Additionally, careful calibration of interrupt nesting levels ensures that the cumulative effect of concurrent interrupts does not compromise the real-time performance of the system. In scenarios that demand extremely high levels of precision, the synchronization strategy may involve the explicit partitioning of shared resources and the segregation of time-sensitive tasks from non-critical processing functions, thereby optimizing overall system throughput while maintaining deterministic response characteristics.

ESP32 For IoT With Arduino Code Snippet

```
#include <Arduino.h>

// Define the interrupt pin and debounce delay (in microseconds)
#define INTERRUPT_PIN 15      // Use digital pin 15 for external
↪   interrupts
#define DEBOUNCE_THRESHOLD 50  // Debounce threshold in microseconds

// Global volatile variables to be used inside the ISR and main loop
volatile unsigned long lastInterruptTime = 0; // Timestamp of the
↪   last valid interrupt
volatile unsigned long interruptCount = 0;     // Count of
↪   processed interrupts
volatile bool eventFlag = false;               // Flag to signal a
↪   processed interrupt event

/*
 * Important Equations and Formulas Referenced:
```

```
 *
 * 1. Interrupt Latency Calculation:
 *    T_latency = current_time - lastInterruptTime
 *    - This calculation determines the delay (in microseconds)
↪     between the triggering of an interrupt
 *       and subsequent time measurements.
 *
 * 2. Clock Frequency Impact on Temporal Resolution:
 *    Given a system clock frequency f_clk, the nominal resolution
↪    (time per tick) is:
 *       T_resolution  1 / f_clk
 *    For example, if f_clk = 80 MHz then T_resolution  0.0125 µs.
 *
 * Debouncing Algorithm:
 *    To avoid spurious activations due to electrical noise, the ISR
↪    only processes a new interrupt if:
 *       (current_time - lastInterruptTime) > DEBOUNCE_THRESHOLD
 *
 * ISR Best Practices:
 *    - Keep the ISR short and non-blocking.
 *    - Avoid heavy calculations and dynamic memory allocations.
 *    - Use the 'volatile' qualifier for variables shared between
↪    the ISR and main code.
 */

// Interrupt Service Routine (ISR) - runs when the defined edge
↪   condition triggers
void IRAM_ATTR handleInterrupt() {
  // Capture the current timestamp (in microseconds)
  unsigned long currentTime = micros();

  // Debounce: process the interrupt only if sufficient time has
  ↪  passed
  if ((currentTime - lastInterruptTime) > DEBOUNCE_THRESHOLD) {
    // Update the timestamp of the last valid interrupt
    lastInterruptTime = currentTime;

    // Increment the count of interrupts received
    interruptCount++;

    // Set flag to inform the main loop that an interrupt event
    ↪  occurred
    eventFlag = true;
  }
}

void setup() {
  // Initialize Serial communication for debugging purposes
  Serial.begin(115200);
  while (!Serial) {
    ; // Wait until Serial is ready
  }
```

```
  Serial.println("ESP32 Interrupt Example with Debounce and Latency
  ↪  Calculation");

  // Configure the interrupt pin as input with an internal pull-up
  ↪  resistor activated
  pinMode(INTERRUPT_PIN, INPUT_PULLUP);

  // Attach the interrupt to the specified pin with rising edge
  ↪  trigger
  attachInterrupt(digitalPinToInterrupt(INTERRUPT_PIN),
  ↪  handleInterrupt, RISING);
}

void loop() {
  // Check if the flag set by the ISR indicates that a new interrupt
  ↪  event has been processed
  if (eventFlag) {
    // Reset the event flag for the next interrupt event
    eventFlag = false;

    // Calculate the latency from the last recorded interrupt (for
    ↪  demonstration)
    unsigned long currentMicros = micros();
    unsigned long T_latency = currentMicros - lastInterruptTime;

    // Output the total interrupt count and the computed latency
    Serial.print("Interrupt Count: ");
    Serial.print(interruptCount);
    Serial.print(" | Latency (us): ");
    Serial.println(T_latency);
  }

  // Perform non-blocking tasks; the delay simulates other periodic
  ↪  processing
  delay(10);
}
```

Chapter 15

Memory Management and Optimization

Memory Architecture of the ESP32

The ESP32's architecture exhibits a bifurcated memory organization that principally separates transient execution requirements from dynamically allocated resources. Central to this organization are two distinct memory realms: the stack and the heap. The stack, allocated in a contiguous block of fast-access on-chip memory, manages local variables and function call contexts through a last-in, first-out (LIFO) discipline. In contrast, the heap caters to dynamically allocated memory, providing a heterogeneous landscape for runtime object instantiation and flexible data structures. This dichotomy, when managed with discipline, serves not only to uphold the deterministic performance requisites of embedded systems but also to ensure optimal use of the constrained resources available on the ESP32 platform.

Stack Memory Management

1   Stack Allocation and Utilization

Stack allocation is inherent to the control flow of any program; each function call engenders an allocation for return addresses, local variables, and saved registers. The deterministic behavior of the stack arises from its disciplined LIFO allocation strategy, which simplifies both the prediction of memory usage and the management of context switches. In the context of the ESP32, allocating an accurate and sufficient stack size for each task is of paramount importance. Meticulous analysis of the call graph combined with a priori estimates of recursion depth ensures that the stack memory allocated is sufficient to sustain the worst-case execution scenario while avoiding the pitfalls of over-provisioning that may impinge on overall system performance.

2 Preventing Stack Overflows and Enhancing Determinism

Given the inherent constraints of embedded architectures, an overflow of stack memory, however transient, can precipitate severe system instability. Preventative mechanisms rely on both static and dynamic analyses to ensure that the maximum stack depth is not inadvertently exceeded. Techniques such as formal verification of function call hierarchies and the empirical monitoring of stack utilization are integral to mitigating risks associated with stack overflow. The explicit design of each task with a carefully calibrated stack size, complemented by runtime surveillance, invariably contributes to enhanced determinism—a linchpin in the firm adherence to real-time operational constraints.

Heap Memory Management

1 Dynamic Allocation Strategies

Dynamic memory allocation on the ESP32 is facilitated by a heap management system that caters to the exigencies of runtime data structure formation. Unlike the stack, the heap supports non-deterministic memory requests, thereby introducing a degree of flexibility that is indispensable for applications with variable memory demands. The allocation strategies implemented—whether based on first-fit, best-fit, or a custom hybrid approach—must be scrutinized under the lens of temporal predictability and computational overhead. This constant trade-off between dynamic flexibility and the inevitability of allocation latency mandates a rigorous assessment of the allocation algorithms employed, ensuring that they are both robust and compatible with the real-time imperatives of the system.

2 Fragmentation and Mitigation Techniques

A prevalent challenge within dynamic memory management is memory fragmentation, a phenomenon where the repetitive cycle of allocation and deallocation leaves behind noncontiguous blocks of free space. Such fragmentation reduces the effective size of allocable memory blocks and may lead to allocation failures even when sufficient cumulative memory exists. Mitigation strategies involve the deployment of memory pooling techniques, which consolidate allocation requests into fixed-size blocks, thereby circumventing the fragmentation issue. Additionally, periodic consolidation of free memory regions and the optimization of memory reuse patterns contribute to sustaining a high degree of allocation efficiency. The vigilance in monitoring and addressing fragmentation is essential to ensure that the system maintains optimal memory utilization over extended periods of operation.

Memory Optimization Strategies

1 Efficient Data Structures and Memory Pools

The selection and design of data structures play a pivotal role in reducing memory overhead. In resource-limited environments, the use of memory pools enables a predictable and speedy allocation process, as fixed-size memory blocks are preallocated and recycled in a controlled fashion. This strategy minimizes the unpredictable behavior typically associated with dynamic memory allocation and alleviates the impact of fragmentation. Moreover, the careful alignment of data structures to utilize spatial locality can significantly reduce cache misses, thereby increasing the overall throughput of memory-intensive operations. The deliberate choice of efficient data structures, in tandem with the implementation of customized memory pools, is critical for optimizing memory usage while preserving high-performance operational characteristics.

2 Resource Allocation and Deallocation Patterns

A methodological approach to both allocation and the subsequent deallocation of memory resources is vital to maintaining system health. The lifecycle of dynamically allocated memory must be orchestrated in a manner that minimizes leakage and ensures the timely recovery of resources. This is achieved through systematic policies that govern the allocation patterns, as well as the judicious timing of deallocation procedures. Techniques such as explicit reference counting, region-based memory management, and deterministic deallocation routines are instrumental in establishing a coherent memory usage model. The interplay between resource allocation and deallocation, when finely tuned, ensures that memory resources are neither starved nor wasted, thereby optimizing the overall resource usage on the ESP32.

Profiling and Diagnostic Techniques for Memory Usage

The continuous profiling of memory usage serves as the diagnostic backbone for preemptively identifying potential bottlenecks and inefficiencies within the memory subsystem. By leveraging statistical analyses of allocation latency, heap utilization trends, and fragmentation rates, it is possible to derive actionable insights into the dynamic behavior of the system's memory management. Instrumentation at the runtime level facilitates the collection of granular data, allowing for a detailed examination of allocation patterns and the subsequent impact on system performance. The assimilation of such diagnostic data into the design process engenders a feedback loop that is indispensable for the iterative refinement of memory management strategies, ensuring that the allocation mechanisms evolve in lockstep with the performance demands of the application.

ESP32 For IoT With Arduino Code Snippet

```
#include <Arduino.h>

// A custom MemoryPool class simulating fixed-size block allocation
↪    to mitigate heap fragmentation
class MemoryPool {
  public:
    // Define block size and total blocks in the pool
    static const int BLOCK_SIZE = 32;    // Each block is 32 bytes
    static const int POOL_BLOCKS = 10;   // Total of 10 blocks
    ↪    available
```

```
MemoryPool() {
  // Initialize all blocks as free
  for (int i = 0; i < POOL_BLOCKS; i++) {
    blockUsed[i] = false;
  }
}

// allocate() implements a first-fit dynamic allocation strategy
// within the pool
void* allocate() {
  for (int i = 0; i < POOL_BLOCKS; i++) {
    if (!blockUsed[i]) {
      blockUsed[i] = true;
      Serial.print("Allocating block ");
      Serial.println(i);
      return (void*)(pool + (i * BLOCK_SIZE));
    }
  }
  Serial.println("MemoryPool: No free blocks available!");
  return NULL; // Return NULL if no blocks are free
}

// free() releases the memory block back into the pool given a
// valid pointer
void free(void* ptr) {
  int index = ((uint8_t*)ptr - pool) / BLOCK_SIZE;
  if (index >= 0 && index < POOL_BLOCKS && blockUsed[index]) {
    blockUsed[index] = false;
    Serial.print("Freed block ");
    Serial.println(index);
  } else {
    Serial.println("MemoryPool: Invalid pointer or block already
    free!");
  }
}

// Returns the number of currently available (free) blocks
int availableBlocks() {
  int count = 0;
  for (int i = 0; i < POOL_BLOCKS; i++) {
    if (!blockUsed[i]) count++;
  }
  return count;
}

// Prints the status of the memory pool (free/total blocks)
void printPoolStatus() {
  Serial.print("MemoryPool status: Free blocks = ");
  Serial.print(availableBlocks());
  Serial.print(" / Total blocks = ");
  Serial.println(POOL_BLOCKS);
}
```

```
  private:
    uint8_t pool[POOL_BLOCKS * BLOCK_SIZE];    // Contiguous memory
    ↪ for the pool
    bool blockUsed[POOL_BLOCKS];               // Boolean array
    ↪ tracking block usage
};

// Global MemoryPool instance for demonstration
MemoryPool memPool;

// Function to simulate dynamic allocation using the ESP32 system
↪ heap
void simulateHeapAllocation() {
  const size_t allocationSize = 50; // Request 50 bytes dynamically
  void *ptr = malloc(allocationSize);
  if (ptr) {
    Serial.print("Heap allocation of ");
    Serial.print(allocationSize);
    Serial.println(" bytes succeeded.");
    // Simulate using the allocated memory
    memset(ptr, 0, allocationSize);
    // Print current free heap size using ESP32 built-in function
    Serial.print("Free heap after allocation: ");
    Serial.println(ESP.getFreeHeap());
    // Free the allocated memory to avoid leakage
    free(ptr);
    Serial.print("Heap memory freed. Free heap: ");
    Serial.println(ESP.getFreeHeap());
  } else {
    Serial.println("Heap allocation failed!");
  }
}

// Function to profile memory usage: calculates percentage of used
↪ heap given an assumed total
void profileMemoryUsage() {
  unsigned int freeHeap = ESP.getFreeHeap();
  // For demonstration, assume a nominal total heap size (this value
  ↪ depends on hardware/configuration)
  unsigned int totalHeap = 240000; // example total heap size in
  ↪ bytes for the ESP32
  float usedHeapPercentage = ((totalHeap - freeHeap) /
  ↪ (float)totalHeap) * 100.0;
  Serial.print("Total free heap: ");
  Serial.print(freeHeap);
  Serial.println(" bytes.");
  Serial.print("Heap usage: ");
  Serial.print(usedHeapPercentage, 2);
  Serial.println("% of total heap.");
}

// The setup() function demonstrates memory allocation,
↪ deallocation, and diagnostic profiling
```

103

```
void setup() {
  Serial.begin(115200);
  delay(2000); // Give time for Serial monitor connection
  Serial.println("ESP32 Memory Management and Optimization Demo");

  // Display initial heap usage and profile
  profileMemoryUsage();

  Serial.println("Demonstrating MemoryPool Allocation:");
  memPool.printPoolStatus();

  // Allocate three blocks from the MemoryPool using first-fit
  ↪  algorithm
  void *block1 = memPool.allocate();
  void *block2 = memPool.allocate();
  void *block3 = memPool.allocate();
  memPool.printPoolStatus();

  // Simulate writing data into allocated blocks (mimicking usage of
  ↪  local variables handled on the stack)
  if (block1) memset(block1, 1, MemoryPool::BLOCK_SIZE);
  if (block2) memset(block2, 2, MemoryPool::BLOCK_SIZE);
  if (block3) memset(block3, 3, MemoryPool::BLOCK_SIZE);

  // Free a block to simulate deallocation and mitigate
  ↪  fragmentation
  memPool.free(block2);
  memPool.printPoolStatus();

  // Demonstrate dynamic heap allocation (complementary to static
  ↪  pool management)
  simulateHeapAllocation();

  // Final memory profile after operations
  profileMemoryUsage();
}

// The loop() function periodically stresses the memory pool and
↪  profiles heap usage,
// showcasing non-blocking operations and callback-based scheduling
↪  using millis().
void loop() {
  static unsigned long lastMillis = 0;
  if (millis() - lastMillis > 5000) { // Every 5 seconds
    lastMillis = millis();
    Serial.println("Loop iteration: Allocating and freeing from
    ↪  MemoryPool");

    // Allocate a block and simulate a brief task then free it
    void *tempBlock = memPool.allocate();
    if (tempBlock != NULL) {
      // Simulate processing delay
      delay(100);
```

```
        memPool.free(tempBlock);
    }
    memPool.printPoolStatus();

    // Re-profile the system heap to detect potential issues with
    ↪  fragmentation
    profileMemoryUsage();
  }
}
```

Chapter 16

Non-volatile Storage with EEPROM

Fundamentals of EEPROM Technology

Electrically Erasable Programmable Read-Only Memory (EEPROM) constitutes a class of non-volatile storage that preserves data in the absence of a continuous power supply. This storage medium operates on the principle of electron tunneling through insulating barriers within floating-gate transistors, thereby allowing selective and reversible alterations of stored charge. The underlying physical processes afford an inherent persistence that is indispensable for retaining critical configuration parameters and system states. Notably, the operational lifecycle of EEPROM cells is typically bounded by approximately 10^5 to 10^6 write cycles, a limitation that imposes constraints on the frequency and method of write operations in embedded applications.

EEPROM Architecture and Electrical Characteristics

The architectural organization of EEPROM is characterized by a byte-addressable structure, often partitioned into discrete pages to facilitate both granular access and block-level management. Each page aggregates a sequence of cells designed to optimize both read and write processes under the constraints of physical and electrical parameters. The programming of EEPROM involves the application of specific voltage levels to induce controlled electron tunneling, while the erasure process similarly requires the careful application of reverse biases. These electrical characteristics dictate not only the speed and energy consumption of memory operations but also the reliability and predictability of data retention. Detailed analysis of these parameters is critical when deploying EEPROM in environments where stringent timing and energy constraints are present.

Persistent Data Storage in IoT Applications

In Internet of Things (IoT) systems, the capacity to store data persistently across power cycles or unexpected interruptions is imperative. EEPROM provides a reliable medium for the retention of configuration settings, calibration data, and transient state information that must survive reboots or power losses. The integration of EEPROM into IoT devices ensures that essential operational parameters are maintained, thereby supporting autonomous network re-establishment and system continuity. By leveraging the intrinsic non-volatility of EEPROM, IoT architectures can uphold robust data integrity while managing the limited available storage space in a manner that is both efficient and resilient.

Best Practices for EEPROM Read/Write Operations via Arduino

The execution of read and write operations on EEPROM within the Arduino ecosystem demands a disciplined approach to safeguard against premature cell degradation and to maintain data integrity. Optimal usage dictates that write operations should be minimized, with writes occurring primarily when significant and persistent alterations in data are detected. This strategy serves to mitigate the impact of the inherent endurance limitations, as excessive or gratuitous write operations risk depleting the cell lifetime. Furthermore, the synchronization of write procedures through batched or staggered operations is recommended to distribute wear evenly across the memory array. Rigorous attention to timing constraints, alongside the implementation of auxiliary integrity checks—such as the incorporation of checksum validations—can substantially enhance reliability. These best practices collectively ensure that EEPROM is leveraged effectively for persistent data storage without compromising system performance, thereby aligning with the operational rigors demanded by IoT applications.

ESP32 For IoT With Arduino Code Snippet

```
#include <EEPROM.h>

// Define the EEPROM size for emulation (adjustable based on ESP32
↪  requirements)
#define EEPROM_SIZE 512
#define CONFIG_START_ADDR 0

// Structure to store non-volatile configuration data
struct IoTConfig {
  int deviceID;          // Unique device identifier
  float threshold;       // Sensor threshold value
  uint8_t mode;          // Operation mode: 0 for standby, 1 for
  ↪  active, etc.
  uint16_t checksum;     // Checksum for data integrity verification
};

// Global configuration instance
IoTConfig config;

// ------------------------------------------------------------
// Function: calculateChecksum
// Description: Calculates the checksum by summing all bytes of the
↪  structure,
// excluding the checksum field itself.
// Equation (in conceptual terms):
//   checksum =  (data[i])
//   where i runs from 0 to (sizeof(IoTConfig) - sizeof(checksum) -
↪  1)
// ------------------------------------------------------------
uint16_t calculateChecksum(const IoTConfig &cfg) {
  const uint8_t *data = (const uint8_t *)&cfg;
  uint16_t sum = 0;
  for (size_t i = 0; i < sizeof(IoTConfig) - sizeof(cfg.checksum);
  ↪  i++) {
    sum += data[i];
  }
  return sum;
}

// ------------------------------------------------------------
```

```
// Function: writeConfigToEEPROM
// Description: Writes the configuration data structure to EEPROM
↪   and commits it.
// -----------------------------------------------------------
void writeConfigToEEPROM(const IoTConfig &cfg) {
  EEPROM.put(CONFIG_START_ADDR, cfg);
  EEPROM.commit();
}


// -----------------------------------------------------------
// Function: readConfigFromEEPROM
// Description: Reads the configuration from EEPROM, verifies the
↪   checksum,
// and returns true if valid, false otherwise.
// -----------------------------------------------------------
bool readConfigFromEEPROM(IoTConfig &cfg) {
  EEPROM.get(CONFIG_START_ADDR, cfg);
  uint16_t storedChecksum = cfg.checksum;
  uint16_t calculatedChecksum = calculateChecksum(cfg);
  if (storedChecksum != calculatedChecksum) {
    return false; // Data integrity check failed
  }
  return true;
}

void setup() {
  Serial.begin(115200);

  // Initialize EEPROM emulation
  if (!EEPROM.begin(EEPROM_SIZE)) {
    Serial.println("EEPROM initialization failed!");
    while (true); // Halt execution if EEPROM cannot be initialized
  }

  // Try to load configuration from EEPROM
  if (!readConfigFromEEPROM(config)) {
    // In case of invalid data or first-time run, initialize default
    ↪   settings
    Serial.println("EEPROM data invalid or uninitialized. Loading
    ↪   default configuration...");
    config.deviceID = 12345;
    config.threshold = 25.5;
    config.mode = 1; // Active mode

    // Calculate checksum for the new configuration based on the
    ↪   algorithm
    config.checksum = calculateChecksum(config);

    // Write the default configuration back to EEPROM
    writeConfigToEEPROM(config);
  } else {
    Serial.println("Valid configuration loaded from EEPROM:");
  }
```

```
  // Display the current configuration parameters
  Serial.print("Device ID: ");
  Serial.println(config.deviceID);
  Serial.print("Threshold: ");
  Serial.println(config.threshold);
  Serial.print("Mode: ");
  Serial.println(config.mode);
}

void loop() {
  // Example update: periodically modify the threshold value to
  ↪  simulate sensor change
  static unsigned long previousMillis = 0;
  const unsigned long updateInterval = 10000; // Update every 10
  ↪  seconds

  if (millis() - previousMillis >= updateInterval) {
    previousMillis = millis();

    // Increment threshold by a small amount to mimic sensor reading
    ↪  change
    config.threshold += 0.1;

    // Recalculate checksum for the updated configuration
    config.checksum = calculateChecksum(config);

    // Write the updated configuration to EEPROM using best
    ↪  practices
    writeConfigToEEPROM(config);

    Serial.println("Configuration updated and written to EEPROM:");
    Serial.print("New Threshold: ");
    Serial.println(config.threshold);
  }
}
```

Chapter 17

Data Formats and Conversion Techniques

Binary Data Representation

In digital systems, data is fundamentally encoded using the binary numeral system. This system represents all information as sequences of binary digits, where each digit, or bit, assumes a value of 0 or 1. The simplicity of the binary system is instrumental in enabling direct manipulation by electronic circuits. In these environments, the numerical value encoded by a string of bits of length n is given by

$$N = \sum_{i=0}^{n-1} b_i \cdot 2^i,$$

where b_i denotes the bit at position i. The efficiency of binary representation is critical in embedded systems, such as those based on the ESP32 architecture, where optimal data storage and rapid logical operations are paramount.

ASCII Encoding

The American Standard Code for Information Interchange (ASCII) is a widely adopted encoding standard that maps textual characters to numerical values. Typically, each character is represented by a 7-bit or 8-bit binary number, which facilitates the consistent exchange of information between disparate systems. The conversion from human-readable text to binary form via ASCII encoding ensures standardized data interpretation, which is essential in environments where communication protocols and data logging require unambiguous textual representation. This encoding scheme supports a broad range of applications in ESP32 platforms, particularly in scenarios involving serial communications and networked data exchanges where clarity and uniformity are essential.

Hexadecimal Notation

Hexadecimal notation provides a compact and convenient alternative for representing large binary values. As a base-16 numeral system, it employs a digit set comprising the symbols 0 through 9 and the letters A through F, where A represents 10, and F represents 15. Binary data can be efficiently grouped into sets of four bits, known as nibbles, with each nibble directly corresponding to a single hexadecimal digit. This grouping is mathematically represented by the conversion of a four-bit binary group $b_3 b_2 b_1 b_0$ into a hexadecimal digit computed as

$$b_3 \times 8 + b_2 \times 4 + b_1 \times 2 + b_0.$$

The succinct representation provided by hexadecimal notation is invaluable in contexts such as memory addressing and debugging, where a concise yet precise portrayal of binary data is demanded.

Conversion Techniques Between Data Formats

Conversion between binary, ASCII, and hexadecimal formats is a fundamental requirement in data handling and processing within embedded systems. The transformation process entails decomposing binary sequences into appropriate groupings that align with the target format. For instance, conversion from binary to ASCII involves partitioning a binary stream into 8-bit segments, with each segment mapped to its corresponding character in the ASCII table. Similarly, converting binary data into hexadecimal format is achieved by dividing the binary string into fixed four-bit groups, each of which is then translated into a single hexadecimal digit as described previously. The mathematical framework governing these conversions relies on base-change formulas and modular arithmetic, ensuring that numerical integrity is maintained during format transformation. These conversion techniques are not only fundamental from a theoretical standpoint but are also critical for precise data manipulation, especially in systems where memory efficiency and processing speed are of utmost importance.

Data Handling Context in ESP32 Platforms

Within the operational context of the ESP32, the interplay between different data formats is pivotal for efficient system performance. The microcontroller's architecture is designed to facilitate rapid binary processing, while various peripherals and communication protocols necessitate the interpretation and conversion of data into human-readable or compact forms. ASCII encoding is essential for textual communication and debugging outputs, whereas hexadecimal notation is frequently utilized for memory operations and sensor data analysis. The conversion mechanisms, which enable seamless transitions between these formats, underpin the reliability of data storage, retrieval, and transmission. Such robust conversion techniques are critical in ensuring that the ESP32 manages data with high fidelity, particularly under constraints imposed by limited computational resources and real-time operational requirements.

ESP32 For IoT With Arduino Code Snippet

```
#include <Arduino.h>

// Function to convert a binary string to a decimal number using the
↪  formula:
// N = sum_{i=0}^{n-1} b_i * 2^i, where b_i is the bit at position i
↪  (LSB at index 0).
long binaryToDecimal(String binStr) {
  long decimal = 0;
  int len = binStr.length();
  for (int i = 0; i < len; i++) {
    // Process bits from right (LSB) to left (MSB)
    char bit = binStr.charAt(len - 1 - i);
    if (bit == '1') {
```

```
      decimal += (1 << i); // (1 << i) computes 2^i
    }
  }
  return decimal;
}


// Function to convert a binary string into its corresponding ASCII
↪  text.
// Assumes the input binary string length is a multiple of 8.
String binaryToASCII(String binStr) {
  String asciiStr = "";
  int len = binStr.length();
  for (int i = 0; i < len; i += 8) {
    // Extract each 8-bit chunk representing a character.
    String byteStr = binStr.substring(i, i + 8);
    char c = (char) binaryToDecimal(byteStr);
    asciiStr += c;
  }
  return asciiStr;
}


// Function to convert a binary string into its equivalent
↪  hexadecimal notation.
// Assumes the binary string length is a multiple of 4.
String binaryToHex(String binStr) {
  String hexStr = "";
  int len = binStr.length();
  for (int i = 0; i < len; i += 4) {
    // Extract each 4-bit group, known as a nibble.
    String nibble = binStr.substring(i, i + 4);
    int value = binaryToDecimal(nibble);
    // Map the value to its corresponding hexadecimal digit.
    if (value < 10) {
      hexStr += char(value + '0');
    } else {
      hexStr += char(value - 10 + 'A');
    }
  }
  return hexStr;
}

void setup() {
  Serial.begin(115200);
  // Wait for the serial connection to establish (useful for native
  ↪  USB boards).
  while (!Serial) { ; }
  delay(2000);

  Serial.println("ESP32 Data Formats and Conversion Techniques
  ↪  Demo");

  // Example 1: Binary to Decimal Conversion using the equation
  // N = sum_{i=0}^{n-1} b_i * 2^i.
```

114

```
String binaryValue = "1010"; // Binary representation; expected
↪   decimal is 10.
long decimalResult = binaryToDecimal(binaryValue);
Serial.print("Binary '");
Serial.print(binaryValue);
Serial.print("' to Decimal: ");
Serial.println(decimalResult);

// Example 2: Binary to ASCII Conversion.
// The binary string represents the characters of "Hello":
// "01001000" -> H, "01100101" -> e, "01101100" -> l, "01101100"
↪   -> l, "01101111" -> o.
String binaryMessage = "0100100001100101011011000110110001101111";
String asciiMessage = binaryToASCII(binaryMessage);
Serial.print("Binary to ASCII: ");
Serial.println(asciiMessage);

// Example 3: Binary to Hexadecimal Conversion.
// Convert the same binary message into hexadecimal format for a
↪   concise view.
String hexMessage = binaryToHex(binaryMessage);
Serial.print("Binary to Hexadecimal: ");
Serial.println(hexMessage);
}

void loop() {
  // No repetitive tasks in this demonstration example.
}
```

Chapter 18

IoT Communication Protocols Overview

Fundamental Networking Architectures and Integration with the ESP32

The ESP32 microcontroller is endowed with a robust networking architecture that supports multiple protocol layers. At the very foundation, the integration of the Internet Protocol (IP) suite with the ESP32 facilitates the handling of both connection-oriented and connectionless communication paradigms. The embedded TCP/IP stack, which adheres to the layered model, is responsible for routing, addressing, and error correction. This architecture enables the ESP32 to interact seamlessly with various network topologies and services, while maintaining the efficiency demanded by low-power, embedded systems. The inherent support for both IPv4 and IPv6 standards further expands the versatility and future-proofing of the device in increasingly interconnected environments.

TCP/IP and Wi-Fi Communication

Wi-Fi stands as the predominant wireless communication medium for the ESP32, supplying efficient and high-throughput connectivity. The Wi-Fi module is built upon the TCP/IP suite, which encapsulates data within reliable, connection-oriented sessions. The transmission control protocol (TCP) reliably manages data segmentation, transmission, acknowledgment, and error recovery so as to ensure complete and accurate delivery of packets. In contrast, the user datagram protocol (UDP) offers a connectionless alternative that minimizes overhead and latency by foregoing error correction and retransmission. The selection of UDP or TCP depends on the application requirements, with TCP being advantageous for data integrity and UDP for real-time or latency-sensitive tasks. The ESP32 architecture leverages hardware accelerations and optimized driver implementations, allowing it to dynamically adapt to fluctuating network conditions and efficiently manage Wi-Fi communications.

Bluetooth and Bluetooth Low Energy (BLE)

The dual-mode capabilities of the ESP32 extend beyond Wi-Fi, incorporating both Bluetooth Classic and Bluetooth Low Energy (BLE) protocols. Bluetooth Classic is oriented toward continuous streaming and relatively high-bandwidth applications, whereas BLE is designed for intermittent, low-power communications. BLE achieves energy efficiency by employing short burst transmissions and a simplified protocol stack, which renders it particularly suited to sensor networks and low-data-rate applications. Both protocols operate under the Bluetooth standard but differ significantly in their operational profiles, message framing, and state management. The ESP32's native support for BLE enables powerful applications involving proximity detection, peer-to-peer data exchange, and real-time monitoring with minimal energy consumption.

MQTT: Lightweight Publish/Subscribe Messaging

The Message Queuing Telemetry Transport (MQTT) protocol is characterized by its lightweight design and suitability for constrained environments. As a publish/subscribe messaging protocol, MQTT decouples message producers from consumers, thereby facilitating scalable and asynchronous communication. The protocol operates over TCP/IP, ensuring reliable delivery through a system of quality of service (QoS) levels. In IoT ecosystems, MQTT is valued for its minimal overhead, small code footprint, and straightforward implementation. Its ability to manage network disruptions, stateful session persistence, and low bandwidth consumption renders it exceptionally well-suited for applications involving numerous low-power sensors and actuators. The ESP32's processing capabilities complement MQTT's design, making it a prototypical choice for real-time telemetry and distributed control systems.

HTTP and RESTful Interfaces

The Hypertext Transfer Protocol (HTTP) remains one of the most ubiquitous communication protocols across networked systems, largely due to its foundational role in the World Wide Web. When paired with Representational State Transfer (REST) architectural principles, HTTP facilitates stateless and scalable interactions between distributed components. The protocol relies on standardized request and response messages that contain headers and a message body, enabling a uniform interface for resource manipulation. In the context of the ESP32, HTTP allows the microcontroller to serve as both a client and a server, supporting applications that range from remote monitoring to providing web-based control interfaces. The inherent compatibility with ubiquitous security mechanisms such as TLS further enhances HTTP's applicability in environments where data integrity and confidentiality are paramount.

CoAP for Constrained Devices

The Constrained Application Protocol (CoAP) is specifically designed for IoT systems with stringent power, bandwidth, and processing limitations. CoAP mirrors the request/response paradigm of HTTP, yet it operates over the User Datagram Protocol (UDP) to reduce transport layer overhead and latency. The protocol facilitates asynchronous message exchanges and includes built-in mechanisms for reliability despite its connectionless foundation. CoAP's design emphasizes resource discovery and efficient multicast support, features that align with the dynamic nature of wireless sensor networks. The ESP32, with its optimizations for real-time operation, can leverage CoAP to implement smart environmental sensing and control solutions that require minimal resource expenditure while maintaining responsive communication channels.

WebSocket: Enabling Real-Time Bidirectional Communication

WebSocket technology provides a persistent, full-duplex communication channel over a single TCP/IP connection. Unlike traditional HTTP interactions, WebSocket facilitates real-time, bidirectional data exchange without the overhead associated with HTTP request/response cycles. This protocol is particularly advantageous for scenarios that demand continuous streaming of data or rapid state updates, as it reduces latency and minimizes connection renegotiation. The ESP32 can capitalize on WebSocket to create responsive and interactive applications in which real-time feedback is crucial. The persistent nature of WebSocket connections, combined with its inherent support for message framing and control, ensures efficient utilization of resources while engaging in complex interactive sessions.

Comparative Considerations for ESP32 Platform Suitability

The suitability of various communication protocols for deployment on the ESP32 platform is determined by a combination of network performance, energy efficiency, and application-specific requirements. The TCP/IP and Wi-Fi protocols offer robust connectivity and high data throughput, yet they incur greater computational and power costs when compared to BLE or CoAP. Bluetooth and BLE serve specialized roles that optimize low-power and near-field communications, although their application scope is constrained by lower bandwidth capacities. MQTT's publish/subscribe paradigm streamlines the management of distributed sensor networks, particularly in contexts where low latency and minimal overhead are essential. Conversely, the HTTP and RESTful interfaces provide a standardized mechanism for accessing web services and controlling remote resources, albeit with higher protocol overhead versus more specialized alternatives. CoAP presents an optimized solution for extremely constrained devices, trading off some reliability in favor of reduced protocol overhead and efficient support for multicast. Lastly, WebSocket caters to applications necessitating real-time, sustained connections, effectively bridging the gap between traditional HTTP communications and the demands of interactive, dynamic systems. Each protocol embodies a set of trade-offs that must be judiciously balanced against the operational parameters and constraints inherent to the ESP32's deployment environment.

ESP32 For IoT With Arduino Code Snippet

```
#include <WiFi.h>
#include <PubSubClient.h>
#include <HTTPClient.h>
#include <ArduinoWebsockets.h>
#include <BLEDevice.h>
#include <BLEServer.h>
#include <WiFiUdp.h>

// Replace with your network credentials
const char* ssid       = "your_ssid";
const char* password   = "your_password";

// MQTT broker details
const char* mqtt_server = "broker.hivemq.com";
const int   mqtt_port   = 1883;

// HTTP endpoint for GET requests
String http_url = "http://example.com/api/data";

// WebSocket server URL
const char* websocket_server = "ws://echo.websocket.org";

// Instantiate WiFi and MQTT clients
WiFiClient espClient;
PubSubClient mqttClient(espClient);

// Instantiate UDP for sending datagrams
WiFiUDP udp;

// BLE definitions
#define SERVICE_UUID        "4fafc201-1fb5-459e-8fcc-c5c9c331914b"
#define CHARACTERISTIC_UUID "beb5483e-36e1-4688-b7f5-ea07361b26a8"
BLEServer *pServer = NULL;

// Timing variable for periodic HTTP requests
unsigned long previousMillis = 0;
const long httpInterval = 10000; // 10 seconds

// WebSocket client from ArduinoWebsockets library
using namespace websockets;
WebsocketsClient webSocket;
```

120

```
// Function to connect to Wi-Fi
void setupWiFi() {
  Serial.print("Connecting to WiFi");
  WiFi.begin(ssid, password);
  while (WiFi.status() != WL_CONNECTED) {
    delay(500);
    Serial.print(".");
  }
  Serial.println("\nWiFi connected");
  Serial.print("IP Address: ");
  Serial.println(WiFi.localIP());
}

// MQTT callback to process incoming messages
void mqttCallback(char* topic, byte* payload, unsigned int length) {
  Serial.print("MQTT Message arrived [");
  Serial.print(topic);
  Serial.print("] ");
  for (unsigned int i = 0; i < length; i++) {
      Serial.print((char)payload[i]);
  }
  Serial.println();
}

// Ensure the MQTT client remains connected (algorithm for
↪    reconnect)
void reconnectMQTT() {
  while (!mqttClient.connected()) {
    Serial.print("Attempting MQTT connection...");
    if (mqttClient.connect("ESP32Client")) {
      Serial.println(" connected");
      // Subscribe to a topic after successful connection
      mqttClient.subscribe("esp32/topic");
    } else {
      Serial.print(" failed, rc=");
      Serial.print(mqttClient.state());
      Serial.println(" try again in 5 seconds");
      delay(5000);
    }
  }
}

// Set up the BLE server to advertise a simple service and
↪    characteristic
void setupBLE() {
  BLEDevice::init("ESP32-BLE");
  pServer = BLEDevice::createServer();
  BLEService *pService = pServer->createService(SERVICE_UUID);
  BLECharacteristic *pCharacteristic =
  ↪    pService->createCharacteristic(
                                      CHARACTERISTIC_UUID,
```

```cpp
                                        ↪   BLECharacteristic::PROPERTY_READ
                                        ↪   |

                                        ↪   BLECharacteristic::PROPERTY_WRITE
                                      );
  // Set an initial value that can be read by clients
  pCharacteristic->setValue("Hello from ESP32");
  pService->start();

  BLEAdvertising *pAdvertising = BLEDevice::getAdvertising();
  pAdvertising->addServiceUUID(SERVICE_UUID);
  pAdvertising->setScanResponse(true);
  // Recommended settings for better advertising response
  pAdvertising->setMinPreferred(0x06);
  pAdvertising->setMinPreferred(0x12);
  BLEDevice::startAdvertising();

  Serial.println("BLE server started and advertising now.");
}

// Initialize and set up the WebSocket client
void setupWebSocket() {
  webSocket.onMessage([](WebsocketsMessage message) {
    Serial.print("WebSocket Message: ");
    Serial.println(message.data());
  });
  webSocket.begin(websocket_server);
  Serial.println("WebSocket client connected.");
}

void setup() {
  Serial.begin(115200);

  // Establish Wi-Fi connection
  setupWiFi();

  // Setup MQTT client with broker settings and callback
  ↪   registration
  mqttClient.setServer(mqtt_server, mqtt_port);
  mqttClient.setCallback(mqttCallback);

  // Start BLE server
  setupBLE();

  // Initialize WebSocket client
  setupWebSocket();
}

void loop() {
  // Maintain MQTT connection
  if (!mqttClient.connected()) {
    reconnectMQTT();
```

```
  }
  mqttClient.loop();

  // Process WebSocket events
  webSocket.poll();

  // UDP communication: send a simple datagram message
  udp.beginPacket("192.168.1.255", 12345); // Broadcast example on
  ↪   port 12345
  udp.print("Hello via UDP");
  udp.endPacket();

  // Periodically perform an HTTP GET request to retrieve data
  unsigned long currentMillis = millis();
  if(currentMillis - previousMillis >= httpInterval) {
    previousMillis = currentMillis;
    HTTPClient http;
    http.begin(http_url);
    int httpCode = http.GET();
    if(httpCode > 0) {
      Serial.printf("HTTP Response code: %d\n", httpCode);
      String payload = http.getString();
      Serial.println("HTTP Response payload: " + payload);
    } else {
      Serial.printf("HTTP GET failed, error: %s\n",
      ↪   http.errorToString(httpCode).c_str());
    }
    http.end();
  }

  // Example: Read an analog sensor value and calculate voltage.
  // Important Equation: voltage = (sensorValue / 4095.0) * 3.3
  int sensorValue = analogRead(34);   // Use ADC1 channel (GPIO34) on
  ↪   ESP32
  float voltage = (sensorValue / 4095.0) * 3.3;
  char sensorMsg[50];
  snprintf(sensorMsg, 50, "Sensor Voltage: %.2f V", voltage);
  // Publish the sensor data to the MQTT topic
  mqttClient.publish("esp32/sensor", sensorMsg);

  delay(1000);
}
```

Chapter 19

Establishing Wi-Fi Connectivity

Architectural Overview of Wi-Fi Connectivity

The *ESP*32 microcontroller incorporates a comprehensive wireless network stack that adheres to the *IEEE* 802.11 standards. This hardware-software integration supports layered functionalities, beginning at the physical and medium access control levels and extending through the encapsulated TCP/IP protocols. The inherent design facilitates precise routing, addressing, and error-control mechanisms necessary for reliable wireless communication. It also supports both IPv4 and IPv6 schemes, which contributes to a versatile operating environment in heterogeneous network infrastructures. The structural organization of the Wi-Fi stack within the *ESP*32 reflects a meticulous balance between computational efficiency and connectivity robustness, making it well suited for a range of embedded IoT applications.

Network Interface Configuration and Parameterization

Configuration of the Wi-Fi interface within the *ESP*32 is predicated upon a detailed parameterization process that integrates both system-wide settings and network-specific credentials. The parameterization involves the careful assignment of the Service Set Identifier ($SSID$), the selection of authentication frameworks such as WPA and $WPA2$, and fine-tuning of radio frequency parameters including channel selection and transmission power settings. These parameters are established through a series of initialization routines that adhere to rigorous protocol specifications. In this context, the configuration process also prioritizes the secure management of network credentials and the implementation of cryptographic measures, ensuring that the association and authentication phases maintain a high level of data integrity and confidentiality.

Dynamic Discovery and Connection Algorithms

The procedural methodology for network discovery on the $ESP32$ involves iterative scanning mechanisms that evaluate the presence and quality of available wireless networks. This iterative process is quantitatively supported by metrics such as the Received Signal Strength Indicator ($RSSI$), measured in dBm, which provides a basis for the selection of the optimal network candidate. The algorithms governing this process incorporate timeout and backoff strategies designed to handle transient network interferences and mitigate connectivity delays. The systematic evaluation of network attributes—including signal quality, security settings, and preconfigured network preferences—ensures that the connection algorithm dynamically adapts to real-time environmental conditions. Such algorithmic structures are implemented within the framework of the device's real-time operating system, thereby maintaining low-latency reconnection and continuous internet access.

Security Considerations in Wi-Fi Configuration

The establishment of a secure wireless connection on the $ESP32$ demands rigorous adherence to protocol-specific authentication and encryption practices. Security measures are enforced through the integration of protocols such as WPA and $WPA2$, which employ robust cryptographic methodologies during the authentication handshake and key exchange processes. These procedures involve the dynamic assignment and refreshment of session keys, thereby reducing the susceptibility to unauthorized access. Further, the entire association process is underpinned by advanced encryption algorithms that guard against eavesdropping and data tampering. The interplay between secure key management and the underlying connection framework is critical in maintaining the integrity of the wireless link, particularly in environments where adversarial threats may be present.

Robustness and Optimization in Wi-Fi Connection Management

Ensuring seamless internet access necessitates the implementation of robustness and optimization strategies within the Wi-Fi connection management routines of the $ESP32$. The system continuously monitors connection quality and implements resilience techniques—such as dynamic adjustment of beacon intervals, modulation schemes, and re-association protocols—to compensate for environmental fluctuations. An adaptive management scheme is employed to detect and recover from transient disconnections, thereby minimizing the impact of interference and signal degradation. The optimization processes are integrated within the real-time operational framework of the microcontroller, ensuring that low-power consumption is balanced with performance efficiency. This combination of proactive monitoring and algorithmic adaptability forms the basis for the resilient and efficient management of wireless connectivity in diverse operational scenarios.

ESP32 For IoT With Arduino Code Snippet

```
#include <WiFi.h>

// Structure for storing known WiFi network credentials
struct WiFiNetwork {
  String ssid;
  String password;
};

// Array of known networks
WiFiNetwork knownNetworks[] = {
  {"MyHomeWiFi", "HomePassword"},
```

```
  {"OfficeWiFi", "OfficePassword"}
};
const int knownNetworkCount = sizeof(knownNetworks) /
↪  sizeof(knownNetworks[0]);

// Global variables to store the selected network credentials after
↪  scanning
String globalSSID = "";
String globalPassword = "";

/*
  Function: getWiFiQuality
  Description:
    Calculates the WiFi signal quality percentage based on the RSSI
    ↪  (in dBm).
    Equation:
      If RSSI <= -100 dBm, then quality = 0%
      If RSSI >= -50 dBm, then quality = 100%
      Otherwise, quality = 2 * (RSSI + 100)
*/
int getWiFiQuality(int rssi) {
  if (rssi <= -100) return 0;
  else if (rssi >= -50) return 100;
  else return 2 * (rssi + 100);
}

/*
  Function: scanAndSelectNetwork
  Description:
    Scans available WiFi networks, evaluates them using the
    ↪  RSSI-based quality formula,
    and selects the best available known network.
    This implements a dynamic discovery algorithm with iterative
    ↪  scanning and evaluation.
*/
void scanAndSelectNetwork() {
  Serial.println("Scanning for WiFi networks...");
  delay(1000);
  int n = WiFi.scanNetworks();

  if (n == 0) {
    Serial.println("No networks found.");
    return;
  }

  int bestQuality = -1;
  String bestSSID = "";
  String bestPassword = "";

  // Iterate over scanned networks to evaluate quality and check
  ↪  against known networks
  for (int i = 0; i < n; i++) {
    String currentSSID = WiFi.SSID(i);
```

127

```
    int rssi = WiFi.RSSI(i);
    int quality = getWiFiQuality(rssi);

    Serial.print("Found: ");
    Serial.print(currentSSID);
    Serial.print(" | RSSI: ");
    Serial.print(rssi);
    Serial.print(" dBm | Quality: ");
    Serial.print(quality);
    Serial.println("%");

    // Compare scanned network with our list of known networks
    for (int j = 0; j < knownNetworkCount; j++) {
      if (currentSSID == knownNetworks[j].ssid) {
        if (quality > bestQuality) {
          bestQuality = quality;
          bestSSID = currentSSID;
          bestPassword = knownNetworks[j].password;
        }
      }
    }
  }

  if (bestSSID != "") {
    Serial.print("Selected network: ");
    Serial.println(bestSSID);
    globalSSID = bestSSID;
    globalPassword = bestPassword;
  } else {
    Serial.println("No known networks found.");
  }
}

/*
  Function: connectToWiFi
  Description:
    Attempts to connect to the specified WiFi network using an
    ↪ exponential backoff algorithm.
    The method retries connection attempts by doubling the delay
    ↪ after each failure until a
    maximum number of retries is reached.
*/
void connectToWiFi(String ssid, String password) {
  int retryCount = 0;
  const int maxRetries = 5;
  int delayTime = 1000; // Initial delay of 1 second

  Serial.print("Attempting to connect to WiFi: ");
  Serial.println(ssid);

  WiFi.mode(WIFI_STA);
  WiFi.begin(ssid.c_str(), password.c_str());
```

128

```
  while (WiFi.status() != WL_CONNECTED && retryCount < maxRetries) {
    Serial.print("Connecting");
    unsigned long startAttemptTime = millis();
    // Wait up to 10 seconds for connection
    while (WiFi.status() != WL_CONNECTED && millis() -
    ↪  startAttemptTime < 10000) {
      Serial.print(".");
      delay(500);
    }

    if (WiFi.status() == WL_CONNECTED)
      break;
    else {
      Serial.println();
      Serial.println("Connection attempt failed. Retrying...");
      retryCount++;
      delay(delayTime);
      delayTime *= 2; // Exponential backoff: double the delay after
      ↪  each attempt
      WiFi.disconnect();
      WiFi.begin(ssid.c_str(), password.c_str());
    }
  }

  if (WiFi.status() == WL_CONNECTED) {
    Serial.println();
    Serial.println("WiFi connected successfully!");
    Serial.print("IP Address: ");
    Serial.println(WiFi.localIP());
  } else {
    Serial.println();
    Serial.println("Failed to connect after multiple attempts.");
  }
}

void setup() {
  Serial.begin(115200);
  delay(1000);

  // Perform dynamic network discovery and select the best known
  ↪  network
  scanAndSelectNetwork();

  // If a known network has been found, attempt to connect using
  ↪  secure and
  // parameterized configuration methods.
  if (globalSSID != "") {
    connectToWiFi(globalSSID, globalPassword);
  }
}

void loop() {
```

```cpp
  // Monitor the WiFi connection and attempt reconnection if the
  ↪  link is lost.
  // This demonstrates robust connection management and
  ↪  optimization.
  if (WiFi.status() != WL_CONNECTED && globalSSID != "") {
    Serial.println("WiFi disconnected. Attempting reconnection...");
    connectToWiFi(globalSSID, globalPassword);
  }

  // Main application logic can be added here.
  // For demonstration, print the current WiFi status every 30
  ↪  seconds.
  Serial.print("Current WiFi status: ");
  Serial.println(WiFi.status() == WL_CONNECTED ? "Connected" :
  ↪  "Disconnected");

  delay(30000);
}
```

Chapter 20

Managing Wi-Fi Networks Programmatically

Scanning Mechanisms and Signal Analysis

A comprehensive examination of wireless network scanning algorithms reveals an intricate process by which the device interrogates the ambient radio frequency environment. In this paradigm, iterative scanning routines catalog available networks, quantifying their respective signal strengths through the measurement of the Received Signal Strength Indicator ($RSSI$), expressed in decibels relative to one milliwatt (dBm). These measured values are converted into a normalized quality metric, such as via the transformation

$$Q = \max\big(0, \min(100, 2(r_{ssi} + 100))\big)$$

which serves to map the raw $RSSI$ values into a standardized scale conducive to comparative analysis. Furthermore, the scanning process concurrently evaluates the channel distribution pursuant to the $IEEE$ 802.11 standard, thereby mitigating the effects of inter-channel interference. The synthesis of these metrics provides a robust framework for the quantitative assessment of network viability in complex and dynamic wireless environments.

Optimal Connection Selection Strategies

The determination of an optimal wireless connection mandates the formulation of a multi-criteria decision model that incorporates both quantitative and qualitative parameters intrinsic to each network. The evaluation process integrates signal quality metrics, security protocol compliance (including adherence to WPA and $WPA2$ standards), and factors indicative of network stability and congestion. One may formalize the selection strategy through an aggregated cost function of the form

$$C = w_1 Q + w_2 S + w_3 R,$$

where Q represents the normalized signal quality, S signifies a metric corresponding to the strength of implemented security protocols, R encapsulates reliability and stability measures, and w_1, w_2, and w_3 are weights determined by empirical assessments. This formalized approach supports the systematic ranking of available networks, thereby facilitating programmatic selection predicated on the minimization (or maximization, as contextually defined) of the cost function. The decision algorithm, therefore, operates at the intersection of quantitative analysis and deterministic selection, ensuring an optimal balance between connectivity quality and security demands.

Dynamic Parameter Management

Subsequent to network selection, the dynamic management of connection parameters emerges as a critical component in sustaining reliable wireless communication. This process involves real-time adjustments to operational parameters, including but not limited to transmission power, channel selection, and frequency of re-association intervals. The adaptive nature of this management strategy is underpinned by continual environmental monitoring and the application of feedback control systems. Re-calibration routines are often implemented using an exponential back-off mechanism, mathematically modeled as

$$T(n) = T_0 \cdot 2^n,$$

where T_0 denotes the initial delay and n the number of successive retries. The underlying protocols, established within the framework of the *IEEE* 802.11 specification, facilitate negotiations between access point and client by dynamically updating parameters to counteract interference and signal degradation. As such, these dynamic management procedures serve as an essential mechanism for maintaining connection integrity under transient and evolving network conditions, thereby ensuring consistent performance across a wide spectrum of deployment scenarios.

ESP32 For IoT With Arduino Code Snippet

```
#include <WiFi.h>

// Wi-Fi connection parameters for demonstration (dummy).
// Note: Replace "your_password" with the correct password if
↪ connecting to a secured network.
const char* password = "your_password";

// Cost function weights
const double w1 = 0.5; // Weight for normalized signal quality (Q)
const double w2 = 0.3; // Weight for security metric (S)
const double w3 = 0.2; // Weight for reliability metric (R)

// Structure to hold information for each scanned network
struct NetworkInfo {
  String ssid;
  int32_t rssi;
  uint8_t encryptionType;
  int channel;
  int quality;      // Normalized Q computed from RSSI using: Q =
  ↪ max(0, min(100, 2*(RSSI + 100)))
  int security;     // Security metric S (100 for secure, 0 for open)
  int reliability;  // Reliability metric R based on channel
  ↪ congestion
  double score;     // Aggregated score = w1*Q + w2*S + w3*R
};

#define MAX_NETWORKS 50
NetworkInfo networksArray[MAX_NETWORKS];
int networkCount = 0;

// Array to count number of networks per channel (channels 1 to 14)
int channelCount[15] = {0};

// Exponential backoff parameters for reconnection attempts
const unsigned long T0 = 500; // Initial delay in milliseconds
const int maxRetries = 5;
```

```
void setup() {
  Serial.begin(115200);
  delay(1000);
  Serial.println("Starting Wi-Fi Scan...");

  // Configure Wi-Fi in station mode and disconnect if already
  ↪  connected
  WiFi.mode(WIFI_STA);
  WiFi.disconnect();
  delay(100);

  // Perform the network scan
  networkCount = WiFi.scanNetworks();
  Serial.print("Number of networks found: ");
  Serial.println(networkCount);

  if(networkCount <= 0 || networkCount > MAX_NETWORKS) {
    Serial.println("No networks found or too many networks -
    ↪  scanning aborted.");
    return;
  }

  // Populate networksArray with scan data and compute normalized
  ↪  metrics
  for (int i = 0; i < networkCount; i++) {
    networksArray[i].ssid = WiFi.SSID(i);
    networksArray[i].rssi = WiFi.RSSI(i);
    networksArray[i].encryptionType = WiFi.encryptionType(i);
    networksArray[i].channel = WiFi.channel(i);

    // Normalize signal quality using:
    // Q = max(0, min(100, 2*(RSSI + 100)))
    int calcQuality = 2 * (networksArray[i].rssi + 100);
    if(calcQuality < 0) calcQuality = 0;
    if(calcQuality > 100) calcQuality = 100;
    networksArray[i].quality = calcQuality;

    // Set security metric S: 0 for open networks, 100 for secure
    ↪  networks
    if (networksArray[i].encryptionType == WIFI_AUTH_OPEN)
      networksArray[i].security = 0;
    else
      networksArray[i].security = 100;

    // Count the number of networks on each channel (channels 1
    ↪  through 14)
    int ch = networksArray[i].channel;
    if(ch >= 1 && ch < 15)
      channelCount[ch]++;
  }

  // Compute reliability metric R for each network based on channel
  ↪  congestion.
```

134

```
// For example: R = max(0, min(100, 100 - (channelCount[channel] -
↪  1) * 10))
for (int i = 0; i < networkCount; i++) {
  int ch = networksArray[i].channel;
  int interference = (channelCount[ch] - 1) * 10;
  int calcReliability = 100 - interference;
  if(calcReliability < 0) calcReliability = 0;
  if(calcReliability > 100) calcReliability = 100;
  networksArray[i].reliability = calcReliability;

  // Compute the aggregated decision metric (score) for network
  ↪  selection:
  // C = w1*Q + w2*S + w3*R
  networksArray[i].score = w1 * networksArray[i].quality +
                           w2 * networksArray[i].security +
                           w3 * networksArray[i].reliability;
}

// Display the scanned networks along with computed metrics
Serial.println("Scanned Networks with Computed Metrics:");
for (int i = 0; i < networkCount; i++) {
  Serial.print(i);
  Serial.print(": SSID=");
  Serial.print(networksArray[i].ssid);
  Serial.print(", RSSI=");
  Serial.print(networksArray[i].rssi);
  Serial.print(" dBm, Quality=");
  Serial.print(networksArray[i].quality);
  Serial.print(", Security=");
  Serial.print(networksArray[i].security);
  Serial.print(", Channel=");
  Serial.print(networksArray[i].channel);
  Serial.print(", Reliability=");
  Serial.print(networksArray[i].reliability);
  Serial.print(", Score=");
  Serial.println(networksArray[i].score);
}

// Select the best network according to the highest aggregated
↪  score
int bestIndex = -1;
double bestScore = -1;
for (int i = 0; i < networkCount; i++) {
  if(networksArray[i].score > bestScore) {
    bestScore = networksArray[i].score;
    bestIndex = i;
  }
}

if(bestIndex == -1) {
  Serial.println("No suitable network found.");
  return;
}
```

```cpp
Serial.println("Best network selected:");
Serial.print("SSID: ");
Serial.println(networksArray[bestIndex].ssid);
Serial.print("Score: ");
Serial.println(networksArray[bestIndex].score);

// Attempt to connect to the selected network with exponential
↪  backoff
bool connected = false;
int retry = 0;
while (!connected && retry < maxRetries) {
  Serial.print("Attempting to connect (Retry ");
  Serial.print(retry);
  Serial.println(")...");

  // Use WiFi.begin() appropriately based on security:
  // Open networks are connected without a password.
  if(networksArray[bestIndex].security == 0)
    WiFi.begin(networksArray[bestIndex].ssid.c_str());
  else
    WiFi.begin(networksArray[bestIndex].ssid.c_str(), password);

  // Allow up to 5 seconds for connection
  unsigned long startTime = millis();
  while (millis() - startTime < 5000) {
    if(WiFi.status() == WL_CONNECTED) {
      connected = true;
      break;
    }
    delay(100);
  }

  if (connected) {
    Serial.println("Connected successfully!");
    Serial.print("IP Address: ");
    Serial.println(WiFi.localIP());
  } else {
    Serial.println("Connection failed.");
    // Dynamic parameter management using an exponential back-off
    ↪  delay:
    // T(n) = T0 * 2^n
    unsigned long backoffDelay = T0 * (1 << retry);
    Serial.print("Waiting for ");
    Serial.print(backoffDelay);
    Serial.println(" ms before retrying.");
    delay(backoffDelay);
    retry++;
  }
}

if (!connected) {
  Serial.println("Failed to connect after maximum retries.");
```

```
  }
}

void loop() {
  // In a real-world application, dynamic adjustments and
  ↪  re-association can be handled here.
  // For demonstration purposes, no periodic tasks are implemented.
}
```

Chapter 21

Creating a Wi-Fi Access Point

Conceptual Foundations and Design Rationale

The operation of an embedded device as a Wi-Fi access point entails configuring the built-in radio transceiver to function autonomously, thereby establishing a localized network environment. In this mode, the device transmits beacon frames that advertise network parameters, including the Service Set Identifier (SSID) and supported data rates, without reliance on an external infrastructure. The intrinsic value of this approach is reflected in the capability to create isolated Internet of Things (IoT) ecosystems wherein communication is confined to proximate devices, thereby reducing network latency and mitigating dependencies on central routers or gateways. The design rationale is reinforced by the need for deterministic performance and predictable wireless channel behavior, given that the access point operates using a prescribed channel from the 2.4 GHz or 5 GHz spectrum according to the prevailing 802.11 standards.

System Architecture and AP Configuration

In the configuration of the ESP32 as a Wi-Fi access point, the system architecture must be systematically arranged to support concurrent client connections and robust management of network resources. The ESP32 integrates a dual-mode radio, which is adept at toggling between station and access point functionalities. The access point mode is activated by reconfiguring the Wi-Fi subsystem to adopt an autonomous broadcast mechanism. Subsequent to mode selection, parameters such as the SSID, beacon interval, and transmission power are defined. The beacon interval, denoted as T_b, is a critical parameter that influences the periodicity of network identification messages. A lower T_b enhances network discovery at the expense of increased channel occupancy, while a higher T_b may impair the rapid detection of network availability. Moreover, the selection of the operating channel is optimized by considering both regulatory constraints and the current electromagnetic spectrum occupancy. The resulting architecture thereby facilitates a deterministic dispatch of management frames that underpin the access point's functionality.

Network Parameterization and Security Considerations

The efficacy of a localized IoT network established via ESP32 access point mode is contingent upon the rigorous definition of network parameters and the implementation of robust security protocols. Paramount among these parameters is the network identifier (SSID), which must be uniquely assigned to ensure proper association of client devices. Additionally, the maximum number of concurrently supported client connections is determined by the available hardware resources and the configuration of underlying network stacks. Concurrently, the access point must implement security measures in adherence to contemporary standards such as WPA and WPA2, thereby ensuring data integrity and confidentiality during wireless transmission. The deployment of encryption algorithms transforms the plain data stream into a secure sequence, typically by employing keys derived via a predefined negotiation process. Channel management strategies also account for potential cross-channel interference, with frequency selection mechanisms being guided by both regulatory mandates and empirical measurements of signal quality. The interplay between these elements defines a comprehensive network configuration that not only promotes connectivity but also safeguards the integrity of localized IoT communications.

ESP32 For IoT With Arduino Code Snippet

```
#include <WiFi.h>

// Access Point configuration parameters
const char* ssid = "ESP32_AP";
const char* password = "strongPassword";   // Minimum 8 characters
↪  for WPA2 security
const int maxClients = 4;                   // Maximum number of
↪  simultaneous client connections

// Beacon interval (T_b) in milliseconds.
// Conceptual equation: T_b = 1 / f_b, where f_b is the beacon
↪  frequency.
// For this demonstration, T_b is set to a default value of 100ms.
unsigned long beaconInterval = 100;

// Define LED pin for heartbeat indication (commonly GPIO2 for ESP32
↪  boards)
const int ledPin = 2;

// Simulated algorithm to select an optimal Wi-Fi channel based on
↪  interference levels.
// In a full application, WiFi.scanNetworks() could be used to
↪  dynamically assess channel occupancy.
int selectOptimalChannel() {
    // Initialize dummy interference values for channels 1 through
    ↪  11 (index 0 is unused)
    int optimalChannel = 1;
    int interference[12] = {999, 999, 999, 999, 999, 999, 999, 999,
    ↪  999, 999, 999, 999};

    // Simulated interference levels (lower value indicates less
    ↪  interference)
    interference[1] = 50;
    interference[2] = 40;
    interference[3] = 35;
    interference[4] = 45;
    interference[5] = 30;
```

140

```
    interference[6] = 10;    // Best candidate due to minimal
    ↳  interference
    interference[7] = 20;
    interference[8] = 25;
    interference[9] = 30;
    interference[10] = 55;
    interference[11] = 30;

    int minInterference = 1000;
    for (int ch = 1; ch <= 11; ch++) {
        if (interference[ch] < minInterference) {
            minInterference = interference[ch];
            optimalChannel = ch;
        }
    }
    return optimalChannel;
}

void setup() {
    Serial.begin(115200);
    delay(1000);

    // Initialize the LED pin for output
    pinMode(ledPin, OUTPUT);

    // Display the conceptual beacon interval formula and its preset
    ↳  value.
    // (T_b = 1 / f_b, with T_b set to 100ms for this demonstration)
    Serial.println("Beacon Interval (T_b) is set to 100ms
    ↳  (default).");

    // Execute the channel selection algorithm to optimize operating
    ↳  parameters.
    int chosenChannel = selectOptimalChannel();
    Serial.print("Optimal channel selected: ");
    Serial.println(chosenChannel);

    // Configure the ESP32 as a Wi-Fi Access Point.
    // This command sets the AP with the specified SSID, password,
    ↳  operating channel, and maximum clients.
    bool apStatus = WiFi.softAP(ssid, password, chosenChannel,
    ↳  false, maxClients);
    if (apStatus) {
        Serial.println("Wi-Fi Access Point created successfully!");
        Serial.print("SSID: ");
        Serial.println(ssid);
        Serial.print("Channel: ");
        Serial.println(chosenChannel);
        Serial.print("AP IP address: ");
        Serial.println(WiFi.softAPIP());
    } else {
        Serial.println("Failed to create Wi-Fi Access Point.");
    }
```

141

```
    // Additional demonstration: Effective Data Transmission Time
    ↪  Calculation
    // Equation: T_tx = Data_Length / (Data_Rate_bytes)
    // where Data_Rate_bytes = Data_Rate (in Mbps) * 1,000,000 / 8
    float dataLength = 1500.0;    // Data packet length in bytes
    float dataRate_Mbps = 24.0;   // Data rate in Mbps
    float dataRate_bytes = dataRate_Mbps * 1000000.0 / 8.0; //
    ↪  Convert Mbps to bytes per second
    float T_tx = dataLength / dataRate_bytes;  // Transmission time
    ↪  in seconds
    Serial.print("Estimated transmission time for 1500 bytes at
    ↪  24Mbps: ");
    Serial.print(T_tx * 1000, 3); // Convert seconds to milliseconds
    ↪  for display
    Serial.println(" ms");
}

void loop() {
    // Simulate a heartbeat mechanism for the AP by blinking the LED
    ↪  with a period derived from the beacon interval.
    digitalWrite(ledPin, HIGH);
    delay(beaconInterval);
    digitalWrite(ledPin, LOW);
    delay(beaconInterval);
}
```

Chapter 22

TCP/IP Communication on ESP32

1 The TCP/IP Protocol Stack in Embedded Systems

The TCP/IP protocol suite underpins modern network communications by organizing functionality into a layered architecture. At the base, the link layer is responsible for handling the physical transmission of data frames over wireless media. Above this, the Internet Protocol (IP) facilitates logical addressing and routing, enabling data packets to traverse disparate networks. The transport layer, where the Transmission Control Protocol (TCP) operates, provides end-to-end communication by establishing reliable connections, implementing error recovery, and managing flow. In many embedded systems such as the ESP32, a lightweight implementation of this suite is employed to balance the constraints of computational resources and the need for robust communication channels. The design of such stacks often adheres to principles of modularity and efficiency, ensuring that each layer interacts seamlessly with adjacent layers while managing the inherent overhead of protocol encapsulation.

2 Integration of TCP/IP Protocols in ESP32 Applications

The incorporation of TCP/IP into the ESP32 ecosystem necessitates a careful alignment of hardware capabilities and network protocol functions. The integrated wireless radio transceiver in the ESP32 extends beyond mere data transmission, providing the critical interface over which TCP/IP protocols are executed. By harnessing an embedded lightweight IP (lwIP) stack, the device is able to convert radio frequency signals into structured data packets conforming to established networking standards. This integration enables the ESP32 to function as both a client and a server within Internet of Things (IoT) ecosystems, thereby facilitating diverse interactions such as remote sensor readings and actuator controls. The layered architecture supports dynamic IP addressing, protocol negotiation, and adaptive error correction without imposing prohibitive overhead on system memory or processing cycles.

3 Ensuring Reliable Data Transfer and Connection Management

Achieving reliability within the TCP/IP framework relies on a confluence of mechanisms engineered to address the variability of wireless networks. Central to this effort is the establishment of a connection via a structured three-way handshake, which employs a sequence of synchronization and acknowledgment messages to ensure that endpoints are ready for communication. Subsequent to connection establishment, data packets are sequenced and monitored through window-based flow control and acknowledgment systems. This methodology not only guarantees ordered delivery but also facilitates retransmission in scenarios where network anomalies or interference cause packet loss. Moreover, built-in congestion control algorithms dynamically adjust transmission parameters by assessing network conditions, thereby optimizing data throughput while mitigating the effects of latency and jitter. Such mechanisms are crucial for maintaining robust data exchange in environments where resource contention and intermittent connectivity are prevalent.

4 Architectural Considerations and Resource Optimization

The deployment of TCP/IP protocols on an embedded platform such as the ESP32 introduces unique challenges in resource management and architectural design. The finite memory available on the device necessitates a streamlined allocation strategy for network buffers and data structures. Parameters such as buffer sizing are optimized to accommodate the maximum expected data load while minimizing wasted memory space. Additionally, the CPU cycles consumed by protocol processing are judiciously balanced against other system tasks, ensuring that network operations do not impede real-time sensor data acquisition or control functions. Performance metrics, including throughput and latency, may be quantified by expressions such as $T = \frac{L \cdot S}{\Delta t}$, where L denotes the number of packets, S the packet size, and Δt the time interval over which transmissions occur. These considerations underline the necessity of a methodical approach to task scheduling and priority assignment, often leveraging real-time operating system (RTOS) capabilities to achieve deterministic performance in multi-threaded environments.

5 Error Handling and Recovery Mechanisms

Within the context of reliable TCP/IP communications, the implementation of robust error handling and recovery protocols is paramount. The transport layer's error detection capabilities, including checksum verification, serve as a first line of defense against data corruption. When discrepancies are detected, retransmission protocols are invoked to restore data integrity without compromising the overall session continuity. The interplay between timeout intervals and acknowledgment signals is calibrated to adapt to varying network conditions, thereby minimizing the latency introduced by recovery procedures. In scenarios where persistent errors occur, the system is engineered to gracefully close connections and release allocated resources, ensuring that sporadic faults do not precipitate a systemic failure. This comprehensive strategy for error management not only reinforces the reliability of network communications but also contributes to the overall resilience of IoT applications deployed in heterogeneous and dynamically evolving environments.

ESP32 For IoT With Arduino Code Snippet

```
#include <WiFi.h>

// WiFi network credentials
const char* ssid     = "YOUR_WIFI_SSID";
const char* password = "YOUR_WIFI_PASSWORD";

// TCP server details (modify with your server's IP and port)
const char* serverIP   = "192.168.1.100";
const uint16_t serverPort = 8080;

WiFiClient client;

// Throughput calculation parameters
// L: Total number of packets to send
// S: Size of each packet in bytes
const int totalPackets = 10;
const int packetSize   = 64;
unsigned long startTime = 0;
unsigned long elapsedTime = 0;
int packetCount = 0;

// Maximum number of retries for each transmission step
const int maxRetries = 3;

// Helper function to generate a string by repeating a character
↪   'count' times
String repeatChar(char c, int count) {
  String result = "";
  for (int i = 0; i < count; i++) {
    result += c;
  }
  return result;
}

// Function to send a packet and wait for an acknowledgement ("ACK")
// It simulates error handling by waiting for a response within a
↪   timeout period.
bool sendPacket(const String &data) {
  if (client.connected()) {
    client.println(data);
    Serial.print("Sent: ");
    Serial.println(data);

    // Define a timeout duration (2 seconds) to wait for an ACK
    unsigned long ackTimeout = millis() + 2000;
    while (millis() < ackTimeout) {
      if (client.available()) {
        String response = client.readStringUntil('\n');
```

```
      response.trim();
      // Check if response contains "ACK"
      if (response.indexOf("ACK") >= 0) {
        Serial.print("Received: ");
        Serial.println(response);
        return true;
      }
    }
    delay(10);
  }
  return false;
}

void setup() {
  Serial.begin(115200);
  delay(1000);

  // Connect to WiFi network
  Serial.print("Connecting to WiFi");
  WiFi.begin(ssid, password);
  while (WiFi.status() != WL_CONNECTED) {
    delay(500);
    Serial.print(".");
  }
  Serial.println("\nWiFi connected");
  Serial.print("IP address: ");
  Serial.println(WiFi.localIP());

  // Establish TCP connection to the server
  Serial.print("Connecting to TCP server ");
  Serial.print(serverIP);
  Serial.print(":");
  Serial.println(serverPort);
  if (!client.connect(serverIP, serverPort)) {
    Serial.println("TCP connection failed!");
    while (true) {
      delay(1000); // Halt execution if connection fails
    }
  } else {
    Serial.println("TCP connection established successfully!");
  }

  // Start the timer for throughput measurement
  startTime = millis();
}

void loop() {
  // If there are packets remaining and the TCP connection is alive,
  // perform the transmission with a simulated three-way handshake.
  if (packetCount < totalPackets && client.connected()) {
    int retries = 0;
    bool success = false;
```

```
// --- Three-Way Handshake Simulation for this Packet ---
// Step 1: Send SYN - Begin handshake
while (retries < maxRetries && !success) {
  if (sendPacket("SYN " + String(packetCount + 1))) {
    Serial.println("SYN acknowledged.");
    success = true;
  } else {
    retries++;
    Serial.println("SYN not acknowledged. Retrying...");
    delay(500);
  }
}
if (!success) {
  Serial.println("Failed SYN handshake for packet " +
  ↪  String(packetCount + 1));
  packetCount++;
  return;
}

// Step 2: Send DATA - Transmit packet payload
retries = 0;
success = false;
String dataPacket = "DATA Packet " + String(packetCount + 1) +
↪  ": " + repeatChar('X', packetSize);
while (retries < maxRetries && !success) {
  if (sendPacket(dataPacket)) {
    Serial.println("DATA acknowledged.");
    success = true;
  } else {
    retries++;
    Serial.println("DATA not acknowledged. Retrying...");
    delay(500);
  }
}
if (!success) {
  Serial.println("Failed DATA transmission for packet " +
  ↪  String(packetCount + 1));
  packetCount++;
  return;
}

// Step 3: Send final ACK - Complete handshake
retries = 0;
success = false;
while (retries < maxRetries && !success) {
  if (sendPacket("ACK " + String(packetCount + 1))) {
    Serial.println("Final ACK acknowledged.");
    success = true;
  } else {
    retries++;
    Serial.println("Final ACK not acknowledged. Retrying...");
    delay(500);
```

```
      }
    }
    if (!success) {
      Serial.println("Failed final ACK for packet " +
      ↪  String(packetCount + 1));
    }
    // -----------------------------------------------------------

    packetCount++;
    delay(1000); // Delay between transmissions
  }
  else {
    // All packets have been processed; calculate throughput based
    ↪  on the formula:
    // T = (L * S) / (Delta t), where Delta t is measured in
    ↪  seconds.
    elapsedTime = millis() - startTime; // Time in milliseconds
    float Delta_t = elapsedTime / 1000.0; // Convert to seconds
    float throughput = (totalPackets * packetSize) / Delta_t; //
    ↪  Throughput in Bytes/sec

    Serial.println("----- Throughput Calculation -----");
    Serial.print("Total Packets Sent (L): ");
    Serial.println(totalPackets);
    Serial.print("Packet Size (S) in bytes: ");
    Serial.println(packetSize);
    Serial.print("Elapsed Time (Delta t in seconds): ");
    Serial.println(Delta_t, 2);
    Serial.print("Calculated Throughput (T in Bytes/sec): ");
    Serial.println(throughput, 2);

    // Close the TCP connection and halt further processing
    client.stop();
    Serial.println("TCP connection closed. End of transmission.");
    while (true) {
      delay(1000);
    }
  }
}
```

Chapter 23

TCP Client-Server Implementation

Architectural Considerations in Client-Server Systems

The client-server paradigm, when implemented over Transmission Control Protocol (TCP), mandates a clear delineation of responsibilities between the two communicating entities. The server functions as a centralized resource provider that listens for incoming connection requests, while the client initiates contact to obtain services or transmit data. In this architecture, the reliability inherent in TCP is leveraged to establish a connection-oriented, stream-based communication channel. The interplay between the transport layer's mechanisms and the underlying network interface is critical, particularly in embedded environments where the constraint on available resources necessitates a compact and efficient design. The modularization of system components, when mapped onto Arduino sketches, benefits from a rigorous separation of concerns. This separation permits the design to adhere to principles of low latency and minimal overhead, ensuring that resource allocation for socket management and data buffering is accomplished in a judicious and systematic manner.

Connection Establishment and Session Management

The establishment of a robust session in TCP client-server communications is predicated on a deterministic handshake mechanism. Initially, the client dispatches a synchronization request to the server, which, upon recognition, responds with an acknowledgment signal. This bilateral exchange, typically characterized as the three-way handshake, lays the groundwork for a synchronized session where sequence numbers and flow control parameters are negotiated. The formalization of this process can be modeled as a finite state machine with transitions defined by the receipt of synchronization and acknowledgment signals. Let S_0, S_1, and S_2 denote the states corresponding to connection initiation, partial synchronization, and fully established connection, respectively. Throughout this sequence, state transitions are governed by protocol-defined timers and acknowledgment conditions that ensure the reliability of the connection. In the context of embedded platforms, the precision of these state transitions is paramount, as sporadic network anomalies require that the handshake mechanism gracefully accommodate retransmissions and timeout-induced resets.

Structured Data Exchange: Message Framing and Parsing

Within the established client-server framework, the structuring of data for transmission is a critical consideration. The process involves the encapsulation of data into discrete messages that are transmitted over the TCP stream. Each message is defined by a specific structure, whereby header fields denote the beginning, payload length, sequence order, and integrity verification elements such as checksums. This form of message framing facilitates the accurate segregation of data packets from the continuous stream of bytes dictated by the TCP protocol. In practice, the design of the framing mechanism must account for variable-length messages and ensure that the beginning and end of a logical data unit are precisely demarcated. The formal representation of throughput within

151

this context is often articulated by the relation

$$T = \frac{L \cdot S}{\Delta t},$$

where L represents the number of packets transmitted, S denotes the size of each packet, and Δt is the time interval allocated to the complete transmission cycle. Accurate message parsing on the receiving end is equally critical, as it enables the reconstruction of the transmitted data with fidelity and correctness.

Reliability Mechanisms and Flow Control Techniques

The reliability of data transfer in a TCP client-server implementation derives from an intertwined network of error detection, acknowledgment strategies, and flow control techniques. On the one hand, checksum algorithms incorporated within the protocol serve as the primary means for detecting data corruption. On the other, sliding window protocols enable the dynamic regulation of outgoing data so that the receiver is not overwhelmed. The cumulative acknowledgment technique allows for both the efficient identification of lost packets and the timely initiation of retransmission protocols. In scenarios involving high variability in network conditions, these mechanisms work in concert to adjust the transmission rate, thereby mitigating the adverse effects of congestion and jitter. The systematic implementation of these flow control techniques ensures that the data stream maintains integrity, an objective that is achieved through cyclic monitoring and adaptive modulation of transmission parameters.

Resource Management and Performance Considerations

When implementing client-server architectures within the constrained environment of an embedded system, the allocation and management of finite computational resources assume critical importance. Memory allocation for dynamically sized buffers must be balanced against the need to preserve system responsiveness. Optimization strategies involve the careful tuning of buffer sizes, task scheduling, and the distribution of CPU cycles among concurrent processes.

Performance metrics, such as latency and throughput, are directly influenced by the efficiency with which these resources are managed. The interplay between network operations and other concurrent processes, such as sensor data acquisition and control signal computation, necessitates the incorporation of task prioritization strategies derived from real-time operating system paradigms. Analytical models can be employed to characterize this relationship, for instance, by considering the computational efficiency C as a function of allocated buffer space B and average task execution time τ, expressed as

$$C = f(B, \tau).$$

Such models provide a theoretical foundation for optimizing system performance in client-server implementations on resource-constrained platforms.

ESP32 For IoT With Arduino Code Snippet

```
#include <WiFi.h>

// WiFi network credentials
const char* ssid     = "your_ssid";
const char* password = "your_password";

// TCP server will listen on this port
WiFiServer server(8080);

// Enum to simulate the three-way handshake states
enum ConnectionState {
  S0,  // Connection initiation
  S1,  // Partial synchronization (after receiving SYN)
  S2   // Fully established connection (after receiving ACK)
};

ConnectionState connectionState = S0;

// Variables for throughput calculation
unsigned int packetCount = 0;      // L in throughput equation
unsigned long totalBytes = 0;      // Total bytes transmitted
  ↪ (accumulated S*L)
unsigned long startTime = 0;       // Starting time of measurement
  ↪ (ms)

// Variables for resource management demo: allocated buffer size (B)
  ↪ and simulated average task execution time ()
unsigned long bufferSize = 1024;   // in bytes
```

```cpp
unsigned long avgTaskExecTime = 10;       // in milliseconds

// Function to compute computational efficiency, C = f(B, )
// For demonstration, we use a simple ratio: efficiency = B / ( + 1)
float computeEfficiency(unsigned long B, unsigned long tau) {
  return (float)B / (tau + 1);
}

// Function to compute a simple checksum - sum of ASCII values
// ↪  modulo 256
uint8_t computeChecksum(const String &data) {
  uint8_t sum = 0;
  for (size_t i = 0; i < data.length(); i++) {
    sum += data[i];
  }
  return sum;
}

// Simulated handshake function using a three-way handshake model
// Client should first send "SYN", then after receiving "SYN-ACK",
// ↪  send "ACK"
void performHandshake(WiFiClient &client) {
  if (client.available()) {
    String handshakeMsg = client.readStringUntil('\n');
    handshakeMsg.trim();
    if (connectionState == SO && handshakeMsg == "SYN") {
      Serial.println("Received SYN from client");
      client.println("SYN-ACK");
      connectionState = S1;
    }
    else if (connectionState == S1 && handshakeMsg == "ACK") {
      Serial.println("Received ACK from client, connection
      ↪  established");
      connectionState = S2;
      startTime = millis(); // Begin timing for throughput
      ↪  calculation
    }
  }
}

// Process incoming message formatted as:
// "SEQ=<sequence>;LEN=<length>;PAYLOAD=<data>;CHK=<checksum>"
void processMessage(WiFiClient &client, const String &msg) {
  // Locate indices of each field
  int seqIndex = msg.indexOf("SEQ=");
  int lenIndex = msg.indexOf("LEN=");
  int payloadIndex = msg.indexOf("PAYLOAD=");
  int chkIndex = msg.indexOf("CHK=");

  // Check all elements exist
  if(seqIndex == -1 || lenIndex == -1 || payloadIndex == -1 ||
  ↪  chkIndex == -1) {
    Serial.println("Malformed message received!");
```

154

```
    return;
  }

  // Extract sequence number
  int seqEnd = msg.indexOf(';', seqIndex);
  String seqStr = msg.substring(seqIndex + 4, seqEnd);

  // Extract length of the payload
  int lenEnd = msg.indexOf(';', lenIndex);
  String lenStr = msg.substring(lenIndex + 4, lenEnd);

  // Extract payload (if there is no ending semicolon, assume
  ↪   end-of-string)
  int payloadEnd = msg.indexOf(';', payloadIndex);
  String payload;
  if(payloadEnd == -1) {
    payload = msg.substring(payloadIndex + 8);
  } else {
    payload = msg.substring(payloadIndex + 8, payloadEnd);
  }

  // Extract checksum value
  String chkStr = msg.substring(chkIndex + 4);
  uint8_t receivedChk = (uint8_t) chkStr.toInt();

  // Verify checksum using the simple checksum algorithm
  uint8_t computedChk = computeChecksum(payload);

  if(computedChk == receivedChk) {
    Serial.println("Checksum verified. Message is valid.");
  } else {
    Serial.println("Checksum mismatch! Data integrity
  ↪     compromised.");
    return;
  }

  // Increment packet count and accumulated bytes based on the
  ↪   provided length field.
  int packetLength = lenStr.toInt();
  packetCount++;
  totalBytes += packetLength;

  Serial.print("Processed packet - Seq: ");
  Serial.println(seqStr);
}

// Calculate throughput using the relation:
// T = (L * S) / t, where L = packetCount, S = average packet size,
↪   t = elapsed time (in sec)
void calculateThroughput() {
  unsigned long currentTime = millis();
  unsigned long elapsed = currentTime - startTime;
```

```
  if(packetCount > 0 && elapsed > 0) {
    float avgPacketSize = (float) totalBytes / packetCount;
    float throughput = (packetCount * avgPacketSize) / (elapsed /
    ↪  1000.0); // bytes/sec
    Serial.print("Current Throughput: ");
    Serial.print(throughput);
    Serial.println(" bytes/sec");
  }
}

void setup() {
  Serial.begin(115200);
  delay(1000);

  // Connect to WiFi network
  WiFi.begin(ssid, password);
  Serial.print("Connecting to WiFi");
  while (WiFi.status() != WL_CONNECTED) {
    delay(500);
    Serial.print(".");
  }
  Serial.println();
  Serial.print("Connected! ESP32 IP Address: ");
  Serial.println(WiFi.localIP());

  // Start TCP Server
  server.begin();
  Serial.println("TCP Server started. Waiting for client
  ↪  connection...");
}

void loop() {
  // Check for an incoming client connection
  WiFiClient client = server.available();

  if (client) {
    Serial.println("Client connected.");
    connectionState = S0; // Reset handshake state for the new
    ↪  connection

    // While the client remains connected
    while (client.connected()) {
      if (connectionState != S2) {
        // Perform the handshake procedure
        performHandshake(client);
      }
      else {
        // Once handshake is complete, start reading messages
        if(client.available()) {
          String msg = client.readStringUntil('\n');
          msg.trim();
          if(msg.length() > 0) {
            processMessage(client, msg);
```

156

```
      }
    }

    // After processing data, periodically calculate throughput
    ↪  and computational efficiency
    if(millis() - startTime > 5000) {  // every 5 seconds
      calculateThroughput();
      float efficiency = computeEfficiency(bufferSize,
      ↪  avgTaskExecTime);
      Serial.print("Computational Efficiency (C = f(B, )): ");
      Serial.println(efficiency);

      // Reset measurements for the next interval
      startTime = millis();
      packetCount = 0;
      totalBytes = 0;
    }
  }
}
Serial.println("Client disconnected.");
client.stop();
  }
}
```

Chapter 24

UDP Communication Fundamentals

Protocol Architecture and Design

The User Datagram Protocol (UDP) is defined as a connectionless, lightweight transport protocol that operates on the Internet Protocol (IP). In contrast to connection-oriented protocols, UDP forgoes the establishment and termination procedures inherent in stateful communication. The protocol encapsulates data into discrete units termed datagrams, each accompanied by a minimal header. This header typically comprises the source port, destination port, length, and checksum fields. The streamlined nature of UDP is particularly advantageous in resource-constrained scenarios, as it reduces processing overhead and minimizes latency. The absence of handshake mechanisms permits immediate data transmission, a property that is invaluable for distributed systems in which temporal efficiency is paramount.

Datagram Structure and Transmission Mechanics

Each UDP datagram maintains clear boundaries, preserving the segmentation of transmitted data. The standard structure of a datagram begins with a header whose fields are succinctly defined, ensuring that the protocol remains computationally efficient. In a typical datagram, if H denotes the header length and P represents the payload size, the total datagram length L is given by

$$L = H + P.$$

The header's checksum field, though modest in its error detection capabilities, serves to verify the integrity of both header and payload. The self-contained nature of each datagram obviates the need for an established connection, thereby enabling rapid, unordered delivery of messages. This quality is particularly salient in scenarios wherein network conditions preclude the latency penalties associated with more robust, stateful data transfer mechanisms.

Trade-offs Between Reliability and Latency

UDP is characterized by an explicit compromise between reliability and transmission speed. The protocol does not implement mechanisms for packet retransmission, flow control, or packet reordering. Instead, the minimal protocol overhead yields a marked reduction in transmission latency. This trade-off is quantified by the throughput formula

$$T = \frac{N \times S}{\Delta t},$$

where T is the throughput achieved, N denotes the number of datagrams transmitted, S represents the average size of each datagram, and Δt is the time interval over which the transmission occurs. By delegating error correction, sequencing, and congestion management to higher-layer protocols or to the application itself, UDP permits a level of efficiency that is highly desirable in systems where prompt data delivery supersedes the necessity for guaranteed delivery. Such design decisions are well suited to Internet of Things scenarios, wherein the rapid exchange of information often takes precedence over absolute reliability.

Applications in ESP32-Based IoT Scenarios

Within the context of ESP32-driven Internet of Things applications, the properties of UDP facilitate highly responsive data transmission schemes. The ESP32 platform benefits from UDP's lightweight nature when executing tasks that involve real-time telemetry, sensor data broadcasting, or the dissemination of control signals. The protocol's reduced computational demands allow the ESP32 to allocate a greater proportion of its limited resources to peripheral activities such as sensor interfacing and signal processing. Moreover, UDP's inherent support for broadcast and multicast communication is particularly advantageous in distributed sensor networks, where simultaneous notification of multiple nodes is required without incurring the overhead associated with connection establishment. The practical implications of utilizing UDP in these scenarios include diminished latency, lower energy consumption, and a protocol design that is inherently compatible with the rapid, transient nature of IoT data exchanges.

ESP32 For IoT With Arduino Code Snippet

```
#include <WiFi.h>
#include <WiFiUdp.h>

// ----- WiFi and UDP Configuration -----
const char* ssid     = "Your_SSID";          // Replace with your
↪   WiFi SSID
const char* password = "Your_PASSWORD";      // Replace with your
↪   WiFi password

// UDP server configuration (adjust the IP as needed)
const char* udpAddress = "192.168.1.100";    // Target UDP server
↪   IP address
const unsigned int udpPort = 4210;           // Target UDP server
↪   port

WiFiUDP udp;

// ----- UDP Datagram Structure Constants -----
const int UDP_HEADER_LENGTH = 8;   // UDP header is typically 8
↪   bytes

// ----- Throughput Measurement Variables -----
// These variables are used to compute the throughput using the
↪   formula:
// T = (N * S) / t
// where: T = throughput (bytes/sec)
//        N = number of datagrams sent
//        S = payload size (bytes)
//        t = elapsed transmission time (seconds)
```

```
unsigned long cycleStartMillis = 0;
unsigned int datagramCount = 0;
unsigned long totalPayloadBytes = 0;  // Sum of payload sizes for
↪  all datagrams sent during a cycle

// ----- Payload for UDP Datagram -----
// This string represents the payload. Its size (in bytes) is used
↪  in computing the datagram size:
// L = H + P, where H is UDP_HEADER_LENGTH and P is the payload
↪  length.
String payloadMessage = "ESP32 UDP Datagram Message";

// ----- Transmission Cycle Settings -----
const unsigned long cycleDurationMillis = 5000;  // Duration for
↪  each transmission cycle (5 seconds)
const unsigned int interPacketDelay = 500;        // Delay (in ms)
↪  between consecutive datagram transmissions

void setup() {
  Serial.begin(115200);
  delay(1000);

  // ----- Connect to WiFi -----
  Serial.println("Connecting to WiFi...");
  WiFi.begin(ssid, password);
  while (WiFi.status() != WL_CONNECTED) {
    delay(500);
    Serial.print(".");
  }
  Serial.println("\nWiFi connected");
  Serial.print("IP Address: ");
  Serial.println(WiFi.localIP());

  // ----- Initialize UDP -----
  // Start UDP on the specified port for sending datagrams.
  udp.begin(udpPort);

  // ----- Initialize Transmission Cycle -----
  cycleStartMillis = millis();
  datagramCount = 0;
  totalPayloadBytes = 0;
}

void loop() {
  unsigned long currentMillis = millis();
  unsigned long elapsedMillis = currentMillis - cycleStartMillis;

  if (elapsedMillis < cycleDurationMillis) {
    // Send UDP datagrams during the cycle
    sendUdpDatagram();
    delay(interPacketDelay);  // Controls transmission frequency
  } else {
    // End of cycle: Calculate and report throughput
```

```
  float elapsedSeconds = (millis() - cycleStartMillis) / 1000.0;
  // Throughput calculation (only using payload size as measure)
  // T = (Total Payload Bytes Sent) / (Elapsed Time in seconds)
  float throughput = totalPayloadBytes / elapsedSeconds;

  Serial.println("--------- Cycle Report ---------");
  Serial.print("Datagrams Sent: ");
  Serial.println(datagramCount);
  Serial.print("Total Payload Bytes Sent: ");
  Serial.println(totalPayloadBytes);
  Serial.print("Elapsed Time (s): ");
  Serial.println(elapsedSeconds, 2);
  Serial.print("Throughput (Bytes/s): ");
  Serial.println(throughput, 2);
  Serial.println("------------------------------");

  // Reset cycle measurements for the next transmission round
  cycleStartMillis = millis();
  datagramCount = 0;
  totalPayloadBytes = 0;
  }
}

// Function to send a UDP datagram and update associated metrics
void sendUdpDatagram() {
  // Determine the payload size (P) and compute the total datagram
  ↪ length (L)
  int payloadSize = payloadMessage.length();  // P = payload size in
  ↪ bytes
  int totalDatagramLength = UDP_HEADER_LENGTH + payloadSize;  // L =
  ↪ H + P

  Serial.print("Sending UDP Datagram with total length (bytes): ");
  Serial.println(totalDatagramLength);

  // Begin constructing and sending the UDP packet
  udp.beginPacket(udpAddress, udpPort);
  udp.print(payloadMessage);
  udp.endPacket();

  // Update metrics for throughput calculation
  datagramCount++;
  totalPayloadBytes += payloadSize;
}
```

Chapter 25

HTTP Client Programming

HTTP Protocol Fundamentals

The HyperText Transfer Protocol (HTTP) constitutes the primary foundation for communication between clients and web services. This protocol operates on a request-response paradigm wherein a client dispatches a request that is subsequently processed by a remote server. The stateless nature of HTTP implies that each request is self-contained, incorporating all information necessary for the server to understand and fulfill the request. Methods such as *GET*, *POST*, *PUT*, and *DELETE* define the intent of the client and prescribe specific semantics in the operation. A nuanced understanding of these methods is essential to appreciate both their inherent benefits and constraints in a resource-centric, embedded environment.

Formulating HTTP Requests in Embedded Environments

Constructing HTTP requests within embedded systems, particularly when utilizing the ESP32 microcontroller, demands careful allocation of limited computational and memory resources. The process entails the precise concatenation of distinct components that collectively form a valid HTTP request. Fundamental to this

163

process is the assembly of the request line, the systematic inclusion of header fields, and the optional integration of a message body. Each component must adhere to the syntax and semantics prescribed by relevant Internet standards, notably those outlined in RFC 7230. A meticulous formulation of the request components mitigates overhead and enhances the efficiency of network transactions conducted over constrained hardware platforms.

Structural Elements of HTTP Requests

An HTTP request is structurally defined by three principal elements: the request line, header fields, and an optional payload. The request line comprises the method identifier, the resource identifier as indicated by the Uniform Resource Identifier (URI), and the HTTP version, typically rendered as $HTTP/1.1$ or $HTTP/2$. Adjacent to the request line, header fields serve to convey metadata such as host identification, content type, connection directives, and user-agent specifications. The optional message body may include serialized data intended for transmission to the server. The design of these structural elements demands rigorous adherence to standard delimiters and line termination conventions, ensuring that the message can be correctly parsed and interpreted by the receiving web service.

Processing HTTP Responses from Web Services

Upon transmission of an HTTP request, the ESP32 receives an HTTP response that encapsulates the outcome of the request. The response is itself composed of a status line, a series of header fields, and an optional response body. The status line provides critical information in the form of a three-digit status code and an accompanying textual reason phrase, facilitating the rapid assessment of the request's success or failure. Status codes in the $2xx$ range generally indicate successful operations, while those in the $4xx$ or $5xx$ ranges denote client-side or server-side errors, respectively. The header fields in the response further detail caching policies, content encoding, and server-specific metadata, all of which contribute to an in-depth understanding of the resultant data stream. Effective processing of these responses is paramount to ensuring that subsequent actions and error handling protocols are executed with precision.

Optimizing HTTP Communications for the ESP32

Optimizing HTTP communications within the constraints of the ESP32 architecture requires an integrative approach that balances performance with resource utilization. This optimization process involves the reduction of excessive header content, the strategic reuse of persistent connections where applicable, and the minimization of dynamic memory operations. The efficiency of HTTP communications is further enhanced by dissecting the relative cost of protocol overhead versus payload delivery, ensuring that non-critical metadata is eschewed in favor of rapid, direct data transmission. The integration of these techniques facilitates a lean communication model that aligns with the operational imperatives of IoT applications, in which rapid, reliable access to web services is critical.

ESP32 For IoT With Arduino Code Snippet

```
#include <WiFi.h>

// Replace with your network credentials
const char* ssid     = "YOUR_SSID";
const char* password = "YOUR_PASSWORD";

// Server settings
const char* host = "www.example.com";
const uint16_t port = 80;

// Function to connect the ESP32 to Wi-Fi
void connectToWiFi() {
  Serial.print("Connecting to ");
  Serial.println(ssid);
  WiFi.begin(ssid, password);

  int retryCount = 0;
  while (WiFi.status() != WL_CONNECTED) {
    delay(500);
    Serial.print(".");
```

```
  if (++retryCount > 20) { // Timeout after several retries
    Serial.println("\nFailed to connect to Wi-Fi");
    return;
  }
}
Serial.println("\nWiFi connected");
Serial.print("IP Address: ");
Serial.println(WiFi.localIP());
}


// Function to build an HTTP request string dynamically
// Constructs the request line, header fields, and terminates
↪   headers properly.
String buildHTTPRequest(const char* method, const char* uri, const
↪   char* hostHeader) {
  String request = "";
  // Request Line: method, URI, and HTTP version
  request += method;
  request += " ";
  request += uri;
  request += " HTTP/1.1\r\n";

  // Essential HTTP header fields
  request += "Host: ";
  request += hostHeader;
  request += "\r\n";

  request += "User-Agent: ESP32-Arduino/1.0\r\n";
  request += "Connection: close\r\n";

  // End of header fields (Empty line)
  request += "\r\n";
  return request;
}

// Function to parse and process the HTTP response
// It reads the status line, extracts the status code, processes
↪   header fields,
// and then prints the body of the response.
void parseHTTPResponse(WiFiClient &client) {
  // Read the first line (status line) from the response
  String statusLine = client.readStringUntil('\n');
  Serial.print("Status Line: ");
  Serial.println(statusLine);

  // Extract the status code from the status line (e.g., "HTTP/1.1
  ↪   200 OK")
  int firstSpace = statusLine.indexOf(' ');
  int secondSpace = statusLine.indexOf(' ', firstSpace + 1);
  String statusCode = "";
  if (firstSpace != -1 && secondSpace != -1) {
    statusCode = statusLine.substring(firstSpace + 1, secondSpace);
  }
```

```
  Serial.print("Status Code: ");
  Serial.println(statusCode);

  // Read and print header fields until an empty line is encountered
  Serial.println("Headers:");
  while (true) {
    String headerLine = client.readStringUntil('\n');
    if (headerLine == "\r") {
      break;
    }
    Serial.print("  ");
    Serial.println(headerLine);
  }

  // Print the response body if available
  Serial.println("Body:");
  while (client.available()) {
    String line = client.readStringUntil('\n');
    Serial.println(line);
  }
}

void setup() {
  Serial.begin(115200);
  delay(1000); // Allow the serial monitor to initialize

  // Connect to the Wi-Fi network
  connectToWiFi();

  WiFiClient client;
  Serial.print("Connecting to ");
  Serial.print(host);
  Serial.print(":");
  Serial.println(port);

  // Establish connection to the HTTP server
  if (client.connect(host, port)) {
    Serial.println("Connected to server");

    // Build the HTTP GET request for the root resource "/"
    String httpRequest = buildHTTPRequest("GET", "/", host);
    Serial.println("HTTP Request:");
    Serial.println(httpRequest);

    // Send the HTTP request to the server
    client.print(httpRequest);

    // Wait for the server response (with a timeout mechanism)
    unsigned long timeout = millis();
    while (client.available() == 0) {
      if (millis() - timeout > 5000) {
        Serial.println(">>> Client Timeout !");
        client.stop();
```

```
      return;
    }
  }

  // Process the received HTTP response
  parseHTTPResponse(client);

  client.stop();
  Serial.println("Disconnected from server");
  } else {
  Serial.println("Connection to server failed");
  }
}

void loop() {
  // No repetitive tasks are needed in loop for this example.
  // Future strategies may include persistent connection reuse and
  ↪   asynchronous processing.
}
```

Chapter 26

Building and Parsing HTTP Requests

HTTP Request Message Composition

The construction of an HTTP request adheres to a stringent structure characterized by the systematic assembly of discrete components. An HTTP request message is principally composed of three segments: the request line, header fields, and an optional message payload. The request line is formed by the sequential concatenation of the method, the Uniform Resource Identifier (URI), and the protocol version, typically represented as $HTTP/1.1$ or $HTTP/2$, with a single space separating each element. The method, indicated by verbs such as GET, $POST$, PUT, and $DELETE$, determines the nature of the operation, while the URI specifies the target resource. Following the request line, header fields convey essential metadata through name-value pairs that are separated by a colon and a space. Each header field is terminated by the carriage return and line feed delimiter, denoted as $\backslash r \backslash n$. In cases where data transmission is required by the request (as with $POST$ or PUT methods), an optional message payload is appended after an empty line that signifies the termination of header fields. Every component of this construction must conform to the syntactic and semantic guidelines defined in established protocol standards.

Techniques for Assembling Request Lines and Header Fields

The meticulous assembly of HTTP request lines and header fields necessitates an approach that preserves both structural integrity and compliance with protocol semantics. The request line is produced by concatenating the method, URI, and protocol version in that precise order, ensuring that single spaces separate these elements to adhere to the protocol's grammar. Header fields follow a similar level of rigor; each field is composed of a field name, a colon, a subsequent space, and the associated value. The use of the \r\n delimiter to separate header fields is critical, as it enables downstream processes to correctly identify the termination of individual fields. The selection and inclusion of header fields are dictated by the operational context, balancing the need to communicate pertinent metadata with the constraints imposed by limited computational and memory resources in embedded environments.

Delimitation and Protocol Compliance in Embedded Contexts

Embedded platforms impose significant constraints on computational capability and memory resources, rendering efficiency in HTTP message construction and parsing paramount. The careful use of delimiters, specifically the \r\n sequence, is not solely a matter of syntactic correctness but also a practical necessity for parsers operating under memory limitations. Each segment of an HTTP message must undergo rigorous validation to ensure that it strictly adheres to the formatting rules specified in protocols such as *RFC* 7230. Such meticulous compliance mitigates the possibility of malformed messages, thereby ensuring unambiguous interpretation by remote web API services. The emphasis on protocol compliance and precise delimitation contributes directly to enhanced interoperability and operational robustness within embedded systems.

Systematic Parsing of HTTP Responses

The parsing of HTTP responses is a process that is as methodical as the construction of the request itself. An HTTP response is divided into a status line, header fields, and an optional message body. The status line, which typically follows the format [HTTP version status code reason phrase], provides immediate insight into the outcome of the request. Extraction of the status code entails isolating the numerical component from the status line, a process that requires precise string manipulation and adherence to standardized criteria. Following the status line, header fields are parsed by identifying the \r\n sequences that denote the end of each header, thereby allowing for the extraction of metadata such as content type, encoding, and server directives. Lastly, the message body is processed based on specifications provided by the header fields; its interpretation relies on an understanding of the indicated content type, whether it be plain text, JSON, XML, or another format.

Computational Strategies for Efficient HTTP Communication

Within resource-constrained embedded environments, the strategies employed for both the construction and parsing of HTTP messages must be optimized to minimize computational overhead. Memory allocation is managed with particular care to allow for the dynamic assembly of message components without leading to fragmentation or excessive latency. Parsing operations utilize string manipulation techniques that are specifically designed to operate efficiently within limited buffer capacities. A detailed analysis of protocol overhead in relation to payload transmission informs selective inclusion of metadata and reduction of extraneous data. Furthermore, rigorous validation procedures at each stage of message handling prevent errors due to misformatted requests or responses, thereby ensuring that interactions with remote web APIs remain reliable and robust.

ESP32 For IoT With Arduino Code Snippet

```
#include <WiFi.h>

// Replace with your network credentials
const char* ssid     = "Your_SSID";
const char* password = "Your_PASSWORD";

// Remote server details
const char* host = "example.com";
const uint16_t port = 80;

// Function to parse and display components from the HTTP response
void parseHTTPResponse(const String &response) {
  Serial.println("\n--- Parsing HTTP Response ---");

  // Extract status line and status code
  int lineEnd = response.indexOf("\r\n");
  if (lineEnd == -1) {
    Serial.println("Malformed response: no status line termination
    ↪ found.");
    return;
  }
  String statusLine = response.substring(0, lineEnd);
  Serial.print("Status Line: ");
  Serial.println(statusLine);

  // Parsing status code: "HTTP/1.1 200 OK" -> 200
  int firstSpace = statusLine.indexOf(" ");
  int secondSpace = statusLine.indexOf(" ", firstSpace + 1);
  if (firstSpace == -1 || secondSpace == -1) {
    Serial.println("Malformed status line.");
  } else {
    String statusCodeStr = statusLine.substring(firstSpace + 1,
    ↪ secondSpace);
    int statusCode = statusCodeStr.toInt();
    Serial.print("Status Code: ");
    Serial.println(statusCode);
  }

  // Extract header fields: they end with the first occurrence of
  ↪ "\r\n\r\n"
  int headerEnd = response.indexOf("\r\n\r\n");
  if (headerEnd != -1) {
    String headerData = response.substring(0, headerEnd);
    Serial.println("\n--- Headers ---");
    Serial.println(headerData);
  } else {
    Serial.println("Headers not properly terminated.");
  }
```

172

```
// Extract message body (if any)
if (headerEnd != -1 && headerEnd + 4 < response.length()) {
  String messageBody = response.substring(headerEnd + 4);
  Serial.println("\n--- Message Body ---");
  Serial.println(messageBody);
} else {
  Serial.println("No message body found.");
}
}

void setup() {
  Serial.begin(115200);
  delay(10);

  // Connecting to Wi-Fi network
  Serial.println();
  Serial.print("Connecting to ");
  Serial.println(ssid);
  WiFi.begin(ssid, password);

  while (WiFi.status() != WL_CONNECTED) {
    delay(500);
    Serial.print(".");
  }

  Serial.println("\nWiFi connected");
  Serial.print("IP Address: ");
  Serial.println(WiFi.localIP());

  WiFiClient client;

  // Connect to the server with the specified host and port
  Serial.print("Connecting to ");
  Serial.print(host);
  Serial.print(":");
  Serial.println(port);
  if (!client.connect(host, port)) {
    Serial.println("Connection failed.");
    return;
  }

  // Build HTTP Request components using important equations and
  ↪    formulas:
  // HTTP Request Equation:
  //    Request-Line = Method + " " + URI + " " + HTTP-Version +
  ↪    "\r\n"
  //    Header Field  = Field-Name + ": " + Field-Value + "\r\n"
  //    Message Payload (optional) preceded by an empty line "\r\n"

  // Constructing the Request-Line
  String method = "GET";
  String uri = "/";
```

173

```
String httpVersion = "HTTP/1.1";
String requestLine = method + " " + uri + " " + httpVersion +
↪    "\r\n";

// Constructing Header Fields; note usage of "\r\n" as delimiters
String headers = "";
headers += "Host: " + String(host) + "\r\n";
headers += "User-Agent: ESP32-Client/1.0\r\n";
headers += "Accept: */*\r\n";
headers += "Connection: close\r\n\r\n"; // The final CRLF signals
↪    end of headers

// Complete HTTP Request Message assembly
String httpRequest = requestLine + headers;

Serial.println("\n--- Sending HTTP Request ---");
Serial.println(httpRequest);

// Send the HTTP Request to the remote server.
client.print(httpRequest);

// Wait for and collect the HTTP Response from the server.
String response = "";
unsigned long timeout = millis() + 5000;  // 5 seconds timeout for
↪    response
while (client.connected() && millis() < timeout) {
    while (client.available()) {
      char c = client.read();
      response += c;
    }
}

// Output the complete HTTP Response
Serial.println("\n--- HTTP Response Received ---");
Serial.println(response);

// Systematic Parsing of the HTTP Response
parseHTTPResponse(response);
}

void loop() {
// No repeated tasks needed; main logic is executed in setup() for
↪    demonstration.
}

/*
Computational Strategies Employed:
- String concatenation is used to assemble the HTTP request
↪    message following the protocol formula:
    "Method + ' ' + URI + ' ' + HTTP-Version + CRLF" for the
    ↪    request line,
    and "Field-Name + ': ' + Field-Value + CRLF" for each header.
```

```
  - The delimiter "\r\n" is rigorously applied to separate the
  ↪   components.
  - Parsing algorithms use indexOf() and substring() to efficiently
  ↪   extract status codes,
    header fields, and message body while working within limited
    ↪   buffer capacities typical in an embedded context.
*/
```
_____

Chapter 27

JSON Parsing and Data Handling

Overview of JSON Structure

JSON, abbreviated from JavaScript Object Notation, constitutes a lightweight data-interchange format defined by a strict syntactic grammar. The format is inherently composed of unordered collections of key-value pairs, designated as objects, and ordered lists of values, termed arrays. Objects are delimited by the characters { and }, while arrays are enclosed by the characters [and]. Each key is represented as a string and is associated with a corresponding value, which may itself be a number, a string, a Boolean, a null, another object, or an array. The rigorous specification of delimiters, such as the colon (:) used to pair keys with values and the comma (,) that separates individual elements, enforces a predictable hierarchical structure. This structure is instrumental in enabling systematic extraction and reconstruction of data during the parsing process. The adherence to formal definitions articulated in standards such as the RFC series ensures that a JSON payload conforms to a deterministic grammar, which is essential when parsing data streams received over network connections in embedded environments.

Methodologies for JSON Parsing

The parsing of JSON data necessitates a multifaceted approach that is both syntactically precise and computationally efficient. At the outset, the data stream is subjected to lexical analysis, wherein individual characters are examined to form tokens that represent the fundamental constructs of the JSON format. The tokenization process identifies strings, numbers, Boolean literals, and structural symbols such as {, }, [, and]. Subsequent to tokenization, a recursive descent parser or an iterative state machine is deployed to analyze the token sequence. A state transition function, denoted as $f : S \times \Sigma \to S$, governs the progression between various parsing states, ensuring that each token aligns with the corresponding element described in the JSON grammar. This analytical method is predicated on the verification of syntactic integrity, where each object and array is recursively inspected to ascertain the correct nesting and closure of delimiters. The parser, therefore, systematically constructs an in-memory representation of the JSON data, mapping keys to their respective values with strict type fidelity. Such a methodology is indispensable in contexts where the network-induced payload may exhibit variability in its structure and size.

Memory Management and Error Recovery in Embedded Contexts

The constraints inherent to embedded systems, notably limited memory capacity and processing power, impose a need for judicious memory management during the parsing process. Allocation and reallocation of memory are performed in a controlled manner, often utilizing pre-allocated buffers to manage the variability in JSON payload sizes. The effective restraint on dynamic memory allocation is critical; if $M_{\max}$ represents the maximum available memory and M_{used} denotes the memory already allocated, then the residual capacity $M_{\text{res}} = M_{\max} - M_{\text{used}}$ must be rigorously monitored to prevent oversubscription during parsing. Error recovery mechanisms are interleaved with the memory management routines to handle anomalies such as incomplete or malformed JSON data. In this context, the parser employs validation techniques that include boundary checks and token re-synchronization to recover from errors without compromising system stability. The incorporation of such strategies minimizes the risk of buffer overflows and ensures that the system remains resilient in the face of unexpected or corrupted network inputs.

Integration of Parsed Data into ESP32 Workflows

Following successful parsing, the translation of JSON data into functional application components is a process governed by both data mapping and type conversion standards. The parsing algorithm produces a structured representation in the form of nested dictionaries and arrays, which must then be integrated with the data flow intrinsic to ESP32 applications. The conversion from textual representations of numbers and strings to their corresponding internal types is accomplished with precision, ensuring that each key-value pair is mapped to an appropriate variable or data structure. This integration is further facilitated by design patterns that promote modularity and separation of concerns, thereby allowing the parsed JSON data to be dispatched readily into the core processing units of the embedded system. Moreover, the synchronization of asynchronous network events with the internal state of the application is achieved by enqueuing parsed objects for processing in a non-blocking manner. Such design considerations ensure that even under conditions of high network latency or variable payload sizes, the system maintains high throughput and operational robustness.

ESP32 For IoT With Arduino Code Snippet

```
/*
 * Comprehensive ESP32 For IoT With Arduino Example
 * This code demonstrates:
 *   - JSON parsing using the ArduinoJson library.
 *   - Error detection and recovery during JSON deserialization.
 *   - Memory management by monitoring free heap and calculating
 *     residual memory using the formula: M_RES = M_MAX - M_USED.
 *   - Integration of asynchronous data processing via FreeRTOS
 ↪   tasks
 *     and queues.
 *
 * The producer task simulates receiving JSON payloads from a
 ↪   network
```

```
 * interface, while the consumer task parses the payload, handles
 ↪   errors,
 * and dispatches the valid data for further processing.
 */

#include <Arduino.h>
#include <ArduinoJson.h>
#include "freertos/FreeRTOS.h"
#include "freertos/task.h"
#include "freertos/queue.h"

// Simulated maximum available memory in bytes for JSON processing
const unsigned long M_MAX = 320000;

// Define a buffer size for JSON payloads
#define JSON_BUFFER_SIZE 256

// FreeRTOS queue handle to pass JSON payloads between tasks
QueueHandle_t jsonQueue;

// -----------------------------------------------------------
// Function: processParsedJson
// Purpose:  Process the parsed JSON document and integrate data
// ↪   into the
//           application workflow. Demonstrates type conversion and
// ↪   data mapping.
// -----------------------------------------------------------
void processParsedJson(JsonDocument &doc) {
  // Check for required keys in the JSON payload
  if (doc.containsKey("sensor") && doc.containsKey("value")) {
    const char* sensor = doc["sensor"];
    float value = 0.0;

    // Determine the type of the "value" field and convert
    // ↪   accordingly
    if (doc["value"].is<float>()) {
      value = doc["value"].as<float>();
    } else if (doc["value"].is<int>()) {
      value = (float)doc["value"].as<int>();
    } else if (doc["value"].is<const char *>()) {
      // Convert string to float if necessary
      value = atof(doc["value"]);
    } else {
      Serial.println("Error: Unexpected data type for sensor
      ↪   value.");
      return;
    }
    Serial.print("Parsed Sensor Data -> Sensor: ");
    Serial.print(sensor);
    Serial.print(", Value: ");
    Serial.println(value);
  } else {
```

```
      Serial.println("Warning: JSON does not contain required keys
      ↪   'sensor' and 'value'.");
  }
}

// ------------------------------------------------------------
// Task: jsonProducerTask
// Purpose: Simulate the reception of JSON payloads from a network
↪   stream.
//          Enqueues the payloads to be processed asynchronously.
// ------------------------------------------------------------
void jsonProducerTask(void * parameter) {
  // Array of sample JSON payloads, including one with an
  ↪   intentionally
  // problematic value to demonstrate error recovery.
  const char* sampleJSONs[] = {
    "{\"sensor\":\"temperature\", \"value\":23.5}",
    "{\"sensor\":\"humidity\", \"value\":45}",
    "{\"sensor\":\"pressure\", \"value\":1013}",
    "{\"sensor\":\"temperature\", \"value\":\"invalid\"}"
  };
  const int numSamples = sizeof(sampleJSONs) /
  ↪   sizeof(sampleJSONs[0]);
  int index = 0;

  while (true) {
    char jsonPayload[JSON_BUFFER_SIZE];
    // Copy the sample JSON string into a local buffer
    strncpy(jsonPayload, sampleJSONs[index], JSON_BUFFER_SIZE - 1);
    jsonPayload[JSON_BUFFER_SIZE - 1] = '\0';

    // Enqueue the JSON payload for the consumer task
    if (xQueueSend(jsonQueue, (void*)&jsonPayload, portMAX_DELAY) !=
    ↪   pdPASS) {
      Serial.println("Error: Failed to send JSON payload to
      ↪   queue.");
    } else {
      Serial.print("Produced JSON payload: ");
      Serial.println(jsonPayload);
    }

    // Cycle to the next sample payload
    index = (index + 1) % numSamples;

    // Delay to simulate network latency
    vTaskDelay(5000 / portTICK_PERIOD_MS);
  }
}

// ------------------------------------------------------------
// Task: jsonConsumerTask
// Purpose: Receive JSON payloads from the queue, parse them, and
↪   perform
```

```
//          memory management calculations using provided formulas.
// -----------------------------------------------------------
void jsonConsumerTask(void * parameter) {
  char receivedJson[JSON_BUFFER_SIZE];

  while (true) {
    // Block until a JSON payload is available in the queue
    if (xQueueReceive(jsonQueue, &receivedJson, portMAX_DELAY) ==
    ↪  pdPASS) {
      Serial.print("Consumed JSON payload: ");
      Serial.println(receivedJson);

      // Create a StaticJsonDocument for parsing the payload.
      StaticJsonDocument<JSON_BUFFER_SIZE> doc;
      DeserializationError error = deserializeJson(doc,
      ↪  receivedJson);

      if (error) {
        // If parsing fails, report the error and skip this payload.
        Serial.print("JSON Parsing Error: ");
        Serial.println(error.c_str());
        continue;
      }

      // Process the parsed JSON data.
      processParsedJson(doc);

      // Memory Management: Monitor available heap memory.
      unsigned long freeHeap = ESP.getFreeHeap();
      // Simulate used memory as the difference between the total
      ↪  available and free memory.
      unsigned long usedMemory = M_MAX - freeHeap;
      // Residual memory computed as: M_RES = M_MAX - M_USED (which
      ↪  approximates freeHeap here).
      unsigned long residualMemory = freeHeap;

      Serial.print("Memory Monitoring -> Total (M_MAX): ");
      Serial.print(M_MAX);
      Serial.print(" bytes, Used (M_USED): ");
      Serial.print(usedMemory);
      Serial.print(" bytes, Residual (M_RES): ");
      Serial.print(residualMemory);
      Serial.println(" bytes");

      Serial.println("--------------------");
    }
  }
}

void setup() {
  Serial.begin(115200);
  delay(1000); // Allow time for serial monitor initialization
```

```
Serial.println("ESP32 For IoT With Arduino - JSON Parsing and Data
↪    Handling Example");

// Create the queue to hold JSON payloads (capacity: 10 items)
jsonQueue = xQueueCreate(10, sizeof(char) * JSON_BUFFER_SIZE);
if (jsonQueue == NULL) {
  Serial.println("Critical Error: Unable to create JSON payload
  ↪    queue.");
  while (true); // Halt execution if the queue cannot be created.
}

// Create the JSON producer task with a stack size of 4096 bytes.
xTaskCreate(
  jsonProducerTask,    // Task function.
  "JSONProducer",      // Name of the task.
  4096,                // Stack size in bytes.
  NULL,                // Task input parameter.
  1,                   // Task priority.
  NULL                 // Task handle.
);

// Create the JSON consumer task with a stack size of 4096 bytes.
xTaskCreate(
  jsonConsumerTask,    // Task function.
  "JSONConsumer",      // Name of the task.
  4096,                // Stack size in bytes.
  NULL,                // Task input parameter.
  1,                   // Task priority.
  NULL                 // Task handle.
);
}

void loop() {
  // The main loop is intentionally left empty as tasks run
  ↪    concurrently.
}
```

Chapter 28

Leveraging RESTful APIs

Fundamental Principles of RESTful Architecture

RESTful APIs are grounded in the architectural style known as Representational State Transfer. This paradigm is characterized by a uniform interface that simplifies interactions between the client and the server. Specifically, the approach mandates that each resource be identified via a unique URI, and that the state transfer occurs by using a predefined set of well-known operations. The statelessness constraint ensures that each interaction contains all of the information necessary for the server to process the request, thereby obviating the need for session storage. The principles of cacheability and a layered system further enhance scalability and system modularity. The uniformity in the communication interface, which primarily utilizes standard HTTP methods, leads to systems where clients and servers can evolve independently, while maintaining a clear separation of concerns.

HTTP Methods and Semantic Data Representation

Within the operational framework of RESTful services, the standard HTTP methods serve as the foundation for resource manipulation. Methods such as *GET*, *POST*, *PUT*, and *DELETE* are used to respectively retrieve, create, modify, and remove resources. Each of these methods encapsulates a distinct semantic meaning that is preserved across diverse applications, ensuring predictability in the interaction with remote services. Data exchanged during this process is typically serialized in a structured format such as JSON, where key-value mapping preserves both semantic meaning and hierarchical organization. The specification of MIME types, for example *application/json*, guarantees that the content adheres to an interoperable format, thereby facilitating seamless communication between heterogeneous systems. The clear delineation of these methods and representations underpins a system in which operations are both intuitive and robust, a quality that is essential in environments with constrained computational resources.

Connectivity Patterns in ESP32-Driven Systems

The ESP32, as a versatile microcontroller with integrated Wi-Fi capabilities, is well-suited for interfacing with remote RESTful services. Establishing a connection between the ESP32 and these external systems involves the identification and allocation of appropriate network resources, accompanied by the proper configuration of the network stack. The process begins with the establishment of a TCP/IP connection, followed by the initiation of an HTTP request that adheres to the syntactic and semantic constraints of RESTful communications. Given that the ESP32 is often deployed in contexts where memory and processing power are limited, the design of connectivity patterns must prioritize both efficiency and reliability. Mechanisms for reconnection, timeout management, and the judicious handling of response payloads are embedded within the system architecture, ensuring that network-induced delays or transient failures do not compromise the operational integrity of the application.

Mechanisms for Data Exchange and Control

The integration of remote RESTful APIs into ESP32 applications facilitates a bidirectional exchange of data and control commands.

At its core, the data exchange mechanism relies on the transformation of device-specific values into standardized HTTP requests, with responses providing the necessary feedback to inform subsequent operational decisions. The transmission of data is achieved through the composition and dispatch of requests that encapsulate structured payloads. These payloads, conforming to the JSON standard, are parsed and translated into native data structures within the ESP32 environment. Conversely, commands or state control messages retrieved from remote endpoints may trigger alterations in the device's configuration or operational state. This integrated approach ensures that remote control directives are executed with high fidelity, preserving the consistency and reliability of system behavior even in the presence of network perturbations.

Robustness and Error Handling in RESTful Interactions

Ensuring robustness in remote service integrations necessitates the incorporation of comprehensive error handling strategies. In the context of RESTful API interactions, error conditions may arise due to network disruptions, malformed requests, or server-side anomalies. The system architecture incorporates mechanisms to validate responses based on HTTP status codes, while also enforcing strict adherence to expected data schemas. Each response is subjected to a rigorous verification process, wherein anomalies in either the structure or content of the payload prompt the activation of predefined recovery protocols. Such mechanisms may include the reissuance of requests, the application of exponential backoff algorithms, or the transition of the system into a safe state pending further communication. The combination of these techniques results in an architecture that is both resilient and adaptive, capable of maintaining operational stability under variable conditions while ensuring that control commands and data exchanges are executed with precision.

ESP32 For IoT With Arduino Code Snippet

```
#include <WiFi.h>
#include <HTTPClient.h>
#include <ArduinoJson.h>

// Wi-Fi network credentials
const char* ssid     = "your_SSID";
const char* password = "your_PASSWORD";

// Server endpoints for GET and POST requests
const char* serverGet  = "http://example.com/api/data";
const char* serverPost = "http://example.com/api/update";

// Exponential backoff parameters
const int maxRetries = 5;
const unsigned long initialBackoff = 1000; // 1 second

/**
 * Function: performGETRequest
 * Description: Sends an HTTP GET request to the server and parses
 ↪   the JSON response.
 */
void performGETRequest() {
  HTTPClient http;
  http.begin(serverGet);
  int httpResponseCode = http.GET();

  if (httpResponseCode > 0) { // Check for successful connection
    Serial.print("GET Response code: ");
    Serial.println(httpResponseCode);
    if (httpResponseCode == 200) {
      String payload = http.getString();
      Serial.println("Response:");
      Serial.println(payload);

      // Parse JSON payload
      StaticJsonDocument<200> doc;
      DeserializationError error = deserializeJson(doc, payload);
      if (!error) {
        // Assuming the JSON contains a key "value"
        int sensorValue = doc["value"];
        Serial.print("Parsed sensor value: ");
        Serial.println(sensorValue);
      } else {
        Serial.println("Error: JSON parsing failed.");
      }
    }
  } else {
    Serial.print("Error on GET request: ");
```

```
    Serial.println(httpResponseCode);
  }
  http.end();
}

/**
 * Function: performPOSTRequest
 * Description: Composes a JSON payload with sensor data and sends
 ↪    it via an HTTP POST request.
 */
void performPOSTRequest() {
  HTTPClient http;
  http.begin(serverPost);
  http.addHeader("Content-Type", "application/json");

  // Create JSON payload
  StaticJsonDocument<200> doc;
  doc["sensorId"]    = 1;
  doc["temperature"] = 25.3;
  doc["humidity"]    = 48.2;

  String requestBody;
  serializeJson(doc, requestBody);

  int httpResponseCode = http.POST(requestBody);

  if (httpResponseCode > 0) {
    Serial.print("POST Response code: ");
    Serial.println(httpResponseCode);
    String responsePayload = http.getString();
    Serial.println("POST Response:");
    Serial.println(responsePayload);
  } else {
    Serial.print("Error on POST request: ");
    Serial.println(httpResponseCode);
  }
  http.end();
}

/**
 * Function: sendGETWithExponentialBackoff
 * Description: Attempts the GET request repeatedly using an
 ↪    exponential backoff strategy
 *              upon encountering failures.
 */
void sendGETWithExponentialBackoff() {
  int retries = 0;
  unsigned long backoffDelay = initialBackoff;
  bool success = false;

  while (retries < maxRetries && !success) {
    Serial.print("GET Attempt ");
    Serial.println(retries + 1);
```

187

```
    HTTPClient http;
    http.begin(serverGet);
    int code = http.GET();

    if (code == 200) {
      success = true;
      Serial.println("GET request successful.");
      String payload = http.getString();
      Serial.println("Response:");
      Serial.println(payload);
    } else {
      Serial.print("GET request failed with code: ");
      Serial.println(code);
      Serial.print("Waiting for ");
      Serial.print(backoffDelay);
      Serial.println(" ms before retrying.");
      delay(backoffDelay);
      backoffDelay *= 2;   // Exponential backoff: delay doubles
      ↪ every retry
    }

    http.end();
    retries++;
  }

  if (!success) {
    Serial.println("GET request failed after maximum retries.");
  }
}

void setup() {
  // Initialize Serial and Wi-Fi
  Serial.begin(115200);
  Serial.println();
  Serial.print("Connecting to WiFi ");

  WiFi.begin(ssid, password);
  while (WiFi.status() != WL_CONNECTED) {
    delay(500);
    Serial.print(".");
  }

  Serial.println();
  Serial.println("WiFi connected successfully.");

  // Perform a GET request with exponential backoff mechanism
  sendGETWithExponentialBackoff();

  // Perform a POST request to send sensor data
  performPOSTRequest();
}
```

```
void loop() {
  // Repeat RESTful interactions at regular intervals
  delay(10000);  // Wait for 10 seconds between interactions

  // Optionally, perform GET and POST requests continuously
  sendGETWithExponentialBackoff();
  performPOSTRequest();
}
```

Chapter 29

Implementing MQTT for IoT Messaging

MQTT Protocol Architecture

The MQTT protocol has emerged as a pivotal mechanism for enabling efficient messaging in constrained and intermittently connected environments. At its core, MQTT adopts a publish/subscribe messaging paradigm which deviates significantly from traditional client-server models. Instead of direct interactions between a sender and receiver, the protocol relies on the abstraction of topics as intermediary channels through which messages are disseminated. This design minimizes coupling between network participants and adheres to principles of loose coupling and scalability. The protocol operates over a minimalistic header structure and leverages the reliable transport provided by TCP, thereby ensuring that the overhead associated with message encapsulation remains negligible. Furthermore, inherent characteristics such as small code footprint and low bandwidth consumption render MQTT particularly well-suited for resource-constrained devices.

Client Configuration and Connection Establishment

Configuring an MQTT client on the ESP32 incorporates critical considerations that extend beyond mere connectivity. The initialization phase is marked by the assignment of a unique client identifier, which functions as a primary means of distinguishing individual clients within a single broker ecosystem. Additionally, parameters including session persistence, keep-alive intervals, and clean session flags are rigorously defined in accordance with application-specific requirements. The connection establishment process involves the initiation of a TCP/IP socket, followed by a protocol-specific handshake with an MQTT broker. During this procedure, the client and broker negotiate settings that impact socket-level stability and message acknowledgment behavior. The emphasis on robust connection initialization protocols is integral to ensuring continuous service delivery in environments where network quality may fluctuate.

The Publish/Subscribe Communication Paradigm

Central to MQTT is the decoupling of publishers and subscribers via topic-based routing. In this model, publishers broadcast messages to topics without the necessity of knowing the identity or number of subscribers. Conversely, subscribers register their interest in specific topics and, once subscribed, they receive all messages published to those topics. Such an arrangement encapsulates an event-driven architecture that inherently supports asynchronous data exchange. The abstraction of topics facilitates multi-level hierarchies, thereby enabling granular control over message filtering and distribution. This semantic division of data flows ensures that critical notifications are disseminated with minimal latency, while simultaneously isolating unrelated message streams. Consequently, the publish/subscribe paradigm under MQTT becomes a cornerstone of scalable and modular system design in IoT deployments.

Quality of Service Levels and Message Delivery Guarantees

MQTT introduces multiple Quality of Service (QoS) levels to modulate the trade-off between delivery assurance and transmission overhead. Specifically, the three QoS levels—denoted as *QoS* 0, *QoS* 1, and *QoS* 2—offer increasing guarantees regarding message delivery. At QoS 0, messages are dispatched without any acknowledgment, operating under a best-effort delivery model. This is particularly advantageous in scenarios where low latency is prioritized over delivery certainty. In contrast, QoS 1 mandates that every message is acknowledged by the recipient, albeit without safeguards against message duplication. Finally, QoS 2 implements a more complex four-step handshake protocol to ensure that messages are received exactly once, thus mitigating any risk of redundancy. The selection of an appropriate QoS level is contingent upon application-specific demands for reliability versus resource conservation.

Session Management and Retained Message Strategies

Effective session management under MQTT involves not only the initiation of reliable client sessions but also the maintenance of state information across disconnections. The use of persistent sessions allows for the retention of subscription information and queued messages, such that transient connectivity losses do not lead to the inadvertent loss of critical data. Additionally, the concept of retained messages provides a mechanism for ensuring that the most recent value associated with a particular topic is readily available to clients who subsequently subscribe to that topic. This functionality is particularly advantageous in sensor networks where periodic updates occur and the latest state must be preserved. The careful orchestration of session parameters and the judicious use of retained messages contribute to a robust communication framework that can adeptly handle volatility in network connectivity.

Error Handling and Reconnection Strategies

In scenarios where network interruptions or transient failures occur, MQTT incorporates a suite of error handling and reconnection techniques designed to preserve system coherence. The protocol's structure allows clients to detect anomalous conditions through explicit status codes and timeouts, prompting an internal reinitialization of network connections. Reconnection strategies typically employ backoff algorithms that incrementally extend the delay between successive reconnection attempts, thereby reducing the likelihood of overwhelming network resources during periods of instability. By integrating these mechanisms into the ESP32's firmware, developers can ensure that message delivery guarantees are maintained even in the face of adverse network conditions. The robustness achieved through these strategies is essential for applications that require high availability and real-time data consistency in IoT messaging contexts.

ESP32 For IoT With Arduino Code Snippet

```
// Comprehensive ESP32 MQTT Example for IoT Messaging
// This code demonstrates the implementation of MQTT on the ESP32
↪   using the Arduino framework.
// It integrates the following key features discussed in the
↪   chapter:
// - WiFi connectivity setup.
// - MQTT client configuration including persistent sessions and
↪   retained messages.
// - Implementation of the MQTT publish/subscribe communication
↪   paradigm.
// - Handling of Quality of Service (QoS) levels:
//      • QoS_0: Best-effort delivery (no acknowledgments).
//      • QoS_1: At least once delivery (acknowledged, possible
↪   duplicates).
//      • QoS_2: Exactly once delivery (via a four-step handshake).
// - Session management to maintain subscriptions and queued
↪   messages.
// - An exponential backoff algorithm for reconnection strategies:
//      Equation: delay = baseDelay * (2^n), where n is the number
↪   of consecutive failures,
//      with baseDelay = 1000 ms, capped at 60000 ms.
//
// Required Libraries:
//   • WiFi.h        - For connecting the ESP32 to a WiFi network.
//   • PubSubClient.h - For handling MQTT operations.

#include <WiFi.h>
#include <PubSubClient.h>

// WiFi network credentials
const char* ssid = "yourSSID";
const char* password = "yourPassword";

// MQTT Broker details (using a public broker example; change as
↪   needed)
```

```cpp
const char* mqtt_server = "broker.hivemq.com";
const int mqtt_port = 1883;

// Create WiFi and MQTT client objects
WiFiClient espClient;
PubSubClient client(espClient);

// Variables for error handling and reconnection strategy
↪   (exponential backoff)
int reconnectAttempt = 0;
unsigned long lastReconnectAttempt = 0;

// Function to calculate exponential backoff delay in milliseconds
unsigned long calculateBackoff(int attempt) {
  const unsigned long baseDelay = 1000; // Base delay of 1000 ms (1
  ↪   second)
  unsigned long delayTime = baseDelay * (1 << attempt); // 1 <<
  ↪   attempt computes 2^attempt
  if(delayTime > 60000) {
    delayTime = 60000; // Cap the delay to a maximum of 60000 ms (60
    ↪   seconds)
  }
  return delayTime;
}

// MQTT callback function to process incoming messages
void callback(char* topic, byte* payload, unsigned int length) {
  Serial.print("Message arrived [");
  Serial.print(topic);
  Serial.print("]: ");
  for (unsigned int i = 0; i < length; i++) {
    Serial.print((char)payload[i]);
  }
  Serial.println();
}

// Function to establish MQTT connection with the broker using a
↪   persistent session
bool reconnect() {
  if (client.connected()) {
    return true;
  }

  // Create a unique client ID based on random hex value for
  ↪   identification
  String clientId = "ESP32Client-";
  clientId += String(random(0xffff), HEX);

  // Attempt connection (the 'false' parameter below implies session
  ↪   persistence)
  if (client.connect(clientId.c_str(), NULL, NULL, NULL, false)) {
    Serial.println("Connected to MQTT broker.");
```

```cpp
    // Subscribe to a topic with QoS level 1 (ensuring messages are
    ↪ at least delivered once)
    if(client.subscribe("esp32/topic", 1)) {
      Serial.println("Successfully subscribed to topic:
      ↪ esp32/topic");
    } else {
      Serial.println("Subscription attempt failed.");
    }
    return true;
  } else {
    Serial.print("MQTT Connection failed, rc=");
    Serial.print(client.state());
    Serial.println(" - will retry using exponential backoff.");
    return false;
  }
}

void setup() {
  Serial.begin(115200);
  delay(10);

  // Initiate connection to WiFi network
  Serial.print("Connecting to WiFi network: ");
  Serial.println(ssid);
  WiFi.begin(ssid, password);

  while (WiFi.status() != WL_CONNECTED) {
    delay(500);
    Serial.print(".");
  }

  Serial.println("\nWiFi connected.");

  // Initialize MQTT server details and callback function
  client.setServer(mqtt_server, mqtt_port);
  client.setCallback(callback);

  // Seed the random number generator for unique client IDs
  randomSeed(micros());
}

void loop() {
  // Ensure the MQTT client remains connected
  if (!client.connected()) {
    unsigned long now = millis();
    // Calculate the delay based on exponential backoff
    unsigned long delayTime = calculateBackoff(reconnectAttempt);

    // Attempt reconnection if sufficient time has elapsed
    if (now - lastReconnectAttempt > delayTime) {
      Serial.println("Attempting MQTT reconnection...");
      if (reconnect()) {
```

```cpp
      reconnectAttempt = 0; // Reset the attempt counter on
      ↪  successful connection
    } else {
      reconnectAttempt++;
      lastReconnectAttempt = now;
    }
  }
} else {
  // Process incoming messages and maintain the connection
  client.loop();

  // Publish a message periodically (every 5 seconds) as an
  ↪  example
  static unsigned long lastPublishTime = 0;
  const unsigned long publishInterval = 5000;
  if (millis() - lastPublishTime > publishInterval) {

    // Example sensor reading: Simulated temperature sensor value
    // Conversion Formula (dummy example): temperature = rawValue
    ↪  * 0.1
    float sensorValue = random(200, 300) / 10.0;

    char message[50];
    snprintf(message, sizeof(message), "Temperature: %.2f C",
    ↪  sensorValue);

    // Publish the message with QoS level 1 and set as retained,
    ↪  so new subscribers immediately get the latest value
    if (client.publish("esp32/topic", message, true)) {
      Serial.print("Published message: ");
      Serial.println(message);
    } else {
      Serial.println("Failed to publish message.");
    }

    lastPublishTime = millis();
  }
}
}
```

Chapter 30

Securing MQTT Communication

Security Threat Model and Communication Vulnerabilities

The MQTT protocol, by design, emphasizes a minimalistic overhead suitable for constrained environments. However, this simplicity introduces an expanded attack surface that must be rigorously examined. In the absence of intrinsic security mechanisms, the protocol is susceptible to adversarial actions including, but not limited to, eavesdropping, unauthorized message injection, and man-in-the-middle exploits. In networks where channel monitoring and passive interception are feasible, attackers may observe plaintext messages and potentially modify or replay packets. Moreover, the lightweight header architecture, though beneficial for low-latency communication, does little to obscure the operational semantics of the transmitted data. Consequently, the threat model necessitates the adoption of additional security layers to mitigate risks associated with data integrity and system intrusion, particularly when sensitive information is relayed over open or public networks.

Secure Transport Channels and Encryption Protocols

Ensuring the confidentiality and integrity of data in transit requires the establishment of secure transport channels. The application of Transport Layer Security (TLS) emerges as a fundamental measure in this regard. By encapsulating MQTT communications within a TLS tunnel, the protocol benefits from robust encryption and authentication mechanisms. The TLS handshake, predicated on asymmetric cryptographic algorithms and digital certificates, guarantees that both endpoints can verify each other's identities prior to data exchange. Once the secure channel is established, symmetric cryptographic algorithms take precedence, providing efficient data encryption while maintaining minimal latency. The careful negotiation of cipher suites and key exchange protocols under TLS ensures that the encryption overhead remains balanced with resource constraints, a critical consideration in IoT deployments featuring devices with limited computational capacity.

Authentication Mechanisms and Session Integrity

Beyond channel encryption, the assurance of session integrity hinges on effective authentication mechanisms. A fundamental security measure involves the assignment of unique credentials to each client, typically in the form of username and password combinations, which are exchanged during the initial connection handshake. This authentication step is pivotal in preventing unauthorized entities from establishing connections with the broker. Furthermore, the use of persistent sessions necessitates a rigorous validation process wherein session states are securely maintained across disconnections. Such mechanisms preempt session hijacking and mitigate replay attacks by enforcing strict credential verification and periodic re-authentication. In addition, auxiliary measures such as token-based authentication and mutual certificate verification are adopted in scenarios demanding higher security guarantees. This comprehensive approach to authentication reinforces the resilience of MQTT communication against unauthorized access and unauthorized message publication or subscription.

Cryptographic Techniques for Data Integrity and Privacy

The preservation of data integrity and privacy during MQTT communication is further enhanced through the application of cryptographic primitives at the message level. Message Authentication Codes (MACs) serve as a critical tool in this context, enabling the recipient to verify that the contents of each message have not been altered during transit. The inclusion of cryptographically derived hashes, such as those produced by the Secure Hash Algorithm (SHA), underpins a verification mechanism that detects any tampering. In parallel, symmetric encryption algorithms, for instance those based on the Advanced Encryption Standard (AES), provide an additional layer of data protection by converting plaintext payloads into ciphered text that remains unintelligible to unauthorized third parties. The judicious selection and application of these cryptographic methods reflect a deliberate trade-off between computational overhead and the imperative for strong security guarantees. This balance is especially critical in settings where IoT devices must operate within strict power and processing constraints, yet the privacy and integrity of the transmitted data cannot be compromised.

ESP32 For IoT With Arduino Code Snippet

```
#include <WiFi.h>
#include <WiFiClientSecure.h>
#include <PubSubClient.h>
#include <mbedtls/sha256.h>

// WiFi and MQTT credentials and server settings
const char* WIFI_SSID     = "yourSSID";
const char* WIFI_PASSWORD = "yourPassword";

const char* MQTT_SERVER   = "mqtt.example.com";
const int   MQTT_PORT     = 8883;
const char* MQTT_USERNAME = "mqttUser";
const char* MQTT_PASSWORD = "mqttPass";

// Root CA certificate for TLS (replace with your broker's actual
↪   certificate)
const char* ca_cert = \
```

```cpp
"-----BEGIN CERTIFICATE-----\n" \
"MIIDdzCCAl+gAwIBAgIEbGPo2zANBgkqhkiG9w0BAQsFADBoMQswCQYDVQQGEwJV\n" \
↪ \
"UzETMBEGA1UECBMKQ2FsaWZvcm5pYTEPMA0GA1UEBxMGU2FudGEgQ2xhcmExETAP\n" \
↪ \
"BgNVBAoTCER1bW15Q28xETAPBgNVBAMTCER1bW15Q0EwHhcNMjAwMTAxMDAwMDAw\n" \
↪ \
"WhcNMzAwMTAxMDAwMDAwWjBoMQswCQYDVQQGEwJVUzETMBEGA1UECBMKQ2FsaWZv\n" \
↪ \
"cm5pYTEPMA0GA1UEBxMGU2FudGEgQ2xhcmExETAPBgNVBAoTCER1bW15Q28xETAP\n" \
↪ \
"BgNVBAMTCER1bW15Q0OEwggEiMA0GCSqGSIb3DQEBAQUAA4IBDwAwggEKAoIBAQC3\n" \
↪ \
"u1QGFwI6x8Dm2SkQr1e9KzWkR7+FThNP5+2pcj/Tl4HJTM7VbmNWFeKixKz9a+FQ\n" \
↪ \
"niE9wD5qmCfxosBNS/Qp9r5Pjdc6pIexKqLeIPgdiiH5O0z3OvfRRSZUaevJDi2d\n" \
↪ \
"f/9TTs1qBvBZ7sJgZNH/Zh0QEx0G6Y8MoAvF16aJfXtUhs4hHPReE1kNaIfqlgiy\n" \
↪ \
"kHy6VD9EF+dflTHzCMqHbrJCORFT3omSXnCoURbk+fiDbSGQO6uONZfDts1FA8Rz\n" \
↪ \
"VBrtnZqJqI3FnANvHnDhvH6u+rYgK1L6Vno7G6cC4Qx0AepAtZX5fl8cRb+cl/72\n" \
↪ \
"YVqB3A/j3t5MBZTmEaRcAgMBAAGjUzBRMB0GA1UdDgQWBBQi6j69a1Jea3r7HlQa\n" \
↪ \
"oYJQGhN4zAfBgNVHSMEGDAWgBQi6j69a1Jea3r7HlQaoYJQGhN4zAPBgNVHRMBAf8E\n" \
↪ \
"BTADAQH/MA0GCSqGSIb3DQEBCwUAA4IBAQB4vRDN/dlKml2jR1XlXlI3OWg7J4YD\n" \
↪ \
"Y/5hPTLq6wuddlRMLs69+JX+3o9BUHniXvLbnquQuhrDiFvzBOOU2WG+hX7QU3B7\n" \
↪ \
"F5hZWZmgClTyoz5kJvsr9VitO+mXG8QuRCo1RyhGJ+Y2/kN8c/qQeDmUbNfQ3wkP\n" \
↪ \
"-----END CERTIFICATE-----\n";

// Instantiate secure WiFi and MQTT client objects
WiFiClientSecure secureClient;
PubSubClient mqttClient(secureClient);

// Function to generate a Message Authentication Code (MAC) using
↪ SHA-256
void generateMAC(const char* message, const char* key, char* macStr)
↪ {
  // Combine the message and key
  String combined = String(message) + String(key);
  const char* input = combined.c_str();
  size_t inputLen = combined.length();

  unsigned char hash[32]; // SHA-256 produces a 256-bit (32-byte)
  ↪ hash
  // Compute SHA-256 hash (0 indicates SHA-256, not SHA-224)
  mbedtls_sha256_ret((const unsigned char*)input, inputLen, hash,
  ↪ 0);
```

```
  // Convert the binary hash into a hex string
  for (int i = 0; i < 32; i++) {
    sprintf(macStr + (i * 2), "%02x", hash[i]);
  }
  macStr[64] = '\0'; // Ensure the string is null-terminated
}

// Function to securely connect to the MQTT broker using TLS
void connectToMQTT() {
  Serial.print("Connecting to MQTT broker");
  while (!mqttClient.connected()) {
    Serial.print(".");
    // Attempt connection with a unique client ID and provided
    ↪ credentials
    if (mqttClient.connect("ESP32Client", MQTT_USERNAME,
    ↪ MQTT_PASSWORD)) {
      Serial.println(" Connected.");
    } else {
      Serial.print("Failed, rc=");
      Serial.print(mqttClient.state());
      Serial.println(" - trying again in 5 seconds");
      delay(5000);
    }
  }
}

void setup() {
  Serial.begin(115200);
  delay(1000);
  Serial.println("ESP32 Secure MQTT Communication Demo");

  // Connect to WiFi network
  WiFi.begin(WIFI_SSID, WIFI_PASSWORD);
  Serial.print("Connecting to WiFi");
  while (WiFi.status() != WL_CONNECTED) {
    delay(500);
    Serial.print(".");
  }
  Serial.println();
  Serial.print("WiFi Connected. IP address: ");
  Serial.println(WiFi.localIP());

  // Configure the secure client with the CA certificate for TLS
  secureClient.setCACert(ca_cert);

  // Set the MQTT server and port for the secure connection
  mqttClient.setServer(MQTT_SERVER, MQTT_PORT);

  // Establish the MQTT connection
  connectToMQTT();
}
```

```
void loop() {
  // Reconnect to MQTT broker if the connection is lost
  if (!mqttClient.connected()) {
    connectToMQTT();
  }
  mqttClient.loop();

  // Example data: sensor reading to be securely transmitted
  const char* sensorData = "Temperature: 25.3°C";
  char mac[65]; // Buffer to hold the 64-character MAC plus null
  ↪  terminator
  // Generate a MAC using SHA-256 to ensure data integrity
  generateMAC(sensorData, "secretKey", mac);

  // Construct the final payload by appending the MAC to the sensor
  ↪  data
  String finalPayload = String(sensorData) + " | MAC: " +
  ↪  String(mac);
  Serial.print("Publishing payload: ");
  Serial.println(finalPayload);

  // Publish the secure payload to the designated MQTT topic
  mqttClient.publish("esp32/sensor", finalPayload.c_str());

  // Wait for 5 seconds before sending the next message
  delay(5000);
}
```

Chapter 31

WebSocket Communication Fundamentals

Theoretical Foundations and Protocol Handshake

The WebSocket protocol introduces a paradigm shift from the traditional request–response model of $HTTP/1.1$ by establishing a persistent, bidirectional channel over a single TCP connection. The protocol is distinguished by its initial handshake mechanism, during which a conventional HTTP request is upgraded to a WebSocket connection. This upgrade is initiated by the client sending an *Upgrade* header alongside a unique key. The key, when concatenated with the globally defined GUID, namely `258EAFA5-E914-47DA-95CA-C5AB0DC85B11`, is subjected to the SHA-1 hashing algorithm. The resulting digest is encoded in base64 to form a response token, which the server returns in the *Sec-WebSocket-Accept* header. This cryptographic exchange not only validates the integrity of the connection request but also serves as the cornerstone for establishing a secure and continuous communication channel. The mathematical formulation for the validation is represented as

$$H = \text{Base64}(SHA\text{-}1(client\_key + GUID))$$

and encapsulates the critical transformation performed during the handshake. Such design decisions ensure that the protocol maintains minimal overhead while providing the necessary framework for two-way communication in environments with stringent resource constraints.

Bidirectional Communication Mechanisms: Architectures and Processes

The fundamental architecture of WebSocket communication is inherently engineered for simultaneous data transmission in both directions. This full-duplex communication channel facilitates real-time exchange of information, thereby eliminating the latency typically associated with establishing separate connections for outbound and inbound data. Once the handshake is successfully executed, the protocol enables asynchronous messaging where both endpoints can send and receive data independently. The continuous connection status also supports an event-driven paradigm, wherein messages can trigger state transitions or processing events without awaiting a synchronous request. In this model, the operational semantics diverge from conventional duplex systems that rely on discrete transactions. Instead, the ability to maintain an open channel is paramount in scenarios involving time-sensitive operations. Such properties are especially critical in applications that demand rapid response times and dynamic adjustments based on incoming data. The architecture is further characterized by its ability to handle fragmented messages, maintain connection persistence through periodic heartbeat messages, and implement efficient error recovery through well-defined close procedures. These mechanisms collectively contribute to a robust framework for real-time interactivity.

Integration of WebSocket Protocol in ESP32 IoT Systems

The adoption of WebSocket communication within ESP32 applications necessitates an intricate balance between advanced protocol features and the inherent resource limitations of embedded systems. The ESP32, with its restricted processing capabilities and memory footprint, must manage buffering, asynchronous I/O, and network error handling in a manner that preserves system stability. In such deployments, the continuous, bidirectional data exchange provided by WebSocket proves advantageous for real-time telemetry and command control scenarios. The protocol's ability to sustain a persistent connection minimizes the computational overhead associated with repeated connection setups, thereby optimizing the utility of the available hardware resources. Integration in this context involves meticulous management of connection states, including the initiation of handshake sequences, monitoring of channel integrity, and execution of non-blocking operations. Hardware-level constraints mandate careful allocation of memory for receive and transmit buffers, while ensuring that state transition mechanisms operate in concurrent environments without leading to deadlocks. The implementation further benefits from leveraging the event-driven nature of the protocol, where callback routines monitor for incoming data packets and trigger appropriate response functions. Thus, the convergence of the WebSocket protocol with the ESP32's capabilities facilitates an efficacious platform for real-time, low-latency communication in intricate IoT ecosystems.

ESP32 For IoT With Arduino Code Snippet

```
#include <WiFi.h>
#include <WiFiClient.h>
#include <WiFiServer.h>
#include <mbedtls/sha1.h>
#include <mbedtls/base64.h>

// Replace with your WiFi network credentials
const char* ssid     = "YOUR_WIFI_SSID";
const char* password = "YOUR_WIFI_PASSWORD";

// Create a WiFiServer object that listens on port 80
WiFiServer server(80);

// The globally defined GUID for WebSocket handshake
const char* websocketGUID = "258EAFA5-E914-47DA-95CA-C5AB0DC85B11";

// Function to generate the Sec-WebSocket-Accept key using SHA-1 and
↪    Base64 encoding
String generateAcceptKey(String clientKey) {
  // Concatenate the client's key with the WebSocket GUID
  String concatenated = clientKey + websocketGUID;
```

```
// Compute the SHA-1 hash of the concatenated string
uint8_t hash[20]; // SHA-1 produces a 20-byte digest
mbedtls_sha1_ret((const unsigned char*)concatenated.c_str(),
↪   concatenated.length(), hash);

// Prepare buffer for Base64 encoded output
size_t encodedLen = 0;
unsigned char encoded[64];
int ret = mbedtls_base64_encode(encoded, sizeof(encoded),
↪   &encodedLen, hash, 20);
if(ret != 0) {
  Serial.println("Error during Base64 encoding");
  return "";
}

// Convert the encoded result into a String
String acceptKey = "";
for(size_t i = 0; i < encodedLen; i++){
  acceptKey += (char) encoded[i];
}
return acceptKey;
}

void setup() {
  Serial.begin(115200);
  delay(1000);
  Serial.println();
  Serial.println("Initializing WiFi...");

  // Connect to WiFi network
  WiFi.begin(ssid, password);
  while(WiFi.status() != WL_CONNECTED) {
    delay(500);
    Serial.print(".");
  }

  Serial.println();
  Serial.print("WiFi connected. IP address: ");
  Serial.println(WiFi.localIP());

  // Start the WebSocket server
  server.begin();
  Serial.println("WebSocket Server started on port 80.");
}

void loop() {
  // Check if a client has connected to the server
  WiFiClient client = server.available();
  if(client) {
    Serial.println("Client connected.");

    // Read the incoming HTTP request
    String request = "";
```

```
uint32_t timeout = millis();
while(client.connected() && millis() - timeout < 2000) {
  while(client.available()) {
    String line = client.readStringUntil('\n');
    request += line + "\n";
    timeout = millis();
    if(line == "\r") { // End of headers
      break;
    }
  }
  if(request.indexOf("\r\n\r\n") != -1) {
    break;
  }
}

Serial.println("Received Request:");
Serial.println(request);

// Look for the 'Sec-WebSocket-Key' in the HTTP headers
int keyIndex = request.indexOf("Sec-WebSocket-Key: ");
if(keyIndex != -1) {
  int keyStart = keyIndex + String("Sec-WebSocket-Key:
  ↪ ").length();
  int keyEnd = request.indexOf("\r", keyStart);
  String clientKey = request.substring(keyStart, keyEnd);
  clientKey.trim();

  Serial.print("Client Key: ");
  Serial.println(clientKey);

  // Generate the response token using the provided algorithm:
  // H = Base64(SHA-1(client_key + GUID))
  String acceptKey = generateAcceptKey(clientKey);
  Serial.print("Generated Accept Key: ");
  Serial.println(acceptKey);

  // Construct the HTTP handshake response required to upgrade
  ↪ to WebSocket
  String response = "HTTP/1.1 101 Switching Protocols\r\n";
  response += "Upgrade: websocket\r\n";
  response += "Connection: Upgrade\r\n";
  response += "Sec-WebSocket-Accept: " + acceptKey + "\r\n\r\n";

  // Send the handshake response to the client
  client.print(response);
  Serial.println("Handshake response sent.");
} else {
  Serial.println("Sec-WebSocket-Key header not found. Sending
  ↪ 400 Bad Request.");
  client.print("HTTP/1.1 400 Bad Request\r\n\r\n");
}

delay(10);
```

```
    client.stop();
    Serial.println("Client disconnected.");
  }
}
```

Chapter 32

Implementing UDP Multicast

Theoretical Foundations of Multicast Communication

UDP multicast is an extension of the connectionless User Datagram Protocol that permits the dissemination of data to a group of receivers concurrently. Unlike unicast transmission, where a single packet is delivered to one endpoint at a time, multicast transmission exploits the network infrastructure to replicate datagrams with minimal additional load. In this paradigm, datagrams are addressed to a multicast group rather than individual destinations. The multicast addressing scheme for IPv4 is defined over the range 224.0.0.0 to 239.255.255.255, while IPv6 utilizes addresses with the prefix $FF00 :: /8$. This addressing framework enables the assignment of a single destination address to represent a collective set of endpoints.

The intrinsic efficiency of UDP multicast lies in its ability to transmit a single packet that is subsequently duplicated by routers or switches for delivery to multiple recipients. In practice, this means that the sender incurs a constant bandwidth cost independent of the number of receiving endpoints. If S denotes the size of the datagram and M the number of recipients, then the cost on the sender side remains approximately S, a substantial improvement over the $M \times S$ cost incurred by traditional unicast transmission.

Mechanics of Data Distribution over UDP Multicast

In multicast communication, data packets are encapsulated within UDP datagrams that maintain their standard header format while utilizing a multicast address as the destination. Upon transmission, intermediate network devices detect the multicast group address embedded in the IP header and replicate the datagram accordingly. This replication process is inherently integrated into network routing protocols that support multicast—ensuring that the same packet reaches all endpoints that have joined the respective multicast group.

The design of UDP multicast is predicated on the absence of connection management mechanisms. A single multicast datagram, dispatched with an appropriate destination address, is simultaneously delivered to all hosts that have expressed interest in that multicast group. Since UDP does not guarantee delivery or order, the protocol inherently favors scenarios that are tolerant of packet loss and do not require the reliability of connection-oriented protocols. Such characteristics render UDP multicast well-suited for applications where real-time performance and reduced latency are paramount.

Multicast Group Addressing and Membership Management

Effective implementation of UDP multicast hinges upon a robust scheme for managing group membership. Hosts indicate their intent to participate in multicast communication by joining a multicast group through established membership protocols. For IPv4, the Internet Group Management Protocol (IGMP) is employed, enabling hosts and adjacent routers to coordinate multicast group memberships. In IPv6, Multicast Listener Discovery (MLD) serves an analogous role. These protocols facilitate the efficient handling of join and leave messages, ensuring that network routers maintain an accurate record of active group members.

A key aspect in this framework is the dynamic nature of group membership. Upon joining a multicast group, a host begins to receive any datagram addressed to the group's dedicated IP address. Conversely, when a host leaves the group, subsequent multicast

210

transmissions no longer reach that endpoint. The agile management of such memberships allows the network to adapt in real time to changing communication patterns without incurring the overhead of individualized connections for each participating host.

Implementation Considerations and Network Dynamics

Implementing UDP multicast within resource-constrained systems necessitates a careful balance between network efficiency and the inherent limitations of the underlying hardware. The stateless nature of UDP multicast simplifies the transmission model; however, it also imposes certain challenges. Among these, the absence of built-in reliability requires that higher-level software layers address issues such as packet loss, ordering, and error correction. In scenarios where data integrity is critical, supplementary protocols or application-level redundancy mechanisms must be employed.

From a network dynamics perspective, the performance of UDP multicast is contingent upon proper buffer management and concurrency handling. Given that datagrams are transmitted without the overhead of connection setup and teardown, the system must allocate sufficient memory for both transmission and reception buffers. Moreover, the multithreaded nature of many IoT deployments often necessitates non-blocking operations so that the processing of multicast datagrams does not impede other critical tasks. These design decisions are influenced by considerations such as data rate, expected latency, and the variability of network conditions.

Finally, the deployment of UDP multicast in a multilayered network architecture requires that routing protocols support multicast forwarding efficiently. Protocols such as Protocol Independent Multicast (PIM) complement the multicast model by dynamically establishing routes that optimize the flow of data to all active endpoints. This integrated approach, grounded in the efficient utilization of bandwidth and computational resources, underscores the advantages of leveraging UDP multicast for simultaneous data transmission across complex IoT ecosystems.

ESP32 For IoT With Arduino Code Snippet

```cpp
#include <WiFi.h>
#include <WiFiUdp.h>

// WiFi network credentials
const char* ssid     = "YOUR_SSID";
const char* password = "YOUR_PASSWORD";

// Multicast configuration
// Use an IPv4 multicast address in the range 224.0.0.0 to
↪   239.255.255.255.
// In this example, we use 239.255.255.250.
const char* multicastAddress = "239.255.255.250";
const int multicastPort = 12345;

// Datagram details
String multicastMessage = "Hello from ESP32 UDP Multicast!";
const int datagramSize = multicastMessage.length(); // S in bytes

// For illustration, assume we have M recipients.
const int numberOfRecipients = 5;

// UDP object instance
WiFiUDP udp;

// Timing for periodic transmission
unsigned long previousMillis = 0;
const long interval = 5000; // Send multicast message every 5000 ms

/*
  Explanation of the cost equation in multicast communication:

  Let S be the size (in bytes) of the UDP datagram.
  Let M be the number of receiving endpoints.

  In UDP multicast:
      Sender Cost  S bytes (since one packet is transmitted once).

  In traditional unicast transmission:
      Sender Cost  M × S bytes (since each recipient gets its own
      ↪   copy).

  This code snippet prints the above comparison for clarity.
*/

// Function prototype for parsing dotted-decimal IP string to
↪   IPAddress
IPAddress parseIP(const char* ipString);
```

```
void setup() {
  Serial.begin(115200);
  delay(1000);

  // Connect to WiFi network
  Serial.println("Connecting to WiFi...");
  WiFi.mode(WIFI_STA);
  WiFi.begin(ssid, password);

  while (WiFi.status() != WL_CONNECTED) {
    delay(500);
    Serial.print(".");
  }
  Serial.println();
  Serial.print("Connected! IP Address: ");
  Serial.println(WiFi.localIP());

  // Begin UDP multicast reception on the specified port.
  // The beginMulticast function binds the UDP instance to the local
  ↪  interface,
  // and subscribes to the multicast group.
  if (udp.beginMulticast(WiFi.localIP(), parseIP(multicastAddress),
  ↪  multicastPort)) {
    Serial.print("UDP multicast started on port ");
    Serial.println(multicastPort);
  } else {
    Serial.println("Failed to start UDP multicast");
  }

  // Print cost analysis: Multicast vs Unicast send cost.
  Serial.println("----------------------------------------");
  Serial.println("Cost Analysis:");
  Serial.print("Datagram size (S): ");
  Serial.print(datagramSize);
  Serial.println(" bytes");
  Serial.print("Number of recipients (M): ");
  Serial.println(numberOfRecipients);
  Serial.print("Multicast Sender Cost: ");
  Serial.print(datagramSize);
  Serial.println(" bytes");
  Serial.print("Unicast Sender Cost (if sent individually): ");
  Serial.print(numberOfRecipients * datagramSize);
  Serial.println(" bytes");
  Serial.println("----------------------------------------");
}

void loop() {
  unsigned long currentMillis = millis();

  // Periodically send the multicast datagram.
  if (currentMillis - previousMillis >= interval) {
    previousMillis = currentMillis;
    sendMulticast();
```

```
}

  // Check for and process any incoming multicast packets.
  receiveMulticast();
}

// Function to send a UDP multicast datagram.
void sendMulticast() {
  Serial.println("Sending UDP multicast message...");

  /*
    Begin a multicast packet.
    The beginPacketMulticast() function requires:
      - The multicast group IP address.
      - The destination port.
      - The local IP interface through which to send.
  */
  udp.beginPacketMulticast(parseIP(multicastAddress), multicastPort,
  ↪  WiFi.localIP());

  // Write the message data into the packet.
  // Note: The underlying sender cost remains ~S bytes regardless of
  ↪  the number of recipients.
  udp.write((const uint8_t*)multicastMessage.c_str(),
  ↪  multicastMessage.length());

  // End the packet and send it.
  if (udp.endPacket() == 1) {
    Serial.println("Message sent successfully.");
  } else {
    Serial.println("Error sending multicast message.");
  }
}

// Function to receive and process any incoming UDP multicast
↪  datagrams.
void receiveMulticast() {
  int packetSize = udp.parsePacket();
  if (packetSize) {
    char incomingPacket[255];
    int len = udp.read(incomingPacket, 254);
    if (len > 0) {
      incomingPacket[len] = '\0'; // Null-terminate the string
    }
    Serial.print("Received packet from ");
    Serial.print(udp.remoteIP());
    Serial.print(":");
    Serial.println(udp.remotePort());
    Serial.print("Contents: ");
    Serial.println(incomingPacket);
  }
}
```

```cpp
// Helper function to convert a dotted-decimal IP string to an
↪   IPAddress object.
IPAddress parseIP(const char* ipString) {
  uint8_t ip[4] = {0, 0, 0, 0};
  int part = 0;
  String ipStr(ipString);
  int startIndex = 0;
  int dotIndex = ipStr.indexOf('.');
  while(dotIndex != -1 && part < 4) {
    ip[part] = ipStr.substring(startIndex, dotIndex).toInt();
    startIndex = dotIndex + 1;
    dotIndex = ipStr.indexOf('.', startIndex);
    part++;
  }
  if (part < 4) {
    ip[part] = ipStr.substring(startIndex).toInt();
  }
  return IPAddress(ip[0], ip[1], ip[2], ip[3]);
}
```

Chapter 33

Bluetooth Low Energy (BLE) Fundamentals

Foundations of Bluetooth Low Energy

Bluetooth Low Energy (BLE) is a wireless communication protocol engineered for applications that demand minimal power consumption while maintaining low latency and robust data throughput. Operating in the 2.4 GHz ISM band, BLE employs frequency hopping spread spectrum to mitigate interference and enhance reliability. The protocol distinguishes itself from legacy Bluetooth implementations by offering both connection-oriented and connectionless communication models. Advertisement and scanning mechanisms form the basis of BLE interactions, allowing devices to broadcast their presence and to detect nearby transmitters with minimal energy expense.

BLE Architecture on the ESP32

The ESP32 integrates a dedicated BLE radio coupled with a complete protocol stack that adheres to established BLE standards. This architecture delineates responsibilities between the controller, which manages low-level radio operations, and the host, which implements high-level protocol features. The system is designed to function in dual roles; it can operate as a peripheral device that periodically broadcasts service information, or as a central device that actively scans for and connects with peripherals. The consolidation of these functionalities in a single chip facilitates concurrent wireless operations, thereby accommodating complex IoT scenarios requiring simultaneous BLE and other protocol support.

BLE Protocol Structures and Data Models

At the core of BLE communication lies the Generic Attribute Profile (GATT), which organizes data into a structured hierarchy of services and characteristics. Each service encapsulates a set of characteristics that represent discrete data points or control commands, all uniquely identified by Universally Unique Identifiers (UUIDs). This architecture enables a standardized method for service discovery and data exchange. Communication procedures such as read, write, and notification operations are defined within the GATT framework, ensuring that data is transmitted reliably within the constraints imposed by a low-power design. The systematic deployment of these data models underpins the flexibility and scalability inherent in BLE implementations.

Programming Techniques in BLE Integration

The integration of BLE functionality on the ESP32 is achieved through an event-driven programming model. Asynchronous events such as connection establishment, disconnection, and data transmission are managed via callback functions that monitor the BLE state machine. This paradigm enables the system to handle assorted events without resorting to blocking operations, thereby preserving responsiveness even under variable network conditions. Programming techniques encompass the configuration of device roles, the specification of advertising parameters, and the dynamic management of connection intervals and scan windows—all tailored to optimize energy efficiency while ensuring reliable communication. The abstraction provided by the BLE API facilitates the mapping of high-level application requirements to underlying protocol operations.

Security and Performance Considerations in BLE Communications

Security within BLE communications on the ESP32 is implemented through a suite of mechanisms that include pairing, bonding, and data encryption. Cryptographic algorithms, such as AES-CCM, are employed at the link layer to safeguard the integrity and confidentiality of transmitted information. Robust key exchange protocols are instituted to prevent unauthorized device access and mitigate potential vulnerabilities. In parallel, performance optimization is achieved through the careful adjustment of parameters such as connection intervals, slave latency, and supervision timeouts. These adjustments are critical in balancing the trade-offs between power consumption and data latency, thereby ensuring that the system operates efficiently even in resource-constrained environments.

ESP32 For IoT With Arduino Code Snippet

```
/*
  This example demonstrates a comprehensive BLE server
  ↪  implementation on the ESP32 using the Arduino framework.

  The code sets up:
    - A BLE server with a custom GATT service and characteristic.
    - Callback functions for handling connection events and
    ↪  characteristic writes.
    - A simple algorithm to calculate an optimal BLE connection
    ↪  interval based on battery voltage and RSSI.

  Important Equation:
    Connection Interval (ms) = 50 + (batteryVoltage * 10) + (|rssi|
    ↪  * 0.5)

  Where:
    - batteryVoltage is measured in Volts.
    - rssi is the Received Signal Strength Indicator in dBm.

  This equation is a demonstration of how performance parameters can
  ↪  be dynamically adjusted
  to optimize BLE communication under variable conditions.
*/

#include <Arduino.h>
```

```cpp
#include <BLEDevice.h>
#include <BLEUtils.h>
#include <BLEServer.h>

// Define the UUIDs for the custom BLE service and its
↪  characteristic.
#define SERVICE_UUID        "4fafc201-1fb5-459e-8fcc-c5c9c331914b"
#define CHARACTERISTIC_UUID "beb5483e-36e1-4688-b7f5-ea07361b26a8"

// Global pointer for the BLE server instance.
BLEServer *pServer = nullptr;

// Callback class to handle BLE Server events such as client
↪  connection and disconnection.
class MyServerCallbacks: public BLEServerCallbacks {
  void onConnect(BLEServer* pServer) {
    Serial.println(">>> Client connected to BLE server.");
  }

  void onDisconnect(BLEServer* pServer) {
    Serial.println(">>> Client disconnected from BLE server.");
    // Restart advertising so that new devices can connect.
    pServer->getAdvertising()->start();
    Serial.println(">>> Advertising restarted.");
  }
};

// Function prototype for the algorithm to calculate the optimal BLE
↪  connection interval.
float calculateOptimalConnectionInterval(float batteryVoltage, int
↪  rssi);

// Callback class to handle characteristic write events.
class MyCallbacks: public BLECharacteristicCallbacks {
  void onWrite(BLECharacteristic *pCharacteristic) {
    std::string rxValue = pCharacteristic->getValue();
    Serial.print(">>> Characteristic Written: ");
    if (rxValue.length() > 0) {
      // Print the received value character by character.
      for (int i = 0; i < rxValue.length(); i++) {
        Serial.print(rxValue[i]);
      }
      Serial.println();
    }

    // Demonstration: When a value is written, perform a calculation
    // to determine a recommended connection interval based on
    ↪  sample parameters.
    float batteryVoltage = 3.7; // Example battery voltage in Volts.
    int rssi = -68;             // Example RSSI value in dBm.
    float connInterval =
      ↪  calculateOptimalConnectionInterval(batteryVoltage, rssi);
```

```
      Serial.print("Calculated Optimal Connection Interval (ms): ");
      Serial.println(connInterval);
  }
};

// Implements the equation for calculating an optimal BLE connection
↪    interval based on battery voltage and RSSI.
// Equation: connectionInterval = 50 + (batteryVoltage * 10) +
↪    (abs(rssi) * 0.5)
float calculateOptimalConnectionInterval(float batteryVoltage, int
↪    rssi) {
  float interval = 50.0 + (batteryVoltage * 10.0) + (abs(rssi) *
  ↪    0.5);
  return interval;
}

void setup() {
  Serial.begin(115200);
  Serial.println("=== Initializing ESP32 BLE Server ===");

  // Initialize BLE and set the device name.
  BLEDevice::init("ESP32_BLE_Server");

  // Create the BLE server and assign server callback functions.
  pServer = BLEDevice::createServer();
  pServer->setCallbacks(new MyServerCallbacks());

  // Create a custom BLE service.
  BLEService *pService = pServer->createService(SERVICE_UUID);

  // Create a BLE characteristic with read and write properties and
  ↪    assign characteristic callbacks.
  BLECharacteristic *pCharacteristic =
  ↪    pService->createCharacteristic(
                                      CHARACTERISTIC_UUID,

                                      ↪    BLECharacteristic::PROPERTY_READ
                                      ↪    |

                                      ↪    BLECharacteristic::PROPERTY_WRITE
                                      ↪    |

                                      ↪    BLECharacteristic::PROPERTY_NOTIFY
                                  );
  pCharacteristic->setCallbacks(new MyCallbacks());

  // Set an initial value for the characteristic.
  pCharacteristic->setValue("Hello BLE!");

  // Start the service.
  pService->start();

  // Configure advertising parameters.
```

220

```
BLEAdvertising *pAdvertising = BLEDevice::getAdvertising();
pAdvertising->addServiceUUID(SERVICE_UUID);
pAdvertising->setScanResponse(true);
// The following settings help to resolve some connection issues
↪  on specific devices.
pAdvertising->setMinPreferred(0x06);
pAdvertising->setMinPreferred(0x12);

// Start advertising the BLE service.
BLEDevice::startAdvertising();
Serial.println(">>> BLE Advertising started.");
}

void loop() {
// The loop is kept minimal as this implementation is
↪  event-driven.
// A delay here simulates other background tasks.
delay(1000);

// For demonstration, simulate sensor data via a sine wave
↪  function.
static float angle = 0.0;
angle += 0.1;
if (angle > 6.28) {
  angle = 0.0;
}
float sensorValue = 50.0 + 10.0 * sin(angle); // Simulated sensor
↪  data.
Serial.print("Simulated Sensor Value: ");
Serial.println(sensorValue);

// Retrieve the BLE characteristic and update its value with the
↪  sensor data.
BLECharacteristic* pCharacteristic =
    pServer->getServiceByUUID(SERVICE_UUID)->
    getCharacteristic(CHARACTERISTIC_UUID);
char sensorStr[8];
dtostrf(sensorValue, 1, 2, sensorStr);
pCharacteristic->setValue(sensorStr);
pCharacteristic->notify();  // Inform connected clients of the
↪  updated value.

// Optional: Additional BLE parameter adjustments or security
↪  routines could be implemented here.
}
```

Chapter 34

BLE Peripheral Programming

Configuring the ESP32 as a BLE Peripheral Device

The configuration of the ESP32 as a Bluetooth Low Energy peripheral device involves the initialization of an embedded BLE stack and the designation of the device's role within the BLE network. This role is characterized by the device's ability to advertize its presence, thus facilitating discoverability by central devices. The configuration process requires the assignment of unique identifiers, typically in the form of Universally Unique Identifiers (UUIDs), and the specification of device attributes such as the device name and advertisement data payload. This arrangement is in strict compliance with the BLE specification, ensuring standardization in device identification and service exposure.

Advertisement Services and Packet Structure

Advertisement services constitute a fundamental aspect of the BLE peripheral paradigm. The peripheral device periodically broadcasts advertisement packets over designated advertising channels in the 2.4 GHz Industrial, Scientific, and Medical (ISM) band.

Each advertisement packet is meticulously structured to incorporate several fields, including flags, complete or partial lists of service UUIDs, and optionally, a short device name. Advertisement intervals, which may be denoted by a parameter I_a, are calibrated to orchestrate an optimal trade-off between energy efficiency and device discovery latency. The precise construction of advertisement packets permits the peripheral device to communicate its available services and characteristics effectively, thereby ensuring prompt and reliable recognition by central devices.

GATT Services and Characteristic Configuration

Central to the operation of BLE peripherals is the General Attribute Profile (GATT), which facilitates the definition and organization of services and their associated characteristics. Each service is composed of one or more characteristics that encapsulate discrete data values or control commands. These characteristics are further defined by properties such as read, write, or notify permissions, and are each uniquely identified by a UUID. The meticulous configuration of GATT services and characteristics enables the peripheral to provide structured access to its capabilities, allowing for both synchronous and asynchronous interactions. Detailed attribute permission settings ensure that data exchanges adhere to established security and operational protocols, thereby maintaining the integrity and reliability of the communication process.

Interplay Between Advertisement and GATT Operations

The dynamic interaction between advertisement mechanisms and GATT operations is a hallmark of the BLE peripheral mode. Advertisement packets serve as the initial mechanism by which a peripheral device makes its GATT services known to potential central devices. Upon establishing a connection, the peripheral transitions to a mode of direct GATT communication wherein service discovery and characteristic interactions are performed. This dual-phase operational strategy demands careful management of both advertisement parameters and connection maintenance protocols. In particular, adjustments to advertisement intervals and payload composition directly influence the responsiveness and energy consumption profiles of the peripheral device. The seamless integration of these functions, facilitated by high-level configuration libraries, exemplifies the robust design capabilities inherent in modern IoT systems based on the ESP32 platform.

ESP32 For IoT With Arduino Code Snippet

```
#include <BLEDevice.h>
#include <BLEUtils.h>
#include <BLEServer.h>

// Define unique UUIDs for the BLE Service and Characteristic
#define SERVICE_UUID        "12345678-1234-1234-1234-1234567890ab"
↪  // Example Service UUID
#define CHARACTERISTIC_UUID "87654321-4321-4321-4321-ba0987654321"
↪  // Example Characteristic UUID

// Advertisement interval boundaries (in milliseconds)
// Note: In BLE, advertisement interval units are typically 0.625
↪  ms,
// but here we use milliseconds for demonstration purposes.
const uint32_t ADV_INTERVAL_MIN = 20;   // Minimum advertisement
↪  interval (ms)
const uint32_t ADV_INTERVAL_MAX = 100;  // Maximum advertisement
↪  interval (ms)

/*
 * Function: calculateAdvInterval
 * -------------------------------
 * Computes the advertisement interval I_a based on a trade-off
 ↪  factor.
 *
 * Equation: I_a = ADV_INTERVAL_MIN + factor * (ADV_INTERVAL_MAX -
 ↪  ADV_INTERVAL_MIN)
 *
 * where 'factor' is a value between 0.0 and 1.0:
 *    - 0.0 -> Indicates a fast advertisement rate (low interval,
 ↪  higher energy consumption)
 *    - 1.0 -> Indicates a slow advertisement rate (high interval,
 ↪  energy efficient)
 */
uint32_t calculateAdvInterval(float factor) {
  if (factor < 0.0) factor = 0.0;
  if (factor > 1.0) factor = 1.0;
  return ADV_INTERVAL_MIN + (uint32_t)(factor * (ADV_INTERVAL_MAX -
  ↪  ADV_INTERVAL_MIN));
}
```

```cpp
// Custom BLE Server Callbacks to handle connection events
class MyServerCallbacks : public BLEServerCallbacks {
  void onConnect(BLEServer *pServer) {
    Serial.println("Central device connected.");
  }

  void onDisconnect(BLEServer *pServer) {
    Serial.println("Central device disconnected.");
    // Restart advertising after disconnection
    pServer->getAdvertising()->start();
    Serial.println("Advertising restarted.");
  }
};

BLECharacteristic *pCharacteristic;

void setup() {
  // Initialize Serial Monitor
  Serial.begin(115200);
  Serial.println("Initializing ESP32 as BLE Peripheral...");

  // Initialize BLE with the device name
  BLEDevice::init("ESP32_BLE_Peripheral");

  // Create a BLE Server and assign our custom callbacks
  BLEServer *pServer = BLEDevice::createServer();
  pServer->setCallbacks(new MyServerCallbacks());

  // Create and configure the BLE Service
  BLEService *pService = pServer->createService(SERVICE_UUID);

  // Create and configure the BLE Characteristic with READ, WRITE,
  ↪    and NOTIFY properties
  pCharacteristic = pService->createCharacteristic(
                      CHARACTERISTIC_UUID,
                      BLECharacteristic::PROPERTY_READ   |
                      BLECharacteristic::PROPERTY_WRITE  |
                      BLECharacteristic::PROPERTY_NOTIFY
                    );

  // Set an initial value for the characteristic
  pCharacteristic->setValue("Initial value from ESP32");

  // Start the BLE Service
  pService->start();

  // Configure BLE Advertising
  BLEAdvertising *pAdvertising = BLEDevice::getAdvertising();
  pAdvertising->addServiceUUID(SERVICE_UUID);
  pAdvertising->setScanResponse(true);
```

```
// Calculate and print the advertisement interval using our
↪   defined algorithm
float energyTradeOffFactor = 0.5; // 0.0 for faster discovery, 1.0
↪   for energy efficiency
uint32_t advInterval = calculateAdvInterval(energyTradeOffFactor);
Serial.print("Calculated Advertisement Interval (ms): ");
Serial.println(advInterval);

// Note: Directly setting the advertisement interval may not be
↪   supported by the default Arduino BLE library.
// This calculation serves as an example of managing advertisement
↪   parameters based on energy/discovery trade-offs.

// Start BLE Advertising
BLEDevice::startAdvertising();
Serial.println("BLE Advertising started.");
}

void loop() {
// Placeholder for main loop operations.
// Simulate dynamic GATT updates by changing the characteristic
↪   value periodically.
delay(2000);

// Update the characteristic value with a counter to mimic data
↪   acquisition and notify connected devices
static int updateCounter = 0;
String updatedValue = "Update " + String(updateCounter++);
pCharacteristic->setValue(updatedValue.c_str());
pCharacteristic->notify();

Serial.print("Notified updated value: ");
Serial.println(updatedValue);
}
```

Chapter 35

BLE Central and Scanning Techniques

Properties of the BLE Central Role

Within the Bluetooth Low Energy (BLE) architecture, the central role is defined by its capacity to initiate and manage connections with multiple peripheral devices. A device operating in central mode is tasked with continuously monitoring the radio frequency spectrum for advertisement packets transmitted by peripherals. This role is inherently characterized by the need to implement robust scanning engines that support asynchronous reception of advertisement data. The central device must execute precise timing and filtering operations to ensure that only packets conforming to predetermined criteria, such as specific service UUIDs or acceptable signal strength levels, are processed. Such operations are critical, as the decision process involves an intricate balance between the scanning duty cycle and energy constraints, where parameters such as the scan interval T_{scan} and the scan window W_{scan} directly influence system performance.

Scanning Methodologies and Algorithmic Considerations

The scanning operation employed by a BLE central device is fundamentally governed by the distinction between passive and active scanning methodologies. In passive scanning, the central device solely listens for advertisement packets without transmitting any scan request messages. Conversely, active scanning involves the transmission of scan request packets to elicit additional information from nearby peripherals. In either approach, the scheduling of scan activities is determined by the periodicity and duration of the scan window. Mathematical models of the scan timing, wherein T_{scan} denotes the periodic repetition interval and W_{scan} indicates the duration of each active scanning period, are applied to optimize the probability of detecting transient advertisement events. The design of these algorithms must account for the statistical distribution of advertisement events across the advertising channels, typically channels 37, 38, and 39, ensuring that the scanning strategy maximizes discovery efficiency while conserving energy.

Technical Implementation of Scanning Procedures

The implementation of scanning procedures in a BLE central device encompasses both hardware configuration and software stack integration. At the hardware level, the radio transceiver is configured to cycle through the designated advertising channels, employing frequency hopping schemes as specified in the BLE standard. The underlying software is then responsible for capturing the advertisement packets that are transmitted. Each captured packet is parsed to extract critical fields, including flags, service UUIDs, and optional data elements such as device names. A sophisticated filtering mechanism is employed to discard extraneous packets and prioritize those that meet specific criteria based on signal strength measurements and preconfigured service identifiers. Given that the reception of advertisement packets is inherently asynchronous, it is necessary to coordinate interrupt service routines with higher-level scanning algorithms that utilize state machines for proper sequencing of operations. This synchronous integration of hardware interrupts and software polling forms the core of the scanning architecture.

Interaction with Peripheral Devices

Upon successful detection of peripheral devices via advertisement scanning, the central device must further process the acquired data to facilitate subsequent interactions. The analysis of advertisement payloads involves a detailed inspection of the packet structure to identify service offerings and capabilities of each peripheral. Policy-based decision algorithms then determine which peripherals qualify for connection initiation based on factors such as signal quality and service priority. Once a potential candidate is selected, the central device initiates a connection sequence through a well-defined protocol handshake. This phase requires precise adherence to timing constraints and protocol specifications, as the connection request is disseminated over the same advertisement channels in which the packet data were originally received. The connection establishment phase is accompanied by additional parameter negotiations that ensure compatibility with the central device's operational requirements. These interactions underscore the critical interplay between scanning operations and connection management, highlighting the need for a unified framework that seamlessly integrates discovery, filtering, and connection protocols within the BLE central role.

ESP32 For IoT With Arduino Code Snippet

```
#include <BLEDevice.h>
#include <BLEUtils.h>
#include <BLEScan.h>
#include <BLEAdvertisedDevice.h>
#include <math.h>

// ****************************************************************
// Explanation:
// ---------------------------------------------------------------
// In this snippet we implement a BLE central scanner on the ESP32
↪    that uses
// both active scanning and basic filtering to discover peripheral
↪    devices.
//
// Two key timing parameters are defined:
//    T_scan    : The overall scan repetition interval in
↪    milliseconds.
//    W_scan    : The duration for which the scanning is actively
↪    performed.
```

229

```cpp
//
// Based on the chapter discussion, the estimated probability of
//   detecting a
// transient advertisement event can be modeled as:
//
//   P(detection) = 1 - exp(- W_scan / T_scan)
//
// These parameters (and the above equation) guide our scheduling:
//   while the
// BLE scan is active for W_scan ms, the code then waits for (T_scan
//   - W_scan) ms
// before the next scan cycle. The BLE library functions
//   (setInterval and setWindow)
// complement these values, with their BLE-standard units.
// ************************************************************


// Define scanning parameters (in milliseconds)
#define SCAN_INTERVAL_MS 5000   // T_scan: Overall scan cycle period
//   (ms)
#define SCAN_WINDOW_MS   2000   // W_scan: Duration of active
//   scanning (ms)

// RSSI threshold for device filtering (-70 dBm is used as a
//   filtering criteria)
#define RSSI_THRESHOLD   -70

BLEScan* pBLEScan = nullptr;

// A callback class to process discovered BLE advertisement packets
class MyAdvertisedDeviceCallbacks : public
    BLEAdvertisedDeviceCallbacks {
  void onResult(BLEAdvertisedDevice advertisedDevice) override {
    // Filter devices based on received signal strength indicator
    //   (RSSI)
    if(advertisedDevice.getRSSI() > RSSI_THRESHOLD) {
      Serial.print("Discovered device: ");
      Serial.println(advertisedDevice.toString().c_str());
    }
  }
};

void setup() {
  // Start serial communication for debugging
  Serial.begin(115200);
  Serial.println("Initializing BLE Central Scanning...");

  // Initialize BLE device with a central role identifier
  BLEDevice::init("ESP32_Central");

  // Retrieve the BLE scanner and assign a callback for
  //   advertisement results
  pBLEScan = BLEDevice::getScan();
```

230

```cpp
pBLEScan->setAdvertisedDeviceCallbacks(new
↪  MyAdvertisedDeviceCallbacks(), false);

// Choose the scanning mode:
// Set active scan to true to allow sending of scan request
↪  packets (active scanning)
// Set to false for passive scanning.
pBLEScan->setActiveScan(true);

// Configure low-level scanning parameters (in BLE specific time
↪  units)
pBLEScan->setInterval(45);    // Time interval between scan windows
pBLEScan->setWindow(30);      // Duration of each scan window (must
↪  be <= interval)

// Calculate and display the estimated detection probability using
↪  the formula:
//    P(detection) = 1 - exp(- W_scan / T_scan)
float detectionProbability = 1 - exp(-((float)SCAN_WINDOW_MS /
↪  (float)SCAN_INTERVAL_MS));
Serial.print("Estimated Detection Probability: ");
Serial.println(detectionProbability, 4);
}

void loop() {
  Serial.println("Starting BLE scan cycle...");

  // Convert scanning window from milliseconds to seconds (BLE
  ↪  library expects seconds)
  uint32_t scanDurationSec = SCAN_WINDOW_MS / 1000;

  // Start active scanning for the duration of the scan window.
  // The second parameter 'false' indicates that the scan is not
  ↪  stopped automatically.
  BLEScanResults foundDevices = pBLEScan->start(scanDurationSec,
  ↪  false);

  Serial.print("Devices found in this cycle: ");
  Serial.println(foundDevices.getCount());

  // Clear the results to free memory for the next scanning cycle.
  pBLEScan->clearResults();

  // Calculate waiting time before next scanning cycle:
  // The device waits for the remainder of the scan interval.
  uint32_t delayDuration = SCAN_INTERVAL_MS - SCAN_WINDOW_MS;
  Serial.print("Waiting for ");
  Serial.print(delayDuration);
  Serial.println(" ms before next scan cycle...");

  // Delay to maintain the overall T_scan period.
  delay(delayDuration);
```

}

232

Chapter 36

Managing Dual Connectivity: Wi-Fi & BLE

Architectural Foundations for Dual Radio Operation

The ESP32 is engineered with an integrated dual radio architecture that permits concurrent execution of Wi-Fi and Bluetooth Low Energy (BLE) protocols. The hardware design incorporates a shared radio frequency front-end equipped with carefully calibrated filtering and isolation circuits. These components are arranged to support time division multiplexing of the radio transceiver, thereby enabling both protocol stacks to access the shared physical medium in a coordinated manner. The architecture capitalizes on a master clock source and dedicated synchronization circuitry to mitigate the challenges associated with switching between wireless standards. This design also supports the partitioning of the available computational resources and ensures that the inherent hardware constraints do not compromise the performance of either connectivity mode.

Radio Frequency Coexistence and Interference Mitigation

Wi-Fi and BLE both operate within the congested 2.4 GHz spectrum, where interference is a significant consideration. The ESP32 employs advanced interference mitigation strategies that encompass both adaptive filtering and dynamic channel selection techniques. By continuously monitoring the relative channel occupancy and signal integrity, the system is capable of adjusting operational parameters in real time. Mathematical models, which describe the duty cycle and power spectral density of the transmissions, are used to establish thresholds that minimize mutual interference. The scheduling routines are designed to separate active transmission and reception intervals between the two protocols, thereby preserving signal quality and ensuring that the overlap of distinct radio events does not result in degradation of network throughput.

Synchronization of Dual-Stack Communications

Accurate synchronization between the Wi-Fi and BLE stacks forms the cornerstone of effective dual connectivity. The architecture enforces a rigorous temporal discipline using a combination of hardware interrupts and software-driven state machines. In this approach, each protocol is assigned its own active period, represented as $W_{\text{Wi-Fi}}$ for Wi-Fi and W_{BLE} for BLE, within a fixed overall cycle duration T_{cycle}. These time windows are allocated such that the likelihood of conflicting radio events is minimized. The synchronization mechanisms rely on precise timing operations that are executed at microsecond resolutions, ensuring that the transition between protocol contexts occurs seamlessly. Formal timing analysis and verification methods contribute to the design, providing guarantees that even under peak load conditions the system adheres to the pre-defined scheduling constraints.

Resource Allocation and System-Level Scheduling

Managing the computational and radio resources required for simultaneous operation demands an intelligent system-level scheduling approach. The dual connectivity paradigm necessitates a dynamic allocation of processing time, memory buffers, and access to the antenna interface. During periods of increased network activity, the scheduler adjudicates access by invoking priority-based policies that are sensitive to both latency and throughput requirements. The dynamic scheduler adjusts the respective operational durations in accordance with real-time measurements, thereby optimizing the effective duty cycles of both Wi-Fi and BLE. Semaphore-based locking mechanisms and non-blocking input/output operations are deployed to prevent resource contention and to ensure that the execution of concurrent tasks remains robust. This approach enables the system to maintain a balanced workload distribution even as demands from both protocols fluctuate.

Coordinated Protocol Stack Integration

The integration of the Wi-Fi and BLE protocol stacks is realized through a modular software architecture that abstracts the complexities of dual connectivity. Each protocol is encapsulated within its dedicated runtime environment, with communication between these environments managed via an event-driven middleware framework. This separation of concerns ensures that the individual protocol operations can be independently optimized and tested while maintaining a synchronized overall functionality. Intertask communication channels are established to propagate critical events, such as connection initiation and data transfer acknowledgments, through a series of well-defined signaling protocols. The modular integration framework leverages a multitasking operating system that supports concurrent execution, thereby enabling both connectivity modes to operate simultaneously without encroaching on each other's operational domains. Detailed system-level scheduling combined with inter-stack decoupling minimizes cross-interference and facilitates a resilient dual connectivity deployment.

ESP32 For IoT With Arduino Code Snippet

```
// Include required libraries
#include <Arduino.h>
#include <WiFi.h>
#include <BLEDevice.h>

// Define overall cycle duration and initial time windows (in
↪   milliseconds)
// These variables represent the equations described in the chapter:
//   T_cycle = w_wifi + w_ble
//   Duty Cycle (Wi-Fi) = (w_wifi / T_cycle) * 100%
unsigned long T_CYCLE = 1000;      // Total cycle duration (ms)
unsigned long w_wifi = 600;        // Wi-Fi active window (ms)
unsigned long w_ble = T_CYCLE - w_wifi;  // BLE active window (ms)

// Global start time of the cycle for synchronization
unsigned long cycleStart = 0;

// Semaphore for coordinating access to the shared radio resource
SemaphoreHandle_t radioSemaphore;

// Function to simulate an interference measurement (value between
↪   0.0 and 1.0)
// In an actual implementation, this would be based on power
↪   spectral density monitoring
float measureInterference() {
  // Simulate interference with a random value
  return random(0, 100) / 100.0;
}

// Adjust the scheduling windows dynamically based on interference
↪   conditions.
// This algorithm demonstrates the application of formulas and
↪   thresholds.
void adjustScheduling() {
  float interference = measureInterference();
  Serial.print("Interference measure: ");
  Serial.println(interference);

  // If interference exceeds threshold (0.5), reduce the Wi-Fi
  ↪   window to mitigate collisions.
  if (interference > 0.5) {
    w_wifi = 500;  // Reduced Wi-Fi active duration (ms)
    Serial.println("High interference detected. Adjusting Wi-Fi
    ↪   window to 500 ms.");
  } else {
    w_wifi = 600;  // Default Wi-Fi window (ms)
    Serial.println("Interference normal. Using default Wi-Fi window
    ↪   of 600 ms.");
```

```
  }
  // Recalculate BLE window based on the updated w_wifi value
  w_ble = T_CYCLE - w_wifi;

  // Calculate duty cycles for each protocol
  float dutyCycleWiFi = ((float)w_wifi / (float)T_CYCLE) * 100.0;
  float dutyCycleBLE = 100.0 - dutyCycleWiFi;
  Serial.print("Duty Cycle - Wi-Fi: ");
  Serial.print(dutyCycleWiFi);
  Serial.print("%, BLE: ");
  Serial.print(dutyCycleBLE);
  Serial.println("%");
}

// Task to handle Wi-Fi specific operations
// This task is active during the Wi-Fi window: [0, w_wifi)
void taskWiFi(void * parameter) {
  for (;;) {
    unsigned long currentTime = millis() - cycleStart;

    if (currentTime < w_wifi) {  // Check if within Wi-Fi active
    ↪ period
      // Acquire semaphore to safely access the shared radio
      ↪ resource
      if (xSemaphoreTake(radioSemaphore, (TickType_t)10) == pdTRUE)
      ↪ {
        Serial.println("Wi-Fi Task: Running Wi-Fi operations");
        // Example operation: Scan for available Wi-Fi networks
        ↪ (simulation)
        int n = WiFi.scanNetworks();
        Serial.print("Found ");
        Serial.print(n);
        Serial.println(" networks.");
        // Simulate processing time
        delay(100);
        // Release the semaphore after completed operation
        xSemaphoreGive(radioSemaphore);
      }
    }
    else {
      // Outside Wi-Fi window, yield to other tasks
      vTaskDelay(50 / portTICK_PERIOD_MS);
    }
  }
}

// Task to handle BLE specific operations
// This task is active during the BLE window: [w_wifi, T_CYCLE)
void taskBLE(void * parameter) {
  for (;;) {
    unsigned long currentTime = millis() - cycleStart;
```

```
    if (currentTime >= w_wifi && currentTime < T_CYCLE) {  // Within
    ↪  BLE active period
      // Acquire the semaphore before using shared radio hardware
      if (xSemaphoreTake(radioSemaphore, (TickType_t)10) == pdTRUE)
      ↪  {
        Serial.println("BLE Task: Running BLE operations");
        // Example operation: Simulate BLE advertising or scanning
        ↪  update
        // In a real scenario, BLE library functions would be
        ↪  invoked here.
        delay(100);
        // Release semaphore
        xSemaphoreGive(radioSemaphore);
      }
    }
    else {
      // Outside BLE window, yield control
      vTaskDelay(50 / portTICK_PERIOD_MS);
    }
  }
}

void setup() {
  // Initialize Serial communication for debugging purposes.
  Serial.begin(115200);
  while (!Serial) { delay(10); }

  // Initialize Wi-Fi in station mode.
  WiFi.mode(WIFI_STA);
  Serial.println("Wi-Fi initialized in STA mode.");

  // Initialize BLE with a device name.
  BLEDevice::init("ESP32-Dual-Connectivity");
  Serial.println("BLE initialized with device name:
  ↪  ESP32-Dual-Connectivity");

  // Create a mutex for managing access to the radio hardware.
  radioSemaphore = xSemaphoreCreateMutex();
  if (radioSemaphore == NULL) {
    Serial.println("Error: Failed to create radio semaphore.");
  }

  // Set the start time for the cycle.
  cycleStart = millis();

  // Create FreeRTOS tasks for handling Wi-Fi and BLE concurrently.
  xTaskCreatePinnedToCore(
    taskWiFi,        // Task function for Wi-Fi
    "Task_WiFi",     // Task name
    4096,            // Stack size (in bytes)
    NULL,            // No parameter is passed
    1,               // Task priority
    NULL,            // Task handle not required
```

```
    1                          // Core ID (pinned to core 1)
  );

  xTaskCreatePinnedToCore(
    taskBLE,        // Task function for BLE
    "Task_BLE",     // Task name
    4096,           // Stack size
    NULL,           // Parameter is NULL
    1,              // Task priority
    NULL,           // No task handle needed
    1               // Running on the same core for demonstration
  );

  Serial.println("Dual connectivity tasks created.");
}

void loop() {
  // Check if the current scheduling cycle has elapsed.
  if (millis() - cycleStart >= T_CYCLE) {
    // Reset the cycle start time and adjust scheduling based on
    ↪  real-time interference.
    cycleStart = millis();
    Serial.println("----- New Cycle -----");
    adjustScheduling();
  }
  // Short delay to yield control and maintain non-blocking
  ↪  behavior.
  delay(50);
}
```

Chapter 37

FreeRTOS Concepts for ESP32

Fundamental Principles of FreeRTOS

FreeRTOS is a deterministic real-time operating system kernel that is architected to serve the needs of embedded applications with stringent timing requirements. At its core, FreeRTOS implements both cooperative and preemptive scheduling policies that enable the concurrent execution of multiple tasks while adhering to real-time constraints. The kernel's minimalistic design centers on a small set of primitives such as tasks, queues, semaphores, and mutexes. These primitives provide the essential infrastructural support for managing process state transitions, inter-task communication, and resource allocation. Tasks, which represent independent units of execution, are assigned priorities denoted by $P_1, P_2, \ldots, P_n$. The scheduler enforces the condition that the task with the highest active priority, mathematically expressed as $\max\{P_1, P_2, \ldots, P_n\}$, receives immediate processor attention. This fundamental principle is critical to ensuring that time-sensitive operations execute within their designated periods.

Integration with the Arduino Core on ESP32

The integration of FreeRTOS with the Arduino core on the ESP32 platform creates a synthesis between a user-friendly programming interface and a robust, real-time scheduling mechanism. In this integrated environment, the Arduino framework operates as an abstraction layer that calls upon the services of the underlying FreeRTOS kernel. Conventional Arduino functions such as setup() and loop() are reinterpreted as tasks within a FreeRTOS-managed execution context. This design facilitates the concurrent execution of multiple routines, where each Arduino function may be scheduled as an independent task. The synergy between the Arduino core and FreeRTOS leverages the dual-core architecture of the ESP32, thereby permitting simultaneous management of both time-critical and background operations. This architectural convergence enables the execution of asynchronous event processing, sensor data acquisition, and communication protocols under a unified runtime environment that is both scalable and responsive.

Multitasking and Scheduling in a Real-Time Environment

Multitasking in a real-time operating system context extends beyond basic concurrent execution; it requires meticulous scheduling and dynamic resource allocation to satisfy diverse timing constraints. The preemptive scheduler incorporated within FreeRTOS on the ESP32 is engineered to evaluate task readiness and refrains from allowing any single task to monopolize processor time. The scheduler partitions processor cycles into discrete time slices or quanta, denoted by q, ensuring that all tasks receive a fair proportion of computational resources. Moreover, the scheduling algorithm is adaptive, dynamically recalculating task orderings based on priority adjustments and the arrival of asynchronous events. Such preemptive strategies ensure that tasks with critical deadlines can preempt lower-priority tasks, thereby fulfilling real-time operational criteria. The deterministic scheduling behavior is analytically modeled using performance metrics such as latency, throughput, and context switch overhead, all of which are optimally minimized to maintain system stability in the face of varying workloads.

Inter-Task Communication and Synchronization Mechanisms

In an environment where concurrent tasks operate in parallel, robust inter-task communication and synchronization become pivotal. FreeRTOS provides a comprehensive suite of mechanisms—queues for buffered communication, semaphores for signaling and mutual exclusion, and mutexes for protecting shared resources—that collectively ensure reliable data transfer and coordination between tasks. Queues allow for asynchronous data exchange between producer and consumer tasks by establishing an ordered buffer that decouples the timing between senders and receivers. Semaphores, both binary and counting, act as gating mechanisms that regulate access to critical sections, thereby preventing race conditions. Mutexes complement these constructs by offering a disciplined approach to resource sharing, ensuring that only one task can access a designated resource at any given time. The formal behavior of these synchronization primitives is characterized by state transition models and queuing theory, where performance parameters such as blocking time and wake-up latency are precisely defined. The integration of these mechanisms within the Arduino framework on the ESP32 enhances the system's capacity to orchestrate complex real-time interactions, ensuring that all concurrently executing tasks maintain high determinism and system integrity.

ESP32 For IoT With Arduino Code Snippet

```
#include <Arduino.h>
#include "freertos/FreeRTOS.h"
#include "freertos/task.h"
#include "freertos/queue.h"
#include "freertos/semphr.h"

// Global Variables and Definitions
// An example array representing task priorities [P1, P2, ..., Pn]
// These values are used to compute the maximum priority following
↪    the formula:
//         max{P1, P2, ..., Pn}
const int ARRAY_SIZE = 5;
int taskPriorities[ARRAY_SIZE] = {2, 4, 3, 5, 1};

// Function to compute maximum priority from an array of priorities.
// This implements the algorithm corresponding to:
//         max{P1, P2, ... , Pn}
int computeMaxPriority(int arr[], int size) {
  int maxPriority = arr[0];
  for (int i = 1; i < size; i++) {
    if (arr[i] > maxPriority) {
      maxPriority = arr[i];
```

```
    }
  }
  return maxPriority;
}


// Declare handles for FreeRTOS inter-task communication.
QueueHandle_t dataQueue;
SemaphoreHandle_t resourceSemaphore;

// Producer Task:
// Generates data periodically and sends it via a FreeRTOS queue to
↪   simulate inter-task communication.
// The delay simulates a time-slice (quantum, q) of 100 ms.
void vTaskProducer(void *pvParameters) {
  int data = 0;
  while (1) {
    data++;   // Simulate data generation
    // Delay to mimic processing time (time slice q)
    vTaskDelay(pdMS_TO_TICKS(100));
    // Send the data to the queue, with a timeout of 10 ticks if
↪    full.
    if (xQueueSend(dataQueue, &data, 10) != pdPASS) {
      Serial.println("Producer: Failed to send data to queue");
    } else {
      Serial.print("Producer: Sent data ");
      Serial.println(data);
    }
  }
}


// Consumer Task:
// Receives data from the queue and processes it safely using a
↪   semaphore for mutually exclusive access.
void vTaskConsumer(void *pvParameters) {
  int receivedData;
  while (1) {
    // Acquire semaphore for exclusive access to shared resource
    if (xSemaphoreTake(resourceSemaphore, pdMS_TO_TICKS(50)) ==
↪    pdTRUE) {
      // If queue has data, retrieve it
      if (xQueueReceive(dataQueue, &receivedData, 0) == pdPASS) {
        Serial.print("Consumer: Received data ");
        Serial.println(receivedData);
      }
      // Release semaphore after processing
      xSemaphoreGive(resourceSemaphore);
    }
    // Delay to simulate context switch and proper time slicing (50
↪    ms)
    vTaskDelay(pdMS_TO_TICKS(50));
  }
}
```

```
// Priority Checker Task:
// Demonstrates the algorithm for evaluating the maximum task
↪   priority using the computeMaxPriority() function.
// It prints the maximum priority periodically (every 500 ms), which
↪   corresponds to the formula:
//        max{P1, P2, ..., Pn}
void vTaskPriorityChecker(void *pvParameters) {
  while (1) {
    int maxP = computeMaxPriority(taskPriorities, ARRAY_SIZE);
    Serial.print("PriorityChecker: Maximum Task Priority = ");
    Serial.println(maxP);
    // Delay to simulate periodic checking (500 ms)
    vTaskDelay(pdMS_TO_TICKS(500));
  }
}

void setup() {
  // Initialize Serial communication for debugging output.
  Serial.begin(115200);

  // Create a queue for inter-task communication with capacity for
  ↪   10 integers.
  dataQueue = xQueueCreate(10, sizeof(int));

  // Create a binary semaphore to protect shared resources.
  resourceSemaphore = xSemaphoreCreateBinary();
  // Initially release the semaphore so tasks can use it.
  xSemaphoreGive(resourceSemaphore);

  // Create FreeRTOS tasks with specified stack sizes and
  ↪   priorities.
  // Note: Priorities here are illustrative and the scheduler will
  ↪   select the highest priority task ready to run.
  xTaskCreate(vTaskProducer, "Producer", 2048, NULL, 2, NULL);
  xTaskCreate(vTaskConsumer, "Consumer", 2048, NULL, 2, NULL);
  xTaskCreate(vTaskPriorityChecker, "PriorityChecker", 2048, NULL,
  ↪   1, NULL);
}

void loop() {
  // The loop is left empty because scheduling and multitasking are
  ↪   managed by FreeRTOS.
}
```

Chapter 38

Implementing FreeRTOS Tasks

Task Creation and Initialization

The FreeRTOS kernel provides a systematic methodology for spawning concurrent units of execution, hereafter referred to as tasks. Each task is instantiated with a dedicated block of memory for its stack and task control structure, which encapsulates essential metadata such as the initial stack pointer, task state, and priority value, denoted as P_i, where i indexes the individual tasks. The initialization phase involves the specification of task parameters, including the designated function that embodies the task's behavior, the stack size required for local variables and function calls, and the relative priority which influences the scheduler's eventual selection mechanism. Within the ESP32 architecture, this process is meticulously optimized to leverage the available hardware resources, ensuring that even tasks with limited computational demands incur minimal overhead during creation.

Task Lifecycle Management

Following initialization, tasks proceed through a well-defined lifecycle characterized by state transitions that include the ready, running, blocked, and suspended states. In the ready state, tasks are queued for execution in accordance with their assigned priorities, while the transition to the running state occurs when the scheduler affords the processor to the selected task. Subsequent transitions to the blocked or suspended states are induced by explicit system calls or resource unavailability, thereby enforcing synchronization constraints and inter-task dependencies. This lifecycle management is governed by precise temporal parameters derived from hardware timer ticks, ensuring that task execution conforms to deterministic scheduling properties. The lifecycle is thus a combined effect of both static configuration and dynamic interaction among tasks, where each transition is meticulously orchestrated to maintain system integrity under varying load conditions.

Preemptive Scheduling and Context Switching

The FreeRTOS kernel employs a preemptive scheduling discipline whereby the execution context is reassigned based on the computed emergent priority set $\{P_1, P_2, \ldots, P_n\}$. The scheduler continuously evaluates tasks in the ready state and assigns the CPU to the task with the highest effective priority, mathematically expressed as $\max\{P_1, P_2, \ldots, P_n\}$. Context switching, defined as the process of saving and restoring task contexts, is a critical operation whose efficiency directly impacts overall system responsiveness. The quantization of processor time into discrete ticks ensures that time slices, denoted by q, are allocated equitably across tasks, while mechanisms such as yielding and forced preemption guarantee that no individual task monopolizes processor resources. The theoretical underpinnings of context switching are rigorously analyzed through parameters including context switch overhead, worst-case latency, and system throughput, all of which are minimized through kernel-level optimizations on the ESP32 platform.

Dynamic Task Management in Resource-Constrained Environments

Dynamic management of tasks is indispensable in scenarios where operational conditions fluctuate, necessitating the creation, suspension, resumption, or deletion of tasks at runtime. In such an environment, the kernel's ability to reassign task priorities and reconfigure scheduling parameters on-the-fly is paramount. The careful orchestration of memory allocation and deallocation for task control blocks and associated stack space minimizes fragmentation and ensures efficient utilization of limited hardware resources. Furthermore, synchronization primitives, which regulate inter-task communication and resource sharing, are intricately linked with dynamic task operations. The concurrent activation and deactivation of tasks are managed by a scheduler that continuously recalibrates its execution order, thereby ensuring that critical tasks receive immediate attention. This dynamic adaptability is crucial to sustaining long-term system stability, particularly in the context of the ESP32 where computational resources are judiciously managed to support real-time responsiveness in complex IoT applications.

ESP32 For IoT With Arduino Code Snippet

```
#include <Arduino.h>

// This code snippet demonstrates key concepts from the chapter
↪    "Implementing FreeRTOS Tasks".
// It showcases FreeRTOS task creation, lifecycle management,
↪    preemptive scheduling,
// context switching, and dynamic task management in an ESP32
↪    environment using Arduino.
//
// Important formulas and ideas include:
// 1. Task priority selection: Given a set of tasks with priorities
↪    {P1, P2, ..., Pn}, the scheduler
//    selects the task with the highest effective priority, i.e.,
↪    max{P1, P2, ..., Pn}.
// 2. Time-slice computation: next_time = current_time + q, where q
↪    is the quantized time slice.

// Global handles for tasks
TaskHandle_t highPriorityTaskHandle = NULL;
TaskHandle_t lowPriorityTaskHandle  = NULL;

// Define task priority constants (P_i)
// Higher numerical value indicates higher priority in this
↪    demonstration.
const UBaseType_t HIGH_PRIORITY = 2;  // P_high = 2
const UBaseType_t LOW_PRIORITY  = 1;  // P_low = 1

// Define a time slice (q) in milliseconds for demonstration
↪    purposes.
const TickType_t timeSlice = pdMS_TO_TICKS(100);

// Function prototypes for task routines.
```

```cpp
void highPriorityTask(void *parameter);
void lowPriorityTask(void *parameter);

void setup() {
  Serial.begin(115200);
  while (!Serial) {
    ; // Wait for serial port to connect. Needed for native USB on
    ↪  some boards.
  }

  Serial.println("ESP32 FreeRTOS Task Demo Starting...");

  // Create the high priority task.
  // Parameters: task function, task name, stack size in words,
  ↪  input parameter (NULL), task priority, task handle.
  xTaskCreate(highPriorityTask, "HighPriorityTask", 2048, NULL,
  ↪  HIGH_PRIORITY, &highPriorityTaskHandle);

  // Create the low priority task.
  xTaskCreate(lowPriorityTask, "LowPriorityTask", 2048, NULL,
  ↪  LOW_PRIORITY, &lowPriorityTaskHandle);
}

void loop() {
  // In this loop, we simulate dynamic task management.
  // For example, every 10 seconds we suspend the low priority task
  ↪  for 2 seconds,
  // then resume it. This demonstrates runtime reconfiguration.

  static uint32_t lastSuspendTime = 0;
  if (millis() - lastSuspendTime > 10000) {
    Serial.println("Main Loop: Suspending Low Priority Task for 2
    ↪  seconds");
    vTaskSuspend(lowPriorityTaskHandle);
    vTaskDelay(pdMS_TO_TICKS(2000));
    Serial.println("Main Loop: Resuming Low Priority Task");
    vTaskResume(lowPriorityTaskHandle);
    lastSuspendTime = millis();
  }

  // Add a short delay so loop() does not consume excessive CPU
  ↪  time.
  vTaskDelay(pdMS_TO_TICKS(100));
}

// High Priority Task: Demonstrates preemptive scheduling and
↪  context switching.
// This task runs a simple loop where it computes a next time slice
↪  using: next = current + q.
void highPriorityTask(void *parameter) {
  while (true) {
    unsigned long currentTime = millis();
```

248

```
    unsigned long nextTimeSlice = currentTime +
    ↪  pdTICKS_TO_MS(timeSlice);  // next = current + q

    Serial.print("HighPriorityTask: Running at ");
    Serial.print(currentTime);
    Serial.print(" ms, Next time slice scheduled at ");
    Serial.print(nextTimeSlice);
    Serial.println(" ms");

    // Simulate task activity for 50ms.
    vTaskDelay(pdMS_TO_TICKS(50));

    // Yield control to allow the scheduler to check for tasks with
    ↪  higher or equal priority.
    taskYIELD();
  }
}

// Low Priority Task: Demonstrates continuous operation under lower
↪  priority.
// This task prints its execution timestamp and simulates a longer
↪  delay.
void lowPriorityTask(void *parameter) {
  while (true) {
    Serial.print("LowPriorityTask: Executing at ");
    Serial.print(millis());
    Serial.println(" ms");

    // Simulate work with a delay of 150ms.
    vTaskDelay(pdMS_TO_TICKS(150));
  }
}
```

Chapter 39

Inter-task Communication with Queues

Fundamentals of Queue Theory in Concurrent Systems

Inter-task communication in real-time operating systems relies on well-defined mechanisms that guarantee both correctness and efficiency when multiple tasks interact concurrently. In this context, queues serve as an indispensable abstraction, facilitating the decoupling of producer and consumer tasks by providing a first-in, first-out (FIFO) data structure. The queue model is formalized by considering a finite sequence of elements, denoted as

$$Q = \{q_1, q_2, \ldots, q_n\},$$

where each element q_i represents encapsulated data or a message generated by a task. Essential performance parameters, such as the data arrival rate λ and the service rate μ, are introduced to ensure that the stability criterion

$$\lambda < \mu$$

is satisfied. The FIFO discipline inherent to queue structures preserves the temporal ordering of messages, which is crucial for maintaining deterministic behavior in systems where the ordering of events significantly affects functionality.

Queue Operations and Synchronization

The primary operations defined on a queue are the enqueue and dequeue operations, which correspond to the insertion and removal of elements, respectively. These operations must be executed atomically to mitigate the risk of race conditions in a concurrent environment. In a system where multiple tasks may simultaneously attempt to modify the queue, synchronization mechanisms such as mutexes or semaphores are employed to ensure mutual exclusion. Consider a task that intends to enqueue an element: it must sequentially read the tail pointer of the queue, write the new element, and update the pointer, all within a critical section. This operation transforms the queue state from

$$Q = \{q_1, q_2, \ldots, q_n\}$$

to

$$Q' = \{q_1, q_2, \ldots, q_n, q_{n+1}\},$$

without any intermediate state being visible to other concurrently executing tasks. The incorporation of such synchronization protocols not only preserves data integrity but also guarantees that inter-task communication remains predictable and reliable under high contention conditions.

Ensuring Data Integrity and Safety Through Queues

Data integrity and safety are paramount in the design of concurrent systems, particularly when multiple tasks rely on shared resources for communication. Queues, by design, enforce a strict ordering of operations that inherently supports the preservation of data integrity. The implementation of atomic operations on queues ensures that each enqueue or dequeue operation is completed in full before another operation intervenes, thereby precluding partial updates that could lead to inconsistencies. The invariant condition for a queue, denoted by

$$I(Q),$$

asserts that for any two elements q_i and q_j, if the enqueue operation for q_i precedes that for q_j, then the corresponding dequeue operations will also reflect this ordering. Such invariants are formally proved using techniques from concurrent algorithm analysis and are critical in environments where tasks have varying levels of priority and execution frequency. Moreover, configurations that support both blocking and non-blocking operations enable tasks to either wait for new messages or poll the queue periodically, each mode being optimized to avoid issues such as deadlock and priority inversion.

Performance Analysis and Deterministic Behavior in Queue Processing

The performance characteristics of queue-based inter-task communication significantly impact the overall system responsiveness, especially in resource-constrained environments. Each queue operation is associated with a certain latency, which must be carefully bounded to meet real-time constraints. Let t_{enqueue} and t_{dequeue} represent the worst-case execution times for the enqueue and dequeue operations, respectively. In a multistage system where data traverses through a sequence of queues, the total latency T_{queue} can be approximated by

$$T_{\text{queue}} \approx \sum_{i=1}^{k} \left(t_{\text{enqueue}}^{(i)} + t_{\text{dequeue}}^{(i)} \right),$$

where k denotes the number of queue stages encountered by the data. The deterministic behavior of such a system is further ensured by an underlying scheduler that allocates processor time based on precise time ticks and carefully calibrated priorities. The design and analysis of these queues incorporate rigorous performance models that account for context switch overheads, synchronization delays, and the dynamic behavior of task scheduling. Such models are instrumental in achieving a predictable throughput and in ensuring that the system adheres to its timing constraints under worst-case conditions.

ESP32 For IoT With Arduino Code Snippet

```
// This example demonstrates inter-task communication using FreeRTOS
↪    queues
// on the ESP32 with Arduino. The code simulates producer and
↪    consumer tasks,
// while referencing key equations and invariants from the chapter.

/*
    Fundamental Queue Model:
    --------------------------
    Let Q = {q_1, q_2, ..., q_n}
    where each q_i is a message produced by a task.
    The stability condition: lambda < mu,
    with lambda being the arrival rate and mu the service rate.

    Invariant, I(Q):
    If enqueue(q_i) happens before enqueue(q_j),
    then dequeue operations will return q_i before q_j.
*/

/*
    Performance Model:
    ------------------
    For each queue stage, the total latency T_queue can be
    ↪    approximated as:
      T_queue    (t_enqueue^(i) + t_dequeue^(i))
    where t_enqueue and t_dequeue represent the worst-case times
    for enqueuing and dequeuing operations respectively.
*/

#include <Arduino.h>

// Queue configuration parameters
const int QUEUE_LENGTH = 10;                // Maximum number of
↪    messages
const int QUEUE_ITEM_SIZE = sizeof(int);    // Size of each
↪    message (integer)
QueueHandle_t messageQueue;                 // FreeRTOS queue
↪    handle

// Simulation parameters for data arrival and service rates
const float lambda = 1.0; // Arrival rate in messages per second
↪    (producer)
const float mu = 2.0;      // Service rate in messages per second
↪    (consumer)
// The stability criterion lambda < mu is satisfied as 1.0 < 2.0

// Producer Task: Enqueues messages into the queue
void producerTask(void *parameter) {
```

253

```cpp
  int message = 0;
  // Delay corresponding to the arrival rate lambda (1 second per
  ↪   message)
  TickType_t producerDelay = pdMS_TO_TICKS(1000);
  for (;;) {
    // Enqueue operation:
    // The following call performs an atomic enqueue, ensuring that
    ↪   the
    // critical section (reading the tail pointer, writing the new
    ↪   element,
    // updating the pointer) is handled within the FreeRTOS queue
    ↪   API.
    if (xQueueSend(messageQueue, &message, portMAX_DELAY) == pdPASS)
    ↪   {
      Serial.print("Enqueued message: ");
      Serial.println(message);
    }
    // The queue state transforms as:
    // Q = {q_1, q_2, ..., q_n}  --->  Q' = {q_1, q_2, ..., q_n,
    ↪   q_{n+1}}
    message++;  // Prepare next message
    vTaskDelay(producerDelay);
  }
}

// Consumer Task: Dequeues messages from the queue
void consumerTask(void *parameter) {
  int receivedMessage;
  // Delay simulating service rate mu (faster processing, 0.5 sec
  ↪   delay)
  TickType_t consumerDelay = pdMS_TO_TICKS(500);
  for (;;) {
    // Dequeue operation: Blocks until a message is available
    if (xQueueReceive(messageQueue, &receivedMessage, portMAX_DELAY)
    ↪   == pdPASS) {
      Serial.print("Dequeued message: ");
      Serial.println(receivedMessage);

      // Additional processing can be simulated here.
      // For performance analysis, one might record the enqueue and
      ↪   dequeue
      // times to compute t_enqueue and t_dequeue per message.

      vTaskDelay(consumerDelay);
    }
  }
}

void setup() {
  Serial.begin(115200);

  // Create the queue to hold integer messages.
  messageQueue = xQueueCreate(QUEUE_LENGTH, QUEUE_ITEM_SIZE);
```

```
if (messageQueue == NULL) {
  Serial.println("Error: Queue creation failed!");
  while (1); // Halt if the queue cannot be created.
}

// Confirm the invariant I(Q): Order is preserved from enqueue to
↪   dequeue.
Serial.println("Queue invariant I(Q) holds: Enqueue order
↪   maintained on dequeue.");

// Create the Producer task.
xTaskCreate(
  producerTask,          // Task function for producing messages
  "ProducerTask",        // Name of the task
  2048,                  // Stack size in bytes
  NULL,                  // Parameter passed to the task
  1,                     // Task priority
  NULL                   // Task handle
);

// Create the Consumer task.
xTaskCreate(
  consumerTask,          // Task function for consuming messages
  "ConsumerTask",        // Name of the task
  2048,                  // Stack size in bytes
  NULL,                  // Parameter passed to the task
  1,                     // Task priority
  NULL                   // Task handle
);
}

void loop() {
  // The main loop remains empty as all operations occur within the
  ↪   tasks.
  vTaskDelay(pdMS_TO_TICKS(1000)); // Yield processor time to tasks.
}
```

Chapter 40

Utilizing Semaphores for Resource Management

Mechanisms of Semaphores in FreeRTOS

Semaphores in FreeRTOS constitute a fundamental synchronization primitive designed to regulate concurrent access to shared resources. At the core of their operation lie atomic routines, typically demarcated as the *take* and *give* operations, which respectively acquire and release access to a resource. In mathematical terms, if S denotes the internal count of a semaphore, then the process of acquiring the semaphore can be modeled by the condition $S > 0$, followed by an update of the state as $S \leftarrow S - 1$. Conversely, the release operation is characterized by $S \leftarrow S+1$, subject to the maximum permissible value that differentiates binary semaphores from counting semaphores. Binary semaphores, constrained with a maximum value of 1, are typically employed to enforce mutual exclusion in accessing a single instance of a resource. Counting semaphores, on the other hand, are utilized in scenarios where multiple instances of the resource are available, thereby managing several concurrent accesses. The design of these mechanisms in FreeRTOS guarantees that operations on the semaphore are performed in an indivisible manner, ensuring that low-level race conditions and context-switch induced inconsistencies are systematically avoided.

Controlling Access to Shared Resources

Within multitasking environments, shared resources such as memory buffers, peripherals, or communication channels must be protected against unsynchronized access that might otherwise result in data corruption or unpredictable behavior. Semaphores serve to serialize access to such resources by allowing only one task, or a specified number of tasks, to enter the critical section at any given time. Formally, consider a resource R that is accessed by a set of tasks. The semaphore associated with R enforces the invariant that if one task is actively using the resource, subsequent tasks must wait until the semaphore is restored to a non-zero state. This condition can be formally expressed as: if task T_i holds the semaphore (implying $S = 0$ in the binary case), then any other task T_j must postpone its access until the operation $S \leftarrow S + 1$ has been executed by T_i. In this manner, the semaphore not only acts as a gatekeeper but also encodes the policy that access to the resource R is granted under strictly controlled conditions, thereby eliminating the hazards intrinsic to concurrent modifications.

Data Integrity through Semaphore Synchronization

Data integrity in concurrent systems is predicated on the ability to maintain consistent state transitions of shared resources. Semaphores are instrumental in realizing this objective by ensuring that modifications to shared data occur within a protected, non-interruptible critical section. Let D represent a shared data structure; the guarantee of data integrity is provided by enforcing that any operation modifying D is bracketed by semaphore acquisition and release procedures. This ensures that while a task is updating D, no other task can concurrently observe or alter an incomplete or inconsistent intermediate state. An invariant, denoted as $I(D)$, is maintained such that the transition from an initial valid state to a subsequent valid state always transpires atomically. The disciplined execution of semaphore operations thereby preserves $I(D)$ by preventing race conditions and ensuring that composite operations on the shared data structure are executed in their entirety before control is transferred to another task.

Synchronization Overheads and Operational Analysis

The integration of semaphores within a real-time scheduling framework introduces a quantifiable overhead due to the atomic operations that are essential for reliable synchronization. Each semaphore operation incurs a latency, here denoted by t_{sem}, which contributes to the overall execution time of critical sections. In scenarios where tasks exhibit high contention for shared resources, the cumulative synchronization overhead becomes a critical parameter in the operational analysis of the system. The total overhead, particularly in a system where semaphore operations are frequent, is given by the summation of individual operation times over all accesses within a given time frame. Moreover, the scheduling algorithm within FreeRTOS must account for blocked tasks that await semaphore availability, thereby influencing the system's response times and throughput. This analysis necessitates a careful balance, wherein semaphores provide the requisite data integrity and mutual exclusion without imposing prohibitive performance penalties. The formal modeling of this overhead, expressed as $T_{\text{sync}} = \sum_{i=1}^{N} t_{\text{sem}}^{(i)}$, is critical for tuning system parameters to meet strict real-time constraints while maintaining robust resource management.

ESP32 For IoT With Arduino Code Snippet

```
#include <Arduino.h>

// Global semaphore handle to regulate resource access
SemaphoreHandle_t xSemaphore;
// Accumulator for synchronization overhead:
// Represents T_sync = (t_sem^(i)) where each t_sem^(i) is the wait
↪    time for a semaphore operation.
volatile unsigned long syncOverhead = 0;

// Simulated shared resource (e.g., a data buffer)
volatile int sharedData = 0;

// Task function that demonstrates semaphore-based access to a
↪    shared resource
void taskFunction(void *pvParameters) {
  // Retrieve the task name from the parameter for logging purposes
  const char* taskName = (const char*) pvParameters;
```

```
// Infinite loop to simulate periodic task execution in a
↪ multitasking environment
for (;;) {
  // Record the current time (in microseconds) before attempting
  ↪ to take the semaphore
  unsigned long startTime = micros();

  // Acquire the semaphore:
  // Condition: if S > 0 then perform S <- S - 1 atomically (this
  ↪ prevents race conditions).
  if (xSemaphoreTake(xSemaphore, portMAX_DELAY) == pdTRUE) {
    // Calculate the wait time incurred by this semaphore take
    ↪ operation
    unsigned long waitTime = micros() - startTime;
    // Add the wait time to our cumulative synchronization
    ↪ overhead
    syncOverhead += waitTime;

    // Begin Critical Section:
    // Access and update the shared resource safely.
    // Reading the shared resource
    int localData = sharedData;
    // Simulate processing/modifying the data (e.g., updating
    ↪ state)
    localData++;  // This operation emulates the update (D -> D +
    ↪ 1)

    // Simulate delay to represent processing time within the
    ↪ critical section,
    // ensuring that tasks exhibit noticeable contention.
    delay(10);

    // Write the updated value back to the shared resource.
    sharedData = localData;
    // End Critical Section

    // Release the semaphore:
    // This operation sets S <- S + 1, allowing waiting tasks to
    ↪ proceed.
    xSemaphoreGive(xSemaphore);

    // Log the update to the Serial monitor
    Serial.print(taskName);
    Serial.print(" updated sharedData to: ");
    Serial.println(sharedData);

    // Delay to simulate periodic invocation of the task
    ↪ (non-critical work)
    delay(100);
  }
}
}
```

259

```cpp
void setup() {
  // Initialize Serial communication for debugging and monitoring.
  Serial.begin(115200);
  // Allow time for the Serial interface to initialize.
  delay(1000);

  // Create a binary semaphore (value constrained to 1) for mutual
  ↪ exclusion.
  xSemaphore = xSemaphoreCreateBinary();
  if (xSemaphore != NULL) {
    // Initially release the semaphore so that its count is set to
    ↪ 1.
    xSemaphoreGive(xSemaphore);
  }

  // Create two tasks to simulate concurrent access to the shared
  ↪ resource.
  // These tasks illustrate the role of semaphores in managing
  ↪ resource integrity.
  xTaskCreate(taskFunction, "Task1", 2048, (void*)"Task 1", 1,
  ↪ NULL);
  xTaskCreate(taskFunction, "Task2", 2048, (void*)"Task 2", 1,
  ↪ NULL);
}

void loop() {
  // Periodically output the accumulated synchronization overhead to
  ↪ the Serial monitor.
  // This overhead is the sum of individual semaphore wait times:
  // T_sync = (t_sem^(i))
  Serial.print("Total Sync Overhead (microseconds): ");
  Serial.println(syncOverhead);

  // Delay between each report to avoid floods in the Serial output.
  delay(5000);
}
```

Chapter 41

Software Timers in a Multitasking Environment

Conceptual Framework of Software Timers

Software timers in FreeRTOS embody a mechanism for managing time-based events that are decoupled from the execution of primary tasks, thereby enabling the scheduling of recurring operations without inducing blocking delays in critical execution paths. At their core, these timers are predicated on the accurate measurement of elapsed time and the timely invocation of callback routines upon the expiration of preconfigured intervals. The underlying theoretical construct can be modeled by a function $f(t)$, where the occurrence of an event is triggered when the temporal condition $t \geq T$ is satisfied, with T being the defined timeout threshold. This formulation establishes a temporal framework in which periodic events are systematically scheduled and executed, maintaining a consistent rhythm in the multitasking environment while adhering to the constraints imposed by the system tick granularity.

Mechanics of Non-blocking Timer Operations

The integration of software timers within the FreeRTOS environment is engineered to preserve the non-preemptive execution of critical operations. Upon the expiration of a timer, the associated callback function is dispatched by a dedicated timer service task. This design paradigm ensures that the invocation of timer callbacks does not encroach upon the processing time of tasks operating with strict real-time requirements. The deferred execution model is governed by a scheduling algorithm that aligns timer callbacks with the system's overall task prioritization scheme. Formally, if the system tick period is denoted by τ, the activation of a timer callback occurs after an interval $N\tau$, where N is an integer such that the desired delay is approximated within the resolution limits of the system. This mathematical representation emphasizes how the architecture inherently guards against blocking operations by compartmentalizing timer-driven activities into a separate execution thread, thereby isolating them from the core critical processes.

Scheduling Recurring Tasks with Timer Reload Mechanisms

Recurrence in software timers is achieved through an automatic reload feature that reinitializes the timer after each expiration event. When configured for periodic operation, the software timer adheres to a recurrence relation expressed as

$$T_{n+1} = T_n + P,$$

where T_n represents the expiration time of the nth callback execution and P denotes the constant period between executions. This recurrence relation ensures that tasks intended to be executed repeatedly are scheduled with mathematical precision, eliminating the need for manual reinvocation. The free-running nature of the timer service task guarantees that these periodic operations are triggered in a timely fashion without causing delay in the responsiveness of higher-priority tasks. In this manner, the hardware-independent timer abstraction supports the implementation of cyclic operations, effectively balancing the competing demands of periodic task scheduling and the preservation of system throughput.

Temporal Accuracy and Overhead Analysis

The precision of software timer-driven events is inherently linked to the resolution of the system tick as well as the scheduling latency of the timer service task. Given a system tick period τ, the timer callback delay can be represented as

$$\delta = k\tau + \epsilon,$$

where k denotes the number of ticks and ϵ represents the additional latency introduced by task scheduling and context switching overhead. This performance parameter ϵ is a critical factor in evaluating the temporal fidelity of the timer mechanism. A rigorous analysis of ϵ involves quantifying the aggregate delay incurred by the processing of timer events, ensuring that the overall impact on system responsiveness remains negligible. The scheduling paradigm within FreeRTOS is designed to minimize such overhead, ensuring that the recurring tasks managed by software timers are executed with a high degree of accuracy. The resultant balance between temporal resolution and system performance facilitates the orchestration of recurring events in a manner that is both precise and efficient, thereby sustaining the real-time operational characteristics of the multitasking environment.

ESP32 For IoT With Arduino Code Snippet

```
// Comprehensive ESP32 code demonstrating the use of software timers
// in a multitasking environment using FreeRTOS with Arduino.
//
// Key Concepts Demonstrated:
// 1. The theoretical model f(t): An event is triggered when t >= T.
//    In our implementation, the timer callback is invoked
↪  periodically
//    after the duration of the timer period.
// 2. Recurrence Relation for Periodic Scheduling:
//    The timer follows the recurrence T_{n+1} = T_n + P, where P is
↪  the period.
```

```
// 3. Non-blocking Timer Operations:
//    The timer callback is executed in a dedicated FreeRTOS timer
↪  service task,
//    ensuring that critical tasks are not blocked.
// 4. Temporal Overhead Representation:
//    The effective delay of the timer callback is given by  = k + ,
//    where   is the system tick period, k is an integer count of
↪  ticks,
//    and   represents additional scheduling overhead.
//
// This demo creates a periodic software timer that triggers every
↪  2000 ms.
// The callback prints a timestamped message to the Serial Monitor
↪  and simulates
// additional processing overhead via a dummy loop.

#include <Arduino.h>
#include "freertos/FreeRTOS.h"
#include "freertos/timers.h"

// Define the period for the software timer (in milliseconds)
#define TIMER_PERIOD_MS 2000

// Global counter to track the number of timer events
volatile unsigned int timerEventCount = 0;

// Timer callback function prototype
void timerCallback(TimerHandle_t xTimer);

// Timer callback function definition
void timerCallback(TimerHandle_t xTimer) {
  // Increment the event counter
  timerEventCount++;

  // Obtain the current system time in milliseconds
  unsigned long currentTime = millis();

  // The conceptual formulation:
  // When current time (t) >= T (threshold), an event is triggered.
  // In a periodic timer, this ensures execution at times:
  //   T_{n+1} = T_n + P, where P is TIMER_PERIOD_MS.

  // Print out the timer event details
  Serial.print("Timer Event ");
  Serial.print(timerEventCount);
  Serial.print(" triggered at ");
  Serial.print(currentTime);
  Serial.println(" ms");

  // Simulate processing overhead () which could be part of the
  ↪  delay:
  //   = k + , where k (number of ticks) is simulated as 1 here,
  // and   represents the loop overhead.
```

264

```cpp
  for (volatile int i = 0; i < 10000; i++) {
    // Dummy computation to simulate processing time overhead
  }
}

void setup() {
  // Initialize serial communication for debugging purposes
  Serial.begin(115200);
  while (!Serial) {;}

  Serial.println("ESP32 FreeRTOS Software Timer Example
  ↪  Starting...");

  // Create a software timer with the following parameters:
  //   - Timer name: "SoftwareTimer" (for debugging purposes)
  //   - Timer period: Converted to ticks using
  ↪    pdMS_TO_TICKS(TIMER_PERIOD_MS)
  //   - Auto-reload flag: pdTRUE for periodic execution
  //   - Timer identifier: Set to (void*) 0
  //   - Timer callback function: timerCallback
  TimerHandle_t softwareTimer = xTimerCreate(
      "SoftwareTimer",                       // Timer name
      pdMS_TO_TICKS(TIMER_PERIOD_MS),        // Timer period in
      ↪  ticks
      pdTRUE,                                // Auto-reload
      ↪  (periodic)
      (void*) 0,                             // Timer ID (not used)
      timerCallback                          // Callback function
  );

  // Verify that the timer was created successfully
  if (softwareTimer == NULL) {
    Serial.println("Error: Timer creation failed!");
  } else {
    // Start the timer with a block time of 0 ticks (non-blocking)
    if (xTimerStart(softwareTimer, 0) != pdPASS) {
      Serial.println("Error: Timer start failed!");
    } else {
      Serial.println("Software Timer started successfully.");
    }
  }
}

void loop() {
  // Main loop can execute other tasks concurrently with the timer.
  // Here, we print a "heartbeat" message every 5 seconds to confirm
  // the main program is responsive.
  static unsigned long lastHeartbeat = 0;
  if (millis() - lastHeartbeat >= 5000) {
    lastHeartbeat = millis();
    Serial.println("Main loop heartbeat...");
  }
```

```
    // Idle in the loop to ensure the FreeRTOS scheduler runs
    ↪  efficiently.
}
```

Chapter 42

Data Logging Techniques in ESP32

Architectural Foundations for Continuous Data Acquisition

The design of data logging mechanisms within the ESP32 framework necessitates a rigorous understanding of both hardware constraints and software architecture. In the context of continuous data acquisition, the underlying workflow is fundamentally characterized by the need to capture sensor outputs as a function of time, denoted by a signal $f(t)$, where t represents continuous temporal evolution. The initiation of data logging is driven by an interfacing layer that captures these sensor outputs and translates them into a discrete sequence of numerical values. This process is formalized by a mapping $L : f(t) \mapsto D$, where D is a dataset structured for further transformation and storage. Critical to this architecture is the consideration of the limited computational resources and memory bandwidth of the ESP32, which requires that the data logging pipeline is both computationally efficient and amenable to real-time operation.

Buffering Strategies and In-Memory Data Aggregation

To bridge the gap between high-frequency sensor data acquisition and relatively slower persistent storage operations, in-memory buffering assumes a central role. Buffer management in this environment is implemented through circular data structures that temporarily hold the continuously sampled data. The buffering mechanism is modeled by the recurrence relation

$$idx = (idx + 1) \mod N,$$

where idx denotes the current position within the buffer and N is the buffer capacity. Such a scheme ensures that the data logging system can cope with variations in data arrival rates and storage latencies, mitigating the risk of data loss. Furthermore, efficient buffer management algorithms employ techniques that balance the temporal coherence of the data stream with the inherent non-determinism of memory write latencies. The stability of the logging process is therefore intimately tied to the optimized management of these transient storage structures.

Persistent Storage Mechanisms

The transition from volatile in-memory buffers to robust, non-volatile storage constitutes the crux of any effective logging strategy. Within the ESP32 ecosystem, several paradigms have been explored, including the use of onboard flash memory and external storage modules, such as SD cards or file systems like SPIFFS and LittleFS. The transformation of the buffered dataset D into a persistent repository S can be expressed as a function

$$S = g(D, \Delta t),$$

where Δt signifies the time interval over which data is aggregated before being committed. This temporal discretization of continuous data streams is instrumental in ensuring that the logging process remains consistent with the limitations imposed by write-cycle endurance and spatial constraints. The implementation of such persistent storage mechanisms must, therefore, reconcile the demands of rapid data capture with the slower, yet more reliable, write operations characteristic of non-volatile memory media.

Temporal Synchronization and Data Integrity

In the realm of continuous data logging, the precise temporal annotation of each logged datum is paramount. The incorporation of accurate timestamps, typically sourced from system clocks with a resolution τ, ensures that the dataset D maintains a coherent temporal structure. By defining a timestamp function $T : D \rightarrow \mathbb{R}$, it becomes possible to assert that each data element is associated with a unique temporal marker, thereby facilitating time-correlated analysis post-capture. In addition to synchronization, maintaining data integrity during both the buffering and storage phases is critical. The application of error-detection algorithms, such as cyclic redundancy checks (CRC) or cryptographic hash functions $H(D)$, serves to authenticate the accuracy of the logged data. This dual emphasis on temporal precision and integrity safeguards the dataset against potential inconsistencies that may arise from buffer overflows or intermittent storage failures.

Optimization and System-Level Considerations

Optimization within the data logging process is achieved by balancing the competing demands of high-frequency data acquisition and the limited throughput of persistent storage interfaces. The logging interval Δt is chosen to maximize data fidelity while minimizing write latency and power consumption, a consideration that is encapsulated in the performance metric

$$\eta = \frac{\text{Data Throughput}}{\text{Storage Latency} + \text{Buffering Overhead}}.$$

System-level optimization further involves the orchestration of logging activities alongside other critical tasks managed by the ESP32. Scheduling algorithms must be designed to accommodate the periodic dumping of buffer contents without compromising the responsiveness of real-time processes. Additionally, the implementation of wear-leveling and efficient garbage collection algorithms ensures that the persistent storage medium sustains longevity in the face of continual write operations. The confluence of these techniques results in a finely tuned data logging subsystem that is capable of reliably capturing and preserving extensive streams of IoT data.

ESP32 For IoT With Arduino Code Snippet

```
#include <Arduino.h>
#include "SPIFFS.h"

// Definitions and constants
const int SENSOR_PIN = 34;        // Analog sensor pin on ESP32
↪ (represents f(t))
const int BUFFER_SIZE = 10;       // Size of circular buffer (N in idx
↪ formula)
const unsigned long LOG_INTERVAL = 1000;  // Logging interval t in
↪ milliseconds

// Structure to hold each logged data entry
struct LogEntry {
  unsigned long timestamp;   // Timestamp T: temporal annotation (in
  ↪ ms)
  int sensorValue;           // Sensor output reading f(t) mapped to
  ↪ numerical value
  uint8_t crc;               // Error detection checksum H(D) for
  ↪ data integrity
};

// Circular buffer to temporarily store data (D from mapping L :
↪ f(t) -> D)
LogEntry dataBuffer[BUFFER_SIZE];
int bufferIndex = 0;              // Current index in the circular
↪ buffer
bool bufferFull = false;          // Indicates if the buffer has wrapped
↪ around
unsigned long lastLogTime = 0;

// Function: Compute a simple checksum (CRC) by combining sensor
↪ value and timestamp
uint8_t computeCRC(const LogEntry &entry) {
  // Simple algorithm: Add lower 8 bits of sensorValue and timestamp
  return ( (entry.sensorValue & 0xFF) + (entry.timestamp & 0xFF) ) &
  ↪ 0xFF;
}

// Function: Flush the content of the circular buffer to persistent
↪ storage (SPIFFS)
// This simulates the conversion S = g(D, t) where data is
↪ aggregated over t
void flushBuffer() {
```

```
  File file = SPIFFS.open("/data_log.txt", FILE_APPEND);
  if (!file) {
    Serial.println("Error: Failed to open persistent storage
    ↪ file.");
    return;
  }

  // Determine number of entries to flush (full buffer if wrapped,
  ↪ else partial)
  int entries = bufferFull ? BUFFER_SIZE : bufferIndex;
  for (int i = 0; i < entries; i++) {
    // Construct log string: "timestamp,sensorValue,crc"
    String logLine = String(dataBuffer[i].timestamp) + "," +
                     String(dataBuffer[i].sensorValue) + "," +
                     String(dataBuffer[i].crc) + "\n";
    file.print(logLine);
  }
  file.close();

  // Reset circular buffer after successful flush
  bufferIndex = 0;
  bufferFull = false;
  Serial.println("Buffer flushed to persistent storage.");
}

void setup() {
  // Initialize serial monitor for debugging output
  Serial.begin(115200);
  while (!Serial) {
    ; // wait for Serial port to initialize
  }

  // Initialize sensor pin (if necessary, as analog input)
  pinMode(SENSOR_PIN, INPUT);

  // Initialize SPIFFS for persistent storage operations
  if (!SPIFFS.begin(true)) {
    Serial.println("Error: SPIFFS Mount Failed");
    return;
  }

  Serial.println("======================================");
  Serial.println("ESP32 Data Logging Initialized");
  Serial.println("Beginning continuous data acquisition...");
  Serial.println("======================================");
}

void loop() {
  unsigned long currentTime = millis();

  // Check if the logging interval t has elapsed for a new sensor
  ↪ read
  if (currentTime - lastLogTime >= LOG_INTERVAL) {
```

271

```
    lastLogTime = currentTime;

    // Read sensor value (simulation of f(t))
    int sensorValue = analogRead(SENSOR_PIN);

    // Form a log entry representing the mapping L : f(t) -> D
    LogEntry entry;
    entry.timestamp = currentTime;      // Temporal annotation T: D
    ↪    ->
    entry.sensorValue = sensorValue;    // Captured analog value
    ↪    from sensor
    entry.crc = computeCRC(entry);      // Compute error-detection
    ↪    checksum H(D)

    // Store the new entry in the circular buffer
    dataBuffer[bufferIndex] = entry;
    // Use recurrence relation: idx = (idx + 1) mod N
    bufferIndex = (bufferIndex + 1) % BUFFER_SIZE;
    if (bufferIndex == 0) {
      bufferFull = true;  // Buffer has wrapped around
    }

    // Debug output to Serial Monitor
    Serial.print("Logged Data -> Timestamp: ");
    Serial.print(entry.timestamp);
    Serial.print(" ms, Sensor Value: ");
    Serial.print(entry.sensorValue);
    Serial.print(", CRC: ");
    Serial.println(entry.crc);

    // If the circular buffer is full, flush it to persistent
    ↪    storage
    if (bufferFull) {
      flushBuffer();
    }
  }
}

// System-level optimization: Other tasks can be interleaved here.
// This ensures real-time responsiveness, aligning with the
↪    performance metric:
//         = Data Throughput / (Storage Latency + Buffering
↪    Overhead)
}
```

Chapter 43

Implementing Circular Buffers for Data Management

Theoretical Foundations of Circular Buffers

Circular buffers are a class of data structures that utilize a fixed-size array arranged in a cyclic fashion. In this configuration, the logical end of the data sequence is conceptually connected to the beginning, thereby forming a continuous loop. This arrangement enables data to be inserted and removed in constant time, effectively meeting the stringent performance requirements of high-frequency data acquisition systems. By exploiting modular arithmetic, the structure inherently simplifies boundary conditions, as the pointer or index is updated according to the relation

$$i_{\text{new}} = (i_{\text{current}} + 1) \quad \text{mod } N,$$

where N represents the capacity of the buffer. Such an approach eliminates the overhead associated with dynamic memory allocation and explicit boundary checking, thereby ensuring a deterministic execution profile.

Design Principles in Resource-Constrained Environments

In environments where computational and memory resources are severely limited, the selection of an appropriate buffering mechanism is critical. Circular buffers provide an attractive solution due to their intrinsic ability to manage a continuous influx of data without resorting to memory reallocation. The fixed-size nature of these buffers guarantees an upper bound on memory usage, which is essential in embedded systems and real-time applications. Moreover, the simplicity of the cyclic data structure minimizes the processing overhead, thus allowing the system to efficiently balance high-frequency data acquisition with subsequent processing or transmission tasks.

Mathematical Modeling and Buffer Dynamics

The operation of a circular buffer can be rigorously modeled using tools from discrete mathematics and modular arithmetic. The progression of the write or read pointer is governed by the recurrence relation

$$i_{\text{new}} = (i_{\text{current}} + 1) \mod N,$$

which succinctly encapsulates the wrap-around characteristic of the buffer. This mathematical model ensures that every new data element is inserted in a deterministic position, and, when the storage capacity is exceeded, the structure gracefully overwrites the oldest data. The invariant maintained by the buffer is critical: at any given time, the distance between the pointers, modulo N, corresponds to the number of valid entries stored. This property affords the system a robust framework for analyzing performance metrics, such as latency and throughput, with respect to the underlying hardware constraints.

Performance Analysis and Memory Efficiency

The efficiency of circular buffers is underscored by their ability to handle continuous streams of data with minimal computational overhead. Operations such as insertion and deletion operate in constant time, $O(1)$, thereby conferring a significant advantage in applications demanding real-time responsiveness. The finite, fixed length of the buffer imposes a known bound on memory consumption, which is essential for rigorous system design in resource-constrained settings. By maintaining a deterministic memory footprint and reducing the need for dynamic allocation, circular buffers contribute to increased system stability. The trade-off, however, lies in the management of data overwriting, which necessitates a careful balance between buffer capacity and data throughput to mitigate potential loss of critical information.

Integration in Real-Time Data Management Systems

When incorporated into a real-time data management framework, circular buffers serve as an effective intermediary between high-frequency data acquisition interfaces and slower persistent storage mechanisms. The cyclic overwriting feature naturally implements a sliding window that preserves the most recent data, thereby ensuring that the system maintains a current state with respect to the incoming information stream. This characteristic is particularly beneficial in applications where immediate insights derived from the latest data are of paramount importance. In resource-constrained environments, the judicious calibration of buffer dimensions relative to the expected data rate and processing latency is imperative. This calibration ensures that the system is capable of sustaining continuous data flows without excessive latency, ultimately harmonizing the dual demands of reliability and performance.

ESP32 For IoT With Arduino Code Snippet

```
#include <Arduino.h>

// Define the capacity of the circular buffer
#define BUFFER_SIZE 10

// CircularBuffer class encapsulating the circular buffer
↪   operations:
```

```cpp
// The update of both head and tail pointers uses modular
↪   arithmetic:
//      i_new = (i_current + 1) mod BUFFER_SIZE
// This ensures the pointer wraps around upon reaching the end of
↪   the buffer.
class CircularBuffer {
  private:
    int buffer[BUFFER_SIZE];
    int head;      // Points to the next insertion index
    int tail;      // Points to the next element to read
    int count;     // Number of valid elements in the buffer

  public:
    // Constructor: Initialize pointers and count
    CircularBuffer() : head(0), tail(0), count(0) {}

    // Check if the buffer is full
    bool isFull() {
      return count == BUFFER_SIZE;
    }

    // Check if the buffer is empty
    bool isEmpty() {
      return count == 0;
    }

    // Insert data into the circular buffer
    void enqueue(int value) {
      if(isFull()) {
        Serial.println("Buffer full, overwriting oldest data");
        // When full, the tail pointer is advanced to make room,
        // implementing the sliding window concept
        tail = (tail + 1) % BUFFER_SIZE;  // Using the formula:
        ↪   (i_current + 1) mod BUFFER_SIZE
        count--;  // Adjust count to reflect the removal of the
        ↪   overwritten data
      }
      buffer[head] = value;
      // Update the head pointer using modular arithmetic
      head = (head + 1) % BUFFER_SIZE;
      count++;
    }

    // Retrieve data from the circular buffer
    int dequeue() {
      if(isEmpty()){
        Serial.println("Buffer is empty!");
        return -1; // Indicate empty buffer
      }
      int value = buffer[tail];
      // Update the tail pointer using modular arithmetic
      tail = (tail + 1) % BUFFER_SIZE;
      count--;
```

```
    return value;
  }

  // Helper function to display the current buffer status
  void printBuffer() {
    Serial.print("Buffer contents: ");
    int idx = tail;
    for (int i = 0; i < count; i++) {
      Serial.print(buffer[idx]);
      Serial.print(" ");
      idx = (idx + 1) % BUFFER_SIZE;
    }
    Serial.println();
  }
};

CircularBuffer circBuf;

void setup() {
  Serial.begin(115200);
  while (!Serial) {
    ; // Wait for serial connection on native USB
  }
  Serial.println("Starting Circular Buffer Demo on ESP32");

  // Simulate high-frequency data acquisition:
  // Insert multiple data items into the circular buffer,
  // illustrating the constant time insertion and cyclic
  ↪ overwriting.
  for (int i = 0; i < 15; i++) {
    // Each data item is computed as i*10 (for demonstration
    ↪ purposes)
    circBuf.enqueue(i * 10);
    // Print the state of the circular buffer after every insertion
    circBuf.printBuffer();
    delay(500); // Simulate a delay between data acquisitions
  }
}

void loop() {
  // In a real-time data management system, data is processed as it
  ↪ becomes available.
  // Dequeue and process one data item at a time from the circular
  ↪ buffer.
  if (!circBuf.isEmpty()) {
    int data = circBuf.dequeue();
    Serial.print("Dequeued data: ");
    Serial.println(data);
    // Print buffer content after removal to observe pointer
    ↪ dynamics
    circBuf.printBuffer();
  }
  // Slow down the processing loop for observation purposes.
```

277

```
  delay(1000);
}
```

Chapter 44

Accessing File Systems in ESP32

Overview of File System Libraries in Resource-Constrained Environments

The implementation of file system libraries in the ESP32 environment facilitates the systematic management of non-volatile storage media through a structured abstraction layer. In this context, file systems such as SPIFFS and LittleFS are employed to mediate between the hardware-specific properties of flash memory and the application-level operations required for data persistence. The architectural design reflects an acute awareness of the limited write cycles intrinsic to flash memory and the necessity for wear leveling algorithms. The system utilizes predefined partitions within the internal flash, which are mounted in accordance with a fixed schema that allows for deterministic allocation of storage resources.

Architectural Integration of File Systems within the Arduino Ecosystem

The ESP32 integrates file system libraries through the Arduino framework by mapping logical file hierarchies onto physical storage partitions. A dedicated initialization routine is responsible for configuring mount points, validating partition integrity, and establishing parameters for file access. The partitioning strategy delineates a distinct area for executable code and a separate segment for file storage, each governed by specific operational constraints. The file system abstraction is implemented as an intermediary layer that translates high-level file I/O requests into low-level operations on flash memory, thereby optimizing both read and write performance under the duress of limited computational and power resources.

Operational Mechanisms for File Input/Output

File I/O operations on the ESP32 are executed via a collection of standardized API routines that encapsulate the underlying hardware interactions. These routines support a comprehensive suite of operations, including file creation, sequential and random access reading, buffered writing, appending, and file deletion. The operational efficiency is enhanced by the use of caching mechanisms that reduce latency and mitigate the variable response times associated with physical flash memory accesses. Moreover, the file system's internal logic employs modular arithmetic in the allocation and management of sectors, thereby ensuring that file operations conform to a predictable performance model. The robustness of the I/O layer is further underscored by the implementation of error detection protocols and transactional integrity checks.

Interfacing File Systems with Arduino Code on the ESP32

Within the Arduino framework, the interfacing with file system libraries is achieved through a well-defined API that abstracts the intricate details of storage management. The integration process involves the configuration of mount points during system initialization, coupled with the dynamic management of file handles and descriptors that represent open files. The API facilitates navigation through directory structures, manipulation of hierarchical file trees, and the execution of atomic operations that guarantee consistency in the event of concurrent access. In doing so, the file system layer effectively decouples the higher-level application logic from the hardware constraints of the storage medium, thereby allowing for more modular and maintainable code structures.

Performance Considerations and Reliability Constraints

The efficiency of file system operations on the ESP32 is a function of both algorithmic approaches and the physical limitations imposed by flash memory technology. Through the employment of fixed-size I/O buffers and a deterministic scheduling of memory accesses, the file system is capable of delivering consistent performance in environments where real-time data handling is imperative. Critical performance metrics such as throughput, latency, and operational overhead are quantified relative to the capacity of the available memory and the operational cycle limits (write cycles) inherent to flash storage. The implementation of wear leveling techniques and error correction routines enhances reliability by mitigating the risk of data corruption and premature medium degradation. These measures are essential for sustaining long-term system stability under intensive read/write cycles.

Challenges in Embedded File System Management

The deployment of file system libraries in embedded systems such as the ESP32 entails addressing a range of challenges unique to resource-constrained environments. The susceptibility to power interruptions, file system fragmentation, and the complexity of ensuring transaction atomicity demand rigorous design considerations. To counter these limitations, the file system incorporates advanced mechanisms for safeguarding data integrity and managing the cyclical nature of flash memory usage. The balance between system performance and reliability is achieved through a meticulous calibration of buffer sizes, sector allocations, and error recovery protocols. These design imperatives converge to form a robust framework that supports the persistence of critical data under the stringent operational conditions prevalent in IoT and real-time applications.

ESP32 For IoT With Arduino Code Snippet

```
#include <SPIFFS.h>

// Simulation constants for wear leveling and sector management
#define MAX_WRITE_CYCLES 100000UL   // Maximum write cycles for
↪    simulation purposes
#define SECTOR_SIZE 4096            // Typical flash sector size in
↪    bytes

// Global counter to simulate persistent write operations
unsigned long writeCounter = 0;

// Function to compute a simple checksum over a given string.
// This serves as an error detection mechanism to verify file
↪    integrity.
unsigned long computeChecksum(const String &data) {
  unsigned long checksum = 0;
  for (int i = 0; i < data.length(); i++) {
    checksum += (unsigned char)data[i];
  }
  return checksum;
}

// Function to compute the number of flash sectors used based on
↪    file size.
// Implements the formula: sectors = ceil(fileSize / SECTOR_SIZE)
unsigned int computeSectorsUsed(size_t fileSize) {
  return (fileSize + SECTOR_SIZE - 1) / SECTOR_SIZE;
}

// Function to update the persistent "counter.txt" file.
// It reads the current write cycle count, increments it, computes a
↪    new checksum,
// and then writes the data transactionally (via a temporary file
↪    and rename operation)
// to simulate atomic file I/O and basic transactional integrity.
void updateDataFile() {
  String filename = "/counter.txt";

  // Read current counter value if the file exists.
  File file = SPIFFS.open(filename, FILE_READ);
  String fileData;
  if (file) {
    fileData = file.readString();
    file.close();
    // Expecting file format: "counter:<value>\nchecksum:<value>\n"
    int idx = fileData.indexOf("counter:");
    if (idx != -1) {
      int endLine = fileData.indexOf("\n", idx);
```

```
    String counterStr = fileData.substring(idx + 8, endLine);
    writeCounter = counterStr.toInt();
  }
} else {
  writeCounter = 0;
}

// Increment the write counter to simulate a new write cycle.
writeCounter++;

// Prepare the new file content, including the counter and its
↪   computed checksum.
String dataLine = "counter:" + String(writeCounter) + "\n";
unsigned long checksum = computeChecksum(dataLine);
dataLine += "checksum:" + String(checksum) + "\n";

// Perform transactional file update:
// 1. Write data to a temporary file.
// 2. Remove the old file if it exists.
// 3. Rename the temporary file to the target filename.
String tempFilename = filename + ".temp";
File tempFile = SPIFFS.open(tempFilename, FILE_WRITE);
if (!tempFile) {
  Serial.println("Failed to open temporary file for writing");
  return;
}
tempFile.print(dataLine);
tempFile.close();

if (SPIFFS.exists(filename)) {
  SPIFFS.remove(filename);
}
if (SPIFFS.rename(tempFilename, filename)) {
  Serial.println("File updated transactionally.");
} else {
  Serial.println("File rename failed.");
}

// Open the updated file to display file size and computed
↪   sectors.
File updatedFile = SPIFFS.open(filename, FILE_READ);
if (updatedFile) {
  size_t fSize = updatedFile.size();
  unsigned int sectors = computeSectorsUsed(fSize);
  Serial.print("Updated File Size: ");
  Serial.print(fSize);
  Serial.print(" bytes, Sectors used: ");
  Serial.println(sectors);
  updatedFile.close();
}

// Simulate wear leveling: calculate the percentage of maximum
↪   write cycles consumed.
```

```cpp
  float wearPercentage = ((float)writeCounter / MAX_WRITE_CYCLES) *
  ↪   100.0;
  Serial.print("Simulated Wear Leveling: ");
  Serial.print(wearPercentage);
  Serial.println("% of max write cycles reached.");
}

// Setup function: initializes Serial communication and mounts
↪   SPIFFS.
// Also creates the initial counter file if it does not exist.
void setup() {
  Serial.begin(115200);
  delay(1000); // Allow time for the Serial Monitor to initialize
  Serial.println("Initializing SPIFFS...");

  if (!SPIFFS.begin(true)) {
    Serial.println("SPIFFS Mount Failed");
    return;
  }
  Serial.println("SPIFFS Mounted Successfully.");

  // Check for the existence of the persistent counter file.
  if (!SPIFFS.exists("/counter.txt")) {
    Serial.println("Creating initial counter file...");
    File file = SPIFFS.open("/counter.txt", FILE_WRITE);
    if (file) {
      String initData = "counter:0\n";
      initData += "checksum:" +
      ↪   String(computeChecksum("counter:0\n")) + "\n";
      file.print(initData);
      file.close();
    } else {
      Serial.println("Failed to create the initial counter file.");
    }
  }
}

// Loop function: periodically updates the persistent data file to
↪   simulate
// continuous file I/O operations, error detection, and
↪   transactional updates.
void loop() {
  updateDataFile();
  delay(5000); // Update every 5 seconds to simulate periodic
  ↪   writes.
}
```

Chapter 45

Event-Driven Programming Paradigms

Fundamental Principles of Asynchronous Event Handling

Asynchronous event handling constitutes a critical paradigm in reactive system design wherein the execution flow is determined by unpredictable external stimuli rather than by a predetermined sequence. In this context, events are modeled as discrete occurrences that encapsulate instantaneous state changes triggered by hardware signals, network interactions, or internal system indicators. These events are characterized by their temporal decoupling from the main execution thread, thereby necessitating an architectural approach based on non-blocking operations. The fundamental theory underpinning asynchronous event handling draws on models of concurrency that utilize dedicated event loops and dispatcher mechanisms to ensure that events are queued, prioritized, and processed in a systematic and deterministic manner.

Event Modeling and Abstraction in IoT Systems

Within the domain of Internet of Things applications, effective abstraction of events is essential for managing the heterogeneity and unpredictability of external stimuli. An event model in this context is constructed to encapsulate key attributes such as event type, timestamp, priority, and contextual metadata that describe the ambient conditions at the time of occurrence. Such a detailed abstraction allows for the integration of diverse data sources into a unified event management framework. The modeling process is often formalized using concepts derived from automata theory, where state transitions are rigorously defined in terms of event occurrences. This facilitates the derivation of transition functions that reliably map the current system state to the next configuration upon receiving a designated event.

Event Dispatch and Processing Mechanisms

The core operational facet of an event-driven system is rooted in the efficiency of its event dispatch and processing mechanisms. A central event loop continuously monitors an event queue, orchestrating the sequencing of incoming events according to predetermined priority and temporal criteria. Upon detection, each event triggers the invocation of its associated handler function, thereby isolating the event-specific logic from the central control flow. The dispatch mechanism is commonly implemented via a non-preemptive scheduling model, ensuring that each event is processed to completion before the subsequent event is handled. In scenarios characterized by high throughput, stochastic models such as the Poisson process are employed to analyze system performance, which in turn informs iterative refinements aimed at minimizing processing latency (L) and maximizing throughput (T).

Concurrency and Synchronization Strategies in Event-Driven Paradigms

The concurrent handling of asynchronous events in a resource-constrained environment, such as those encountered in IoT deployments, necessitates robust strategies for managing simultaneous event triggers. Concurrency in event-driven systems is often achieved through cooperative multitasking, wherein event handlers are designed to yield control to the central dispatcher following the completion of localized processing. This prevents any single routine from monopolizing processor resources. In addition, the potential for race conditions and resource contention is addressed by incorporating synchronization primitives—such as mutexes and semaphores—that regulate access to shared data structures. The theoretical framework for these synchronization strategies is grounded in formal concurrency theory, which emphasizes critical section analysis and deadlock avoidance. The interplay between concurrent event processing and effective synchronization ensures that system responsiveness is enhanced while preserving the integrity and determinism of state transitions in a non-deterministic operational environment.

ESP32 For IoT With Arduino Code Snippet

```
#include <Arduino.h>

#define MAX_EVENTS 10   // Maximum number of events in the queue

// Define event types for simulation purposes
enum EventType {
  EVENT_TYPE_A, // For example: Sensor Reading
  EVENT_TYPE_B, // For example: Network Message
  EVENT_TYPE_C  // For example: System Alert
};

// Event structure encapsulating the event model attributes
struct Event {
  EventType type;          // Identifier for the event type
  unsigned long timestamp; // Time (in ms) when event occurred
  int priority;            // Priority level (1 to 10)
  String data;             // Metadata or descriptive data
};
```

287

```
// Global event queue and counter to simulate FIFO processing
Event eventQueue[MAX_EVENTS];
int eventCount = 0;

// Adds an event to the queue if space permits
void addEvent(Event evt) {
  if (eventCount < MAX_EVENTS) {
    eventQueue[eventCount++] = evt;
  } else {
    Serial.println("Warning: Event queue full!");
  }
}

// Dispatches an event by invoking the appropriate handler based on
↪   event type
void dispatchEvent(Event evt) {
  Serial.print("Dispatching Event: ");
  Serial.print((int)evt.type);
  Serial.print(" | Timestamp: ");
  Serial.print(evt.timestamp);
  Serial.print(" | Priority: ");
  Serial.println(evt.priority);

  // Event handling logic based on event type
  switch(evt.type) {
    case EVENT_TYPE_A:
      Serial.println("-> Handling Event Type A: Sensor Reading");
      break;
    case EVENT_TYPE_B:
      Serial.println("-> Handling Event Type B: Network Message");
      break;
    case EVENT_TYPE_C:
      Serial.println("-> Handling Event Type C: System Alert");
      break;
    default:
      Serial.println("-> Unknown Event Type");
      break;
  }

  // Calculate processing latency: L = current time -
  ↪   event.timestamp
  unsigned long latency = millis() - evt.timestamp;
  Serial.print("Event Latency (ms): ");
  Serial.println(latency);
}

// Processes all events in the global queue using FIFO order
void processEventQueue() {
  for (int i = 0; i < eventCount; i++) {
    dispatchEvent(eventQueue[i]);
  }
  // Clear the queue after processing all events
```

```
    eventCount = 0;
}

// Global variables for event generation and performance metrics
unsigned long lastEventGenTime = 0;
const unsigned long eventGenInterval = 1000;   // Generate an event
↪  every 1000ms (1 s)
int totalEventsProcessed = 0;

// Setup function: initializes serial communication and seeds the
↪  RNG
void setup() {
  Serial.begin(115200);
  Serial.println("ESP32 Event-Driven Programming Example");
  // Seed the random number generator using an analog input
  randomSeed(analogRead(0));
}

// Loop function: main event-driven loop simulating asynchronous
↪  event generation,
// dispatch, and performance monitoring.
void loop() {
  unsigned long currentTime = millis();

  // Asynchronously generate a new event at defined intervals
  if (currentTime - lastEventGenTime >= eventGenInterval) {
    lastEventGenTime = currentTime;

    // Construct a new event with random type and priority
    Event newEvent;
    newEvent.type = (EventType)(random(0, 3)); // Randomly picks 0,
    ↪  1, or 2
    newEvent.timestamp = currentTime;
    newEvent.priority = random(1, 11);          // Priority between 1
    ↪  and 10
    newEvent.data = "Sample Event Data";

    addEvent(newEvent);
    Serial.print("Event Added. Queue Size: ");
    Serial.println(eventCount);
  }

  // Check if there are pending events; if so, process them
  if (eventCount > 0) {
    processEventQueue();

    // Update the count of processed events
    totalEventsProcessed++;

    // Calculate throughput (T) as events processed per second:
    // T = totalEventsProcessed / (elapsed time in seconds)
    float throughput = (totalEventsProcessed * 1000.0) /
    ↪  (float)currentTime;
```

```
    Serial.print("Throughput (events/sec): ");
    Serial.println(throughput);
  }

  // Short delay to yield control (simulating cooperative
  ↪ multitasking)
  delay(10);
}
```

Chapter 46

Implementing State Machines in IoT Applications

Foundational Concepts and Theoretical Underpinnings

The formalism of state machines provides a rigorous framework for representing and controlling the sequential behavior of systems subject to a stream of events. At its core, a state machine is defined as a quintuple $M = (S, \Sigma, \delta, s_0, F)$ where S denotes a finite set of states, Σ is the set of possible input events, $\delta : S \times \Sigma \to S$ is the transition function that deterministically maps a given state and input to a subsequent state, $s_0 \in S$ is the designated initial state, and $F \subseteq S$ represents a set of terminal states. The mathematical precision afforded by this model ensures that sequential event-driven behavior is captured completely, thereby facilitating an unambiguous description of system dynamics. Within the domain of IoT, this abstraction is paramount, as the interplay between asynchronous external events and internal state evolution demands a disciplined architectural approach.

Modeling Sequential Events for Complex Logic

Complex logic in embedded systems is often realized through the orderly progression of states, each corresponding to a distinct operational mode within the overall system. In this context, the processing of sequential events is modeled by considering that each event $e_i \in \Sigma$ triggers a state transition through the mapping $\delta(s, e_i)$ where $s \in S$. Such a formulation allows for the encapsulation of intricate temporal sequences and conditional responses without ambiguity. By representing each possible configuration and transition explicitly in a state diagram, it becomes feasible to visualize not only the immediate response to every event but also the cascading effects on future system behavior. This level of systematic detail is particularly crucial in ESP32-based applications, where real-time responsiveness and efficient handling of asynchronous triggers directly impact the reliability of the IoT deployment.

Design Patterns for ESP32-Based State Machines

Adopting established design patterns for state machines ensures that the complexity of sequential logic is managed effectively in resource-constrained environments. Hierarchical state machines, for instance, enable the encapsulation of nested states, thereby isolating sub-behaviors within broader operational contexts. In such models, a composite state may itself be decomposed into a lower-level state machine, allowing for encapsulation and reuse of common logic patterns. Additionally, the employment of transition tables or decision matrices aids in the clear specification of state transitions, enhancing both scalability and maintainability. Emphasis is placed on a modular design framework in which each state is self-contained, with clearly defined entry and exit criteria. This systematic partitioning of functionality proves advantageous when addressing the multifaceted control-flow requirements inherent in ESP32-centric IoT applications.

Execution Semantics and Performance Considerations

The execution semantics of state machines in the realm of real-time IoT systems are characterized by stringent requirements for determinism and low-latency responses. The synchronization between asynchronous event triggers and state transitions is managed so as to preserve the integrity of the overall system state. Every transition is subject to careful validation, often measured in terms of the processing latency L, where L is defined as the difference between the event generation time and the time at which the subsequent state change is fully realized. Particular attention is devoted to scenarios that involve concurrent events, where the selection of an appropriate scheduling policy ensures that no single event monopolizes processing resources. Optimization of the state evaluation routines is thus critical; these routines are streamlined to eliminate redundant computations while ensuring that the dispatch of transitions remains both predictable and timely. The resulting architecture not only guarantees adherence to strict performance metrics but also reinforces the inherent reliability required for sophisticated IoT deployments based on the ESP32 platform.

ESP32 For IoT With Arduino Code Snippet

```
// ESP32 IoT State Machine Implementation in Arduino
// Based on the formal model: M = (S, , , s0, F)
// S: {STATE_INIT, STATE_WIFI_CONNECT, STATE_MEASURE,
↪   STATE_TRANSMIT, STATE_SLEEP, STATE_ERROR}
// : {EVENT_INIT_COMPLETE, EVENT_WIFI_CONNECTED,
↪   EVENT_MEASURE_COMPLETE,
//    EVENT_TRANSMIT_SUCCESS, EVENT_TIMEOUT, EVENT_ERROR_OCCURED}
// : Defined by the function stateTransition()
// s0: STATE_INIT (initial state)
// F: For this example, STATE_SLEEP acts as a terminal state before
↪   restarting

#include <Arduino.h>

// Define the set of states S
enum State {
  STATE_INIT,
  STATE_WIFI_CONNECT,
```

```
  STATE_MEASURE,
  STATE_TRANSMIT,
  STATE_SLEEP,
  STATE_ERROR
};

// Define the set of events
enum Event {
  EVENT_INIT_COMPLETE,
  EVENT_WIFI_CONNECTED,
  EVENT_MEASURE_COMPLETE,
  EVENT_TRANSMIT_SUCCESS,
  EVENT_TIMEOUT,
  EVENT_ERROR_OCCURED
};

// Global variable to store the current state, starting at s0 =
↪   STATE_INIT
State currentState = STATE_INIT;

// Variable to timestamp the entry of each state, used to compute
↪   latency L
// where L = (current time - state entry time)
unsigned long stateStartTime = 0;

// Simulated sensor value (for demonstration purposes)
int sensorValue = 0;

// Transition function (s, e)
// This function returns the next state based on the current state
↪   and the event encountered.
State stateTransition(State current, Event event) {
  switch (current) {
    case STATE_INIT:
      if (event == EVENT_INIT_COMPLETE) {
        return STATE_WIFI_CONNECT;
      }
      break;
    case STATE_WIFI_CONNECT:
      if (event == EVENT_WIFI_CONNECTED) {
        return STATE_MEASURE;
      } else if (event == EVENT_TIMEOUT) {
        return STATE_ERROR;
      }
      break;
    case STATE_MEASURE:
      if (event == EVENT_MEASURE_COMPLETE) {
        return STATE_TRANSMIT;
      }
      break;
    case STATE_TRANSMIT:
      if (event == EVENT_TRANSMIT_SUCCESS) {
        return STATE_SLEEP;
```

294

```
      }
      break;
    case STATE_SLEEP:
      // After sleep, reinitialize the cycle by transitioning as if
      ↪ initialization completed.
      if (event == EVENT_INIT_COMPLETE) {
        return STATE_WIFI_CONNECT;
      }
      break;
    case STATE_ERROR:
      // In an error scenario, perform recovery and transition back
      ↪ to Wi-Fi connection.
      if (event == EVENT_INIT_COMPLETE) {
        return STATE_WIFI_CONNECT;
      }
      break;
    default:
      break;
  }
  // If no transition condition is satisfied, remain in the current
  ↪ state.
  return current;
}

void setup() {
  Serial.begin(115200);
  // Set the initial timestamp for the state machine.
  stateStartTime = millis();
  Serial.println("State Machine Starting: STATE_INIT");
}

void loop() {
  unsigned long currentTime = millis();
  unsigned long elapsed = currentTime - stateStartTime;
  Event eventOccurred;  // Variable to hold the event generated
  ↪ based on current state

  switch (currentState) {
    case STATE_INIT:
      // Simulate initialization tasks.
      if (elapsed >= 2000) { // After 2 seconds, consider
      ↪ initialization complete.
        Serial.println("Event: INIT_COMPLETE");
        eventOccurred = EVENT_INIT_COMPLETE;
        currentState = stateTransition(currentState, eventOccurred);
        stateStartTime = currentTime; // Reset timer for the new
        ↪ state.
        Serial.println("Transitioned to STATE_WIFI_CONNECT");
      }
      break;

    case STATE_WIFI_CONNECT:
      // Simulate Wi-Fi connection attempt.
```

```
  if (elapsed >= 3000) { // Assume Wi-Fi connects successfully
  ↪  in 3 seconds.
    Serial.println("Event: WIFI_CONNECTED");
    eventOccurred = EVENT_WIFI_CONNECTED;
    currentState = stateTransition(currentState, eventOccurred);
    stateStartTime = currentTime;
    Serial.println("Transitioned to STATE_MEASURE");
  }
  // Uncomment the following block to simulate a connection
  ↪  timeout and error:
  /*
  else if (elapsed >= 4000) {
    Serial.println("Event: TIMEOUT");
    eventOccurred = EVENT_TIMEOUT;
    currentState = stateTransition(currentState, eventOccurred);
    stateStartTime = currentTime;
    Serial.println("Transitioned to STATE_ERROR");
  }
  */
  break;

case STATE_MEASURE:
  // Simulate sensor data measurement.
  if (elapsed >= 1500) { // After 1.5 seconds, assume the sensor
  ↪  reading is complete.
    // For an actual ESP32, use analogRead(pin) (example:
    ↪  analogRead(34))
    sensorValue = analogRead(34);
    Serial.print("Sensor Value: ");
    Serial.println(sensorValue);
    Serial.println("Event: MEASURE_COMPLETE");
    eventOccurred = EVENT_MEASURE_COMPLETE;
    currentState = stateTransition(currentState, eventOccurred);
    stateStartTime = currentTime;
    Serial.println("Transitioned to STATE_TRANSMIT");
  }
  break;

case STATE_TRANSMIT:
  // Simulate data transmission over a network.
  if (elapsed >= 2000) { // After 2 seconds, assume transmission
  ↪  is successful.
    Serial.println("Transmitting data...");
    // Here you would typically integrate Wi-Fi client code,
    ↪  HTTP/MQTT calls, etc.
    Serial.println("Event: TRANSMIT_SUCCESS");
    eventOccurred = EVENT_TRANSMIT_SUCCESS;
    currentState = stateTransition(currentState, eventOccurred);
    stateStartTime = currentTime;
    Serial.println("Transitioned to STATE_SLEEP");
  }
  break;
```

```
case STATE_SLEEP:
  // Simulate low-power sleep mode operation.
  if (elapsed >= 1000) { // After 1 second, wake up from sleep.
    Serial.println("Device is in sleep mode...");
    Serial.println("Waking up from sleep. Reinitializing...");
    eventOccurred = EVENT_INIT_COMPLETE;
    currentState = stateTransition(currentState, eventOccurred);
    stateStartTime = currentTime;
    Serial.println("Transitioned to STATE_WIFI_CONNECT");
  }
  break;

case STATE_ERROR:
  // Error handling and recovery routine.
  if (elapsed >= 3000) { // After 3 seconds, attempt recovery.
    Serial.println("Attempting error recovery...");
    eventOccurred = EVENT_INIT_COMPLETE;
    currentState = stateTransition(currentState, eventOccurred);
    stateStartTime = currentTime;
    Serial.println("Recovered. Transitioned to
    ↪  STATE_WIFI_CONNECT");
  }
  break;

  default:
    break;
}
}
```

Chapter 47

Implementing Callback Mechanisms

Defining the Callback Paradigm

In formal terms, a callback function is an executable unit that is supplied as a parameter to another function, thereby enabling deferred execution in response to particular events or conditions. Mathematically, if one considers a primary function $F : X \to Y$ that operates on an input domain X to yield an output in Y, then a callback is represented as a function $g : A \to B$ that is registered with F and invoked when a specified condition or event from the set E is satisfied. This abstraction encapsulates the mechanism by which control flow is transferred asynchronously, thereby removing the dependence on linear execution order and allowing for the division of computational responsibilities.

Callback Functions in Asynchronous Event Handling

The asynchronous nature of event-driven systems mandates that certain operations must occur in a non-blocking fashion, such that the main execution thread is not hindered by time-consuming tasks. Callback mechanisms provide a robust solution by decoupling event generation from event processing. When an asynchronous event is triggered, the system enqueues an identifier corresponding to that event, and at an appropriate juncture, the registered callback function is executed to handle the event. This process is formally describable by considering that if $e \in E$ represents an event and $\gamma : E \to$ {Registered Callbacks} is the mapping that associates each event with its handler, then the asynchronous execution is governed by the composite function $\gamma(e)(\cdot)$, which is invoked once e is detected. Emphasis on such modular interaction facilitates the creation of responsive systems, where the timely processing of events is critical to overall system performance.

Enhancing Modularity through Callbacks

The introduction of callback functions into system architecture inherently promotes modularity by segregating event detection from event handling logic. This design pattern permits a clear abstraction boundary between the core operational framework and the reactive response mechanisms. Formally, if the overall system behavior is denoted by a function H that is decomposable as $H = H_{\text{core}} \circ H_{\text{callback}}$, then the independent evolution of each component can be assured. Such decoupling facilitates not only the isolation of fault domains, but also simplifies testing and verification procedures. In addition, the adoption of callbacks contributes to improved reusability of code modules since specific event responses become encapsulated in self-contained functions that can be repurposed across disparate contexts within an application.

Design Considerations and Theoretical Analysis

The architectural integration of callbacks necessitates rigorous consideration of timing, concurrency, and resource management. An essential aspect is ensuring that the callback registration mechanism preserves determinism in the presence of asynchronous stimuli, particularly when multiple callbacks are concurrently eligible for execution. If the set of callback functions is denoted as $\mathcal{G} = \{g_1, g_2, \ldots, g_n\}$, then designing an efficient scheduling policy, represented as $\sigma : 2^{\mathcal{G}} \to \mathcal{G}$, is crucial to prevent race conditions and ensure predictable behavior. Furthermore, callbacks must be designed with regard to potential reentrant behavior and memory management constraints inherent to resource-limited environ-

299

ments. A formal treatment of these issues might involve modeling the invocation sequence as a partially ordered set, where the dependencies between asynchronous events and callback invocations are explicitly captured. Such analysis underpins the theoretical guarantees that callback mechanisms provide in mitigating latency and improving overall system throughput.

Analytical Framework for Callback Utilization

The implementation of callback mechanisms can be further elucidated by adopting an analytical framework that considers both the temporal and causal relationships inherent in event-driven systems. When a callback function g is invoked as a result of an event e, the temporal delay incurred can be quantitatively expressed as $\Delta t = t_{\text{callback}} - t_e$, where t_e is the time at which the event occurred and t_{callback} is the time of callback execution. This metric is integral to evaluating the responsiveness of the system, especially in scenarios where low-latency processing is paramount. In parallel, the causal link between event and handler is maintained by a well-defined mapping that preserves the invariant that every registered callback is correctly associated with its triggering condition. Such formalisms, when rigorously applied, not only enhance the modular architecture but also provide a solid foundation for reasoning about correctness and performance in complex IoT deployments.

ESP32 For IoT With Arduino Code Snippet

```
// This example demonstrates a callback mechanism on the ESP32 using
↪   Arduino,
// incorporating key equations and scheduling ideas discussed in the
↪   chapter.
// The core idea is to simulate asynchronous event handling, measure
↪   the delay,
// and select between multiple callback functions based on a simple
↪   scheduling policy.
//
// Formal Equation (for delay measurement):
//      t = t_callback - t_event
//
```

```cpp
// In this code, when an event occurs (every 5 seconds), we record
↪    its timestamp,
// then after a simulated processing delay (100 ms), we call a
↪    selected callback.
// Two callbacks (callbackOne and callbackTwo) are registered
↪    implicitly, and a
// simple scheduling rule (alternating based on event count) is used
↪    to choose which
// callback to execute.

#include <Arduino.h>

// Define a type for callback functions that receive the event
↪    timestamp.
typedef void (*CallbackFunction)(unsigned long eventTime);

// Forward declarations for the callback functions.
void callbackOne(unsigned long eventTime);
void callbackTwo(unsigned long eventTime);

// Global configuration and state variables.
unsigned long eventInterval = 5000;   // Time interval (ms) between
↪    simulated events.
unsigned long lastEventTime = 0;      // Timestamp of the last event.
int eventCount = 0;                   // Counter to alternate between
↪    callbacks.

void setup() {
  Serial.begin(115200);
  // Wait for the serial port to connect (useful for native USB
  ↪    boards).
  while (!Serial) {
    ; // Do nothing until Serial is ready.
  }
  Serial.println("ESP32 Callback Mechanism Demo");
  Serial.println("-------------------------------");
}

void loop() {
  // Check if the event interval has elapsed.
  if (millis() - lastEventTime >= eventInterval) {
    // Record the event's occurrence time.
    unsigned long eventTimestamp = millis();
    Serial.print("Event triggered at: ");
    Serial.println(eventTimestamp);

    // Scheduling function: choose a callback based on the event
    ↪    count.
    // This implements a simple scheduling policy : 2^{G} → G.
    CallbackFunction scheduledCallback;
    if (eventCount % 2 == 0) {
      scheduledCallback = callbackOne;
      Serial.println("Scheduling callbackOne");
```

301

```
  } else {
    scheduledCallback = callbackTwo;
    Serial.println("Scheduling callbackTwo");
  }

  // Simulate processing delay before callback invocation
  ↪ (non-blocking equivalent).
  // Here, we use delay() to simulate asynchronous task
  ↪ scheduling.
  delay(100);  // Simulated delay of 100 ms

  // Capture the time immediately before the callback is invoked.
  unsigned long callbackInvocationTime = millis();
  // Calculate the delay t = t_callback - t_event.
  unsigned long deltaT = callbackInvocationTime - eventTimestamp;
  Serial.print("Measured callback delay (ms): ");
  Serial.println(deltaT);

  // Invoke the scheduled callback with the original event
  ↪ timestamp.
  scheduledCallback(eventTimestamp);

  // Increment the event counter.
  eventCount++;
  // Update the last event time for the next iteration.
  lastEventTime = millis();

    Serial.println("-------------------------------");
  }
}


// Callback function that processes the event (Callback One).
void callbackOne(unsigned long eventTime) {
  unsigned long currentTime = millis();
  // Compute delay: t = t_now - eventTime.
  unsigned long delayMeasured = currentTime - eventTime;
  Serial.print("Callback One executed at: ");
  Serial.print(currentTime);
  Serial.print(" ms (Delay: ");
  Serial.print(delayMeasured);
  Serial.println(" ms)");
  // Additional processing may be added here for real IoT use cases.
}

// Callback function that processes the event (Callback Two).
void callbackTwo(unsigned long eventTime) {
  unsigned long currentTime = millis();
  // Compute delay: t = t_now - eventTime.
  unsigned long delayMeasured = currentTime - eventTime;
  Serial.print("Callback Two executed at: ");
  Serial.print(currentTime);
  Serial.print(" ms (Delay: ");
  Serial.print(delayMeasured);
```

```
    Serial.println(" ms)");
    // Additional processing may be added here for real IoT use cases.
}
```

Chapter 48

Scheduling Periodic Tasks with Callbacks

Foundations of Callback-Driven Perioding

Periodic task scheduling in embedded systems is achieved by employing callback functions as the fundamental mechanism for triggering recurring actions. In this framework, a callback (represented by a function $g : T \to R$) is registered with a scheduler that activates it once a predetermined temporal condition is met. The formulation of periodicity hinges on the definition of a recurrence interval Δt, such that the set of scheduled invocation times is given by

$$E = \{t_0, t_1, t_2, \dots\}, \quad \text{with} \quad t_{i+1} = t_i + \Delta t.$$

The deterministic execution of these callbacks underpins the timing guarantees necessary for reliable operation, ensuring that each task associated with a given callback is activated without deviation from the intended schedule.

Mathematical Formulation of Recurring Callback Invocation

The periodic activation of tasks through callbacks can be rigorously described using a formal mathematical model. Let E denote the sequence of event times at which the periodic tasks are scheduled. The mapping from each event time $t_i \in E$ to its respective callback is captured by a function

$$C : E \to F,$$

where F represents the set of available callback routines. Formally, the invocations satisfy the condition

$$\forall t_i \in E, \quad C(t_i) = f_i,$$

with $f_i \in F$ being the callback function executed when the scheduling predicate $P(t)$, defined as

$$P(t) \equiv (t \mod \Delta t = 0),$$

evaluates to true. The correctness of the model is ensured by maintaining the invariant that the inter-invocation interval

$$\delta t = t_{i+1} - t_i,$$

remains constant and equivalent to Δt. The deviation between the scheduled and actual invocation times, denoted as Δt_{error}, is given by

$$\Delta t_{\text{error}} = |t_{\text{actual}} - t_i|,$$

and must be minimized to conform to the real-time constraints required by time-sensitive applications.

Temporal Dynamics and Reliability Metrics

The reliability of a periodic scheduling mechanism is critically dependent on the temporal dynamics of callback execution. During each periodic interval, the registered callback is expected to execute within a controlled latency. Denote the callback delay as

$$\delta t_{\text{callback}} = t_{\text{callback}} - t_i,$$

where t_{callback} is the time at which the callback is actually executed. The system is designed to satisfy

$$\delta t_{\text{callback}} \leq \epsilon,$$

305

with ϵ representing the maximum allowable latency for the given application. An analysis of the cumulative latency over N invocations may be expressed as

$$L = \sum_{i=0}^{N-1} \delta t_{\text{callback}}^{(i)},$$

where maintaining a low aggregate latency is paramount for the deterministic behavior of the scheduling system. The rigorous control of these temporal metrics ensures that the scheduled tasks maintain high fidelity with respect to their intended periodic activation, despite the asynchronous nature of callback-based processing.

Efficiency Considerations in Resource-Constrained Environments

Embedded architectures, such as the ESP32, impose stringent restrictions on computational and memory resources, necessitating an efficient implementation of the callback scheduling mechanism. The overhead associated with the management of callbacks, denoted by O, directly influences the overall performance of the scheduler. The efficiency of the system can be quantified by the ratio

$$S = \frac{O}{\Delta t},$$

where a lower value of S signifies that the scheduler operates with minimal resource consumption relative to the given time interval. A critical objective in the design of such systems is the reduction of O, thereby allowing the underlying scheduler to devote the majority of available processing capacity to the execution of the periodic tasks. Additionally, the integration of a deterministic task dispatcher—governed by a policy function

$$\sigma : \mathcal{P}(F) \rightarrow F,$$

where $\mathcal{P}(F)$ is the power set of callback functions—facilitates the prioritization of callbacks based on criteria such as frequency of occurrence and computational load. This strategy not only affords a modular separation between task initiation and task execution but also promotes rigorous adherence to the time constraints dictated by the periodic schedule.

ESP32 For IoT With Arduino Code Snippet

```
#include <Arduino.h>

// Define the LED pin (typically built-in LED for ESP32 is on GPIO2)
#define LED_PIN 2

// Scheduling parameters
const unsigned long DELTA_T = 1000;      // Recurrence interval in
↪    milliseconds
const unsigned long EPSILON = 10;        // Maximum allowable latency
↪    in milliseconds

// Global variables to track scheduling and performance
unsigned long nextSchedule = 0;          // Next scheduled invocation
↪    time (t_i)
unsigned long cumulativeLatency = 0;     // Cumulative latency over
↪    invocations (L)
unsigned long invocationCount = 0;       // Number of times the
↪    callback has been executed
unsigned long callbackOverhead = 0;      // Overhead of the callback
↪    function measured in microseconds

// Define a callback function type to allow flexible registration
typedef void (*CallbackFunction)();
CallbackFunction registeredCallback = NULL;

// Example periodic task callback function (f_i)
// This function simulates work by toggling the LED and performing a
↪    simple arithmetic task.
void periodicTask() {
  // Record start time to measure callback execution overhead
  unsigned long startMicros = micros();

  // Toggle LED state to mimic a real task
  digitalWrite(LED_PIN, !digitalRead(LED_PIN));

  // Simulate computational work (simple arithmetic as a
↪    placeholder)
  int a = 10;
  int b = 20;
  int c = a + b;  // Basic operation to simulate processing load

  // Additional processing could be added here (e.g., sensor
↪    readings, communication routines)

  // Measure end time and compute the overhead (O)
  unsigned long endMicros = micros();
  callbackOverhead = endMicros - startMicros;
}
```

```
// Function to register a callback function for periodic invocation.
void registerCallback(CallbackFunction cb) {
  registeredCallback = cb;
}

void setup() {
  // Initialize serial communication for debugging and metric
  ↪  printouts.
  Serial.begin(115200);
  delay(1000); // Allow time for the serial monitor to connect

  // Set up the LED pin as OUTPUT
  pinMode(LED_PIN, OUTPUT);
  digitalWrite(LED_PIN, LOW);

  // Register the periodic callback function (f_i)
  registerCallback(periodicTask);

  // Initialize the next scheduled invocation time t_0
  nextSchedule = millis() + DELTA_T;
  Serial.println("Starting periodic task scheduling...");
}

void loop() {
  // Get the current system time (t)
  unsigned long currentTime = millis();

  // Check the scheduling predicate: Is the current time at or past
  ↪  the scheduled time?
  if (currentTime >= nextSchedule) {
    // Compute the deviation (t_error) between the scheduled time
    ↪  (t_i) and the actual callback time.
    unsigned long t_actual = currentTime;
    long deltaTimeError = (long)t_actual - (long)nextSchedule;
    if (deltaTimeError < 0) {
      deltaTimeError = 0;   // Ensure non-negative error
    }

    // Store latency per callback invocation (t_callback = t_actual
    ↪  - t_i)
    cumulativeLatency += deltaTimeError;

    // Print timing metrics for debugging
    Serial.print("Scheduled Time (t_i): ");
    Serial.print(nextSchedule);
    Serial.print(" ms, Actual Time: ");
    Serial.print(t_actual);
    Serial.print(" ms, t_error: ");
    Serial.print(deltaTimeError);
    Serial.println(" ms");
```

```cpp
  // Check if the callback delay violates the maximum allowed
  ↪  latency ()
  if (deltaTimeError > EPSILON) {
    Serial.println("Warning: Callback latency exceeded acceptable
    ↪  threshold ()!");
  }

  // Execute the registered callback function if it exists
  if (registeredCallback != NULL) {
    registeredCallback();

    // Print the measured overhead (O) of the callback execution
    Serial.print("Callback Overhead (O): ");
    Serial.print(callbackOverhead);
    Serial.println(" microseconds");
  }

  // Increment the invocation counter
  invocationCount++;

  // Schedule the next invocation (t_{i+1} = t_i + t)
  nextSchedule += DELTA_T;

  // Optionally, every 10 invocations, print cumulative metrics
  ↪  and efficiency ratio
  if (invocationCount % 10 == 0) {
    Serial.print("Cumulative Latency (L) after ");
    Serial.print(invocationCount);
    Serial.print(" invocations: ");
    Serial.print(cumulativeLatency);
    Serial.println(" ms");

    // Calculate efficiency: S = (O / t) where a lower ratio
    ↪  denotes minimal resource usage
    float efficiency = ((float)callbackOverhead) / DELTA_T;
    Serial.print("Efficiency Ratio (S = O/t): ");
    Serial.println(efficiency, 4);
  }
}

// Additional non-blocking tasks can be handled here, maintaining
↪  overall system responsiveness.
}
```

Chapter 49

Time Management in ESP32 Programming

Overview of System Timers in Embedded Architectures

In embedded systems, precise timekeeping is paramount for efficient task management and deterministic behavior. The ESP32, operating within the Arduino ecosystem, furnishes system timer functions that have become integral to the orchestration of timing-dependent operations. In particular, the functions $millis()$ and $micros()$ serve as the foundational tools for temporal measurement. The function $millis()$ yields an unsigned long integer representing the number of milliseconds elapsed since system initialization, whereas $micros()$ provides a higher resolution measure by returning the elapsed time in microseconds. These functions establish a virtual timeline against which events are scheduled and delays are quantified, thereby enabling precise control over the execution order of tasks.

Scheduling and Delay Mechanisms via System Timers

Temporal scheduling in the ESP32 environment relies on system timers to determine the appropriate instants for task initiation. A common paradigm involves defining a reference time t_0 and scheduling subsequent events at discrete intervals. Let the intended time for the ith event be expressed as

$$t_i = t_0 + i \cdot \Delta t,$$

where Δt denotes a predetermined time interval. The system continuously monitors the current time, as obtained from $millis()$ or $micros()$, and compares it with the scheduled event times. If the current timestamp fulfills the condition $t \geq t_i$, the corresponding task is initiated. This mechanism obviates the need for blocking delay routines, thereby maintaining system responsiveness. Additionally, the elapsed time difference

$$\delta t = |t_{\text{actual}} - t_i|$$

can be computed to assess the scheduling precision, ensuring that the inherent latency remains within acceptable limits for time-critical operations.

Temporal Resolution and Rollover Considerations

The selection between $millis()$ and $micros()$ is deeply influenced by the requirements for time resolution and the implications of timer rollover. Although $millis()$ offers a coarser granularity compared to $micros()$, it is capable of tracking time over significantly longer durations. For instance, given that the $millis()$ function typically operates over a 32-bit counter, the maximum representable time span is approximately $2^{32} - 1$ milliseconds, corresponding to nearly fifty days before a rollover occurs. In contrast, $micros()$, with its finer resolution, experiences rollover at much shorter intervals. The periodic nature of these rollovers necessitates the use of modular arithmetic when computing time differences. In scenarios where two timestamps, t_a and t_b, are compared, the elapsed duration may be determined by

$$\Delta t = (t_b - t_a) \bmod M,$$

where M represents the modulus appropriate for the timer in use. Such considerations are critical in applications that demand high precision, as they ensure continuity in time tracking despite the intrinsic limitations of fixed-width counters.

Implications for Time-Critical Task Execution

In environments where time-sensitive operations are paramount, the deployment of system timers enables a non-blocking, deterministic approach to task execution. The ability to measure elapsed time with either millisecond or microsecond granularity facilitates the scheduling of tasks that depend on stringent timing constraints. Let ϵ denote the maximum allowable latency for a time-critical task. The temporal correctness of such a task is maintained if the inequality

$$\delta t \leq \epsilon$$

holds consistently across executions. This framework supports a variety of high-priority operations, ranging from sensor data acquisition to real-time communication, by providing a reliable basis for latency measurement and management. The continuous assessment of the time differential between scheduled and actual task execution allows the system to dynamically adjust its scheduling strategy, thereby ensuring that temporal anomalies are minimized. The interplay between the measured delays and the predetermined scheduling intervals underpins the robust performance of the ESP32 in applications where microsecond-level precision can be pivotal.

ESP32 For IoT With Arduino Code Snippet

```
#include <Arduino.h>

// Constants for scheduling and latency management
const unsigned long INTERVAL_MS = 1000;   // t: Time interval
↪   between events (1 second)
const unsigned long MAX_LATENCY = 50;      // : Maximum allowable
↪   scheduling latency in milliseconds

// Global variables for time tracking and event scheduling
unsigned long startTime      = 0;  // t: Initial reference time in
↪   milliseconds (from millis())
unsigned long nextEventTime  = 0;  // t: Scheduled time for the
↪   next event
unsigned long eventCount     = 0;  // Counter used to compute the
↪   ideal scheduled time: t = t + i·t
```

```
void setup() {
  Serial.begin(115200);
  // Wait for Serial to initialize (for boards with native USB)
  while (!Serial) {
    ; // Do nothing until serial port connects.
  }

  // Initialize the reference time and schedule the first event
  startTime = millis();                    // Record system initialization
  ↪   time
  nextEventTime = startTime + INTERVAL_MS;  // First event scheduled
  ↪   at t + t

  Serial.println("ESP32 Time Management Scheduler Started.");
}

void loop() {
  unsigned long currentTime = millis(); // Get current system time
  ↪   in milliseconds

  // Check if the current time has reached (or surpassed) the
  ↪   scheduled event time.
  // Using signed arithmetic ensures correct behavior during timer
  ↪   rollover.
  if ((long)(currentTime - nextEventTime) >= 0) {
    // An event is due. Compute the scheduling error (t) as:
    // t = | t_actual - t |, here t_actual is currentTime.
    unsigned long latency = currentTime - nextEventTime;

    // Output event details: scheduled time, actual execution time,
    ↪   and latency.
    Serial.print("Event ");
    Serial.print(eventCount + 1);
    Serial.print(" scheduled at: ");
    Serial.print(nextEventTime);
    Serial.print(" ms, executed at: ");
    Serial.print(currentTime);
    Serial.print(" ms, latency: ");
    Serial.print(latency);
    Serial.println(" ms");

    // Compare measured latency against maximum allowable threshold
    ↪   ()
    if (latency > MAX_LATENCY) {
      Serial.println("Warning: Latency exceeds threshold!");
    }

    // For applications requiring higher temporal resolution,
    ↪   demonstrate using micros():
    // Expected high-resolution time is computed as: (t + i·t) ×
    ↪   1000, converting ms to µs.
```

```
    unsigned long expectedMicros = (startTime + eventCount *
    ↪   INTERVAL_MS) * 1000UL;
    unsigned long actualMicros   = micros();
    Serial.print("High-resolution timing: expected ");
    Serial.print(expectedMicros);
    Serial.print(" μs, actual ");
    Serial.print(actualMicros);
    Serial.println(" μs");

    // Update event counter and schedule the next event using the
    ↪   formula: t = t + i·t
    eventCount++;
    nextEventTime = startTime + eventCount * INTERVAL_MS;
  }
}
```

Chapter 50

Data Packet Construction and Parsing

Fundamental Principles of Packet-Based Communication

In modern communication systems, data is typically transmitted in discrete units known as packets. A packet is an ordered collection of bits that encapsulates both control information and application data, thereby establishing a modular paradigm for communication across heterogeneous networks. The conceptual framework for packet-based communication is predicated on the separation of concerns; information necessary for routing, synchronization, and integrity checking is segregated from the primary payload. This segregation facilitates independent manipulation and verification of both control and data components. Packet structures are often abstracted as a concatenation of segments, expressed mathematically as

$$P = H \parallel D \parallel T,$$

where H represents the header, D denotes the payload, and T signifies the trailer. Such a formulation emphasizes the importance of modular design, allowing each segment to be processed according to its unique requirements.

Structural Components of Data Packets

The construction of a data packet involves the meticulous allocation of bits into distinct fields that collectively enable efficient transmission and reliable reception. The header, typically a fixed-length segment, is designed to carry control information such as packet identification, source and destination addresses, and protocol version indicators. It performs the critical role of establishing context for the data that follows. Embedded within or following the header, optional fields may convey additional metadata including time stamps and priority flags necessary for dynamic routing. The payload, which contains the substantive information intended for the recipient, may vary in length and is demarcated either by an explicit length field or by well-defined delimiter sequences. Embedded at the end of the packet, the trailer usually contains error-detection or error-correction codes, such as a cyclic redundancy check, which enable the verification of data integrity after transmission. Representing the lengths of these segments as L_H, L_D, and L_T respectively, the overall packet length L_P is given by

$$L_P = L_H + L_D + L_T.$$

This formalism underscores the need for precise delineation between packet components to ensure robust processing and validation at the receiver end.

Techniques for Data Packet Construction

The process of constructing data packets for transmission involves a systematic synthesis of several key elements, each of which must adhere to the protocol specifications governing the communication medium. Packet construction begins with the assembly of the header, wherein critical routing and control parameters are encoded in a predetermined format. These parameters include unique identifiers, sequence numbers, and timing information, all of which contribute to the efficacy of data reassembly and ordering upon receipt. Following header construction, the payload is inserted into the packet, often preceded or followed by auxiliary fields that indicate the payload's length. In protocols where the payload length is variable, the inclusion of a length field, denoted as L_D, is indispensable. In certain instances, packet formats necessitate the application of framing techniques, which may involve the insertion of sentinel byte sequences at the beginning and end of the packet to provide clear demarcation. In these cases, the framing process is governed by transformation functions that may include bit stuffing or byte insertion to preserve synchronization. The ultimate stage in packet construction is the appending of the trailer, which houses error-detection codes. These codes are computed over the aggregated contents of the header and payload, and are essential for detecting anomalies introduced during transmission. The mathematical rigor underlying these construction techniques ensures precise adherence to protocol specifications and optimizes the overall communication efficiency.

Parsing Techniques for Data Packet Reception

The parsing of incoming data packets is a critical function in ensuring that transmitted information is accurately interpreted and processed. Parsing routines are architected to operate on continuous streams of data, systematically identifying and demarcating the constituent segments of each packet. The initiation of the parsing process is frequently predicated on the detection of unique start-of-packet identifiers, which signal the onset of a new packet within the bit stream. State machine models are commonly employed to manage the transition between the expected fields, such as the header, payload, and trailer. As the parser traverses a packet, it engages in the extraction of individual fields based on predetermined lengths or delimiter sequences. Simultaneously, it performs integrity checks by recalculating error-detection codes over the retrieved header and payload segments and comparing the result to the received trailer contents. An illustrative example involves the computation of a checksum C as

$$C = \left(\sum_{i=1}^{L} b_i \right) \bmod N,$$

where b_i represents the ith byte of the data and N is a modulus defined by the protocol. Discrepancies between the computed checksum and the received verification code indicate the presence of transmission errors, prompting subsequent error-handling procedures. Parsing algorithms are further refined to account for conditions such as overlapping packets and variable-length payloads by employing sliding window techniques. The concurrent application of these techniques results in robust and resilient parsing methodologies that are capable of reconstituting the logical data structure from raw bit streams even under adverse transmission conditions.

ESP32 For IoT With Arduino Code Snippet

```
#include <Arduino.h>

// This example demonstrates packet creation and parsing based on
↪   the chapter's concepts.
// Packet structure: P = H  D  T, where:
//   H: Header
//   D: Payload (Data)
//   T: Trailer (Checksum)
// Overall packet length: L_P = L_H + L_D + L_T

// Define segment sizes
const int HEADER_SIZE  = 5;      // Fixed-length header (e.g., 5
↪   bytes)
const int TRAILER_SIZE = 1;      // Trailer holds checksum (1 byte)
const char payloadData[] = "Hello ESP32 IoT!";   // Sample payload
↪   data
const int PAYLOAD_SIZE = sizeof(payloadData) - 1; // Exclude the
↪   null terminator

// Compute overall packet size: L_P = L_H + L_D + L_T
const int PACKET_SIZE = HEADER_SIZE + PAYLOAD_SIZE + TRAILER_SIZE;

// Global packet buffer
byte packet[PACKET_SIZE];

// Computes checksum using: C = (sum(b_i) mod N)
// Here N is chosen as 256 for a one-byte checksum.
byte computeChecksum(const byte* data, int length, byte modValue) {
  unsigned int sum = 0;
  for (int i = 0; i < length; i++) {
    sum += data[i];
  }
  return sum % modValue;
}

// Constructs the data packet by concatenating header, payload, and
↪   trailer
void constructPacket() {
  // --- Header Construction ---
  // Define the header with pre-determined fields:
```

```
    // [Start Identifier, Protocol Version, Packet Identifier, Payload
    ↪  Length, Sequence Number]
    byte header[HEADER_SIZE] = { 0xAA, 0x01, 0xBB, (byte)PAYLOAD_SIZE,
    ↪  0x01 };
    // Copy header into packet buffer
    memcpy(packet, header, HEADER_SIZE);

    // --- Payload Insertion ---
    // Copy payload data right after the header.
    memcpy(packet + HEADER_SIZE, payloadData, PAYLOAD_SIZE);

    // --- Trailer Addition ---
    // Compute checksum over header and payload for integrity
    ↪  verification.
    byte checksum = computechecksum(packet, HEADER_SIZE +
    ↪  PAYLOAD_SIZE, 256);
    // Append the checksum as the trailer.
    packet[HEADER_SIZE + PAYLOAD_SIZE] = checksum;
}

// Parses the incoming packet, verifies structure, and performs
↪  checksum validation.
bool parsePacket(const byte* packet, int packetSize) {
    // Validate packet length: must be at least header + trailer
    ↪  length.
    if (packetSize < HEADER_SIZE + TRAILER_SIZE) {
      Serial.println("Error: Packet too short.");
      return false;
    }

    // Extract payload length from header (we placed it in the 4th
    ↪  byte of the header).
    byte extractedPayloadLength = packet[3];
    // Confirm overall packet length matches L_P = L_H + L_D + L_T.
    if (HEADER_SIZE + extractedPayloadLength + TRAILER_SIZE !=
    ↪  packetSize) {
      Serial.println("Error: Payload length mismatch.");
      return false;
    }

    // Recalculate checksum over header and payload.
    byte computedChecksum = computechecksum(packet, HEADER_SIZE +
    ↪  extractedPayloadLength, 256);
    byte receivedChecksum = packet[HEADER_SIZE +
    ↪  extractedPayloadLength];

    // Validate checksum.
    if (computedChecksum != receivedChecksum) {
      Serial.println("Error: Checksum mismatch. Data corruption
      ↪  detected.");
      return false;
    }
```

319

```
// Output parsed components for verification.
Serial.print("Header: ");
for (int i = 0; i < HEADER_SIZE; i++) {
  Serial.print(packet[i], HEX);
  Serial.print(" ");
}
Serial.println();

Serial.print("Payload: ");
for (int i = 0; i < extractedPayloadLength; i++) {
  Serial.print((char)packet[HEADER_SIZE + i]);
}
Serial.println();

Serial.print("Checksum: ");
Serial.println(receivedChecksum, HEX);

return true;
}

void setup() {
  Serial.begin(115200);
  while (!Serial) { ; } // Wait for Serial to be ready

  Serial.println("Constructing Packet...");
  constructPacket();

  Serial.println("Constructed Packet (Hex):");
  for (int i = 0; i < PACKET_SIZE; i++) {
    Serial.print(packet[i], HEX);
    Serial.print(" ");
  }
  Serial.println();

  Serial.println("Parsing Packet...");
  if (parsePacket(packet, PACKET_SIZE)) {
    Serial.println("Packet parsed successfully!");
  } else {
    Serial.println("Packet parsing failed!");
  }
}

void loop() {
  // Main loop remains empty as packet construction and parsing are
  ↪   demonstrated in setup().
}
```

Chapter 51

Data Serialization Techniques

Conceptual Foundations

Data serialization is the systematic process of transforming complex data structures and objects into a linear sequence of bytes suitable for storage or network transmission. In formal terms, this process can be modeled as an encoding function

$$E : \mathcal{D} \to \mathbb{B}^*,$$

where $\mathcal{D}$ is the domain of structured data and $\mathbb{B}^*$ represents the set of all finite-length binary strings. This mapping facilitates the conversion of in-memory representations to a canonical form that maintains essential structural and type information. The serialized representation may include metadata that defines the boundaries and interpretation of individual data elements, thereby permitting reconstruction without loss of fidelity.

Representational Formalisms and Structured Encoding

Serialization techniques may employ either binary or textual representations, each with inherent trade-offs between compactness, ease of parsing, and human readability. Binary serialization formats tend to optimize for compactness and rapid processing, encapsulating information through fixed-length fields or variable-length encoding schemes. This can be formally captured by considering a serialized data object $s \in \mathbb{B}^*$ that adheres to a predetermined schema σ, such that the mapping

$$E_\sigma : \mathcal{D}_\sigma \to \mathbb{B}^*$$

is both injective and, ideally, bijective over the appropriate subdomain $\mathcal{D}_\sigma \subset \mathcal{D}$. In contrast, text-based serialization formats represent data using standardized character sets, and are typically self-describing to varying degrees, allowing for implicit type interpretation and schema evolution. The formalism underlying such representations must account for an additional layer of syntactic structure, often modeled as a transformation from $\mathcal{D}$ to a language defined by a context-free grammar.

Deserialization Processes and Data Integrity Assurance

The inverse operation, deserialization, is defined as the reconstruction of original data structures from their serialized forms. This process is represented by the decoding function

$$D : \mathbb{B}^* \to \mathcal{D},$$

subject to the condition that for every $d \in \mathcal{D}$ serialized by E, it holds that $D(E(d)) = d$. To ensure the fidelity of this round-trip transformation, the serialized data often incorporates additional integrity checks such as checksums or cryptographic hashes. If a checksum C is computed over the serialized content, then during deserialization, verification is achieved by comparing the computed checksum

$$C' = \text{checksum}(s')$$

of the received data s' with the expected value embedded within s'. Any discrepancy between C' and the embedded checksum triggers error-handling mechanisms that may include request retransmission or controlled degradation of service.

Efficiency Considerations in Network Communication

In the realm of network communications, the efficiency of serialization techniques is paramount. Given that serialized data represents the payload for transmission over potentially constrained networks, minimizing the length $L(s)$ of the serialized form $s \in \mathbb{B}^*$ is essential. This optimization is subject to the dual constraints of computational complexity and data integrity. Specifically, the objective is to minimize $L(s)$ while ensuring that both E and D operate with time complexities that are linear or near-linear in the size of the data structure. In mathematical terms, if $T_E(n)$ and $T_D(n)$ denote the time complexities of the encoding and decoding functions respectively for an input of size n, efficient serialization requires that

$$T_E(n), T_D(n) \in \mathcal{O}(n).$$

Furthermore, serialized representations designed for network communication must be resilient to transmission errors and sensitive to bandwidth limitations. Techniques such as data compression and adaptive field allocation are commonly employed to balance the competing demands of expressiveness, compactness, and resilience. The trade-off between verbosity and computational overhead in serialization ultimately defines the practical limits of efficient networked data exchange.

ESP32 For IoT With Arduino Code Snippet

```
// Comprehensive ESP32 IoT with Arduino Code Snippet
// This code demonstrates the process of serializing and
↪    deserializing sensor data,
// reflecting key equations and algorithms from this chapter.
//
// Key Concepts:
// 1. Encoding Function E: D -> B^*
//     - Converts sensor data (domain D) to a binary representation
↪    (B^*),
//       where the data packet comprises temperature, humidity, and a
↪    checksum.
// 2. Decoding Function D: B^* -> D
//     - Reconstructs original sensor data from the binary packet,
//       ensuring that for any d in D, D(E(d)) = d.
```

```
// 3. Checksum Calculation for Data Integrity:
//     - Checksum, C = sum(data_bytes) mod 256, is computed to verify
↪    the data.
// 4. Efficiency:
//     - Both serialization and deserialization operations run in
↪    O(n) time.
//
// Data Packet Layout:
// [Temperature (4 bytes)] [Humidity (4 bytes)] [Checksum (1 byte)]
// Total Packet Length = 9 bytes

#include <Arduino.h>
#include <string.h>

// Define a structure for sensor data
struct SensorData {
  float temperature;  // Temperature in degrees Celsius
  float humidity;     // Humidity in percentage
};

// Function to compute checksum over a given data buffer
uint8_t computeChecksum(const uint8_t* data, size_t len) {
  uint8_t checksum = 0;
  for (size_t i = 0; i < len; i++) {
    checksum += data[i]; // Sum modulo 256 occurs automatically with
    ↪    uint8_t arithmetic
  }
  return checksum;
}

// Serialization function implementing the encoding: E : D -> B^*
// This converts sensor data into a canonical binary format with an
↪    appended checksum.
void serializeData(const SensorData &sensor, uint8_t *buffer, size_t
↪    &length) {
  length = 0;
  // Copy the temperature value (4 bytes)
  memcpy(buffer + length, &sensor.temperature,
  ↪    sizeof(sensor.temperature));
  length += sizeof(sensor.temperature);
  // Copy the humidity value (4 bytes)
  memcpy(buffer + length, &sensor.humidity,
  ↪    sizeof(sensor.humidity));
  length += sizeof(sensor.humidity);
  // Compute checksum over the 8 bytes of sensor data
  uint8_t cs = computeChecksum(buffer, length);
  // Append checksum (1 byte) to the buffer
  buffer[length] = cs;
  length += 1;
}

// Deserialization function implementing the decoding: D : B^* -> D
```

324

```cpp
// It verifies the integrity of the received data via the checksum
//   before reconstructing the sensor data.
bool deserializeData(const uint8_t *buffer, size_t length,
↪  SensorData &sensor) {
  // Verify that the length matches the expected packet size
  if (length != sizeof(sensor.temperature) + sizeof(sensor.humidity)
↪  + 1) {
    return false;
  }
  // Extract the received checksum (last byte)
  uint8_t receivedChecksum = buffer[length - 1];
  // Compute the checksum over the data (excluding the checksum
↪  byte)
  uint8_t computedChecksum = computeChecksum(buffer, length - 1);

  // Verify integrity: if mismatched, return false to indicate error
  if (receivedChecksum != computedChecksum) {
    return false;
  }

  size_t index = 0;
  // Deserialize temperature (first 4 bytes)
  memcpy(&sensor.temperature, buffer + index,
↪  sizeof(sensor.temperature));
  index += sizeof(sensor.temperature);
  // Deserialize humidity (next 4 bytes)
  memcpy(&sensor.humidity, buffer + index, sizeof(sensor.humidity));
  return true;
}

void setup() {
  Serial.begin(115200);
  delay(1000); // Wait for Serial communication to initialize

  // Simulated sensor data reading
  SensorData reading;
  reading.temperature = 23.75;
  reading.humidity = 55.20;

  // Buffer for serialized data
  uint8_t serializedBuffer[20];
  size_t serializedLength = 0;

  // Serialize the sensor data into binary form
  serializeData(reading, serializedBuffer, serializedLength);

  Serial.println("Serialized Data Packet (in HEX):");
  // Print each byte of the serialized packet in HEX format
  for (size_t i = 0; i < serializedLength; i++) {
    if (serializedBuffer[i] < 16) {
      Serial.print("0");
    }
    Serial.print(serializedBuffer[i], HEX);
```

```
  Serial.print(" ");
}
Serial.println();

// Attempt to deserialize the binary packet
SensorData recoveredReading;
if (deserializeData(serializedBuffer, serializedLength,
↪  recoveredReading)) {
  Serial.println("Deserialization Successful:");
  Serial.print("Temperature: ");
  Serial.println(recoveredReading.temperature);
  Serial.print("Humidity: ");
  Serial.println(recoveredReading.humidity);
} else {
  Serial.println("Error: Checksum verification failed. Data is
↪  corrupt.");
}
}

void loop() {
// In a real-world IoT scenario, sensor data may be periodically
↪  collected,
// serialized, transmitted, and then deserialized on receipt.
// For demonstration purposes, no repeating operations are
↪  implemented here.
}
```

Chapter 52

Implementing Cloud Data Integration

Cloud Service Integration Paradigms

Cloud data integration for the ESP32 encompasses a range of methodological approaches that establish a seamless connection between embedded sensor networks and remote cloud infrastructures. The process can be conceptualized as a transformation of locally acquired data from an application domain, denoted as $\mathcal{D}$, into a structured repository within a cloud-based storage space, symbolized by $\mathcal{S}$. This transformation supports both unidirectional and bidirectional exchanges, wherein the intrinsic data is encapsulated by an encoding mechanism prior to transmission. The paradigms adopted in this integration process involve variations of synchronous and asynchronous messaging frameworks, each designed to contend with factors such as inherent latency, network variability, and the power constraints of the ESP32 environment. A core aspect of these paradigms is the requirement to serialize native data structures into standardized formats that are accepted by remote service endpoints, thereby ensuring reliability and consistency in the subsequent data retrieval and manipulation cycles.

Architectural Considerations for Cloud Communication

The architecture underpinning cloud communication necessitates a detailed consideration of multilayered system interactions and the dynamics of data flow. A robust architectural framework decouples sensor data acquisition from the complex interplay of network protocols and remote application services. The overall data transmission can be mathematically abstracted by a composite function

$$C(d) = A(T(E(d))),$$

where $d \in \mathcal{D}$ represents the sensor data, E is the encoding function that transforms the data into a transmittable format, T encapsulates the operational dynamics of the network transmission layer, and A characterizes the application layer processing conducted by the cloud service. Such an abstraction underscores the necessity for each component to be meticulously engineered, ensuring that issues pertaining to transmission delays, error correction, and resource management are rigorously addressed. The modular separation of responsibilities facilitates not only scalability but also the adaptability of the overall system architecture to evolving network conditions and service specifications.

Interfacing with Cloud APIs for Remote Data Storage and Interaction

The integration of ESP32 applications with cloud platforms is principally facilitated through well-defined application programming interfaces (APIs). These APIs, which typically adhere to standardized protocols such as HTTPS or MQTT, establish a formal interaction model for remote data storage and command exchange. The transmitted payloads, often serialized into formats such as JSON or XML, must conform to predefined schemas that allow the cloud service to accurately parse and persist the incoming information. In this context, the formulation of a request can be represented by the function

$$R = f(E(d), \theta),$$

where $E(d)$ denotes the encoded representation of the sensor data and θ comprises session-specific parameters including authentication tokens and contextual metadata. The remote service processes such requests to update the state of the cloud repository, enabling functionalities that range from data visualization to complex analytical processing. This interfacing methodology ensures that data stored in the cloud remains accessible for real-time interaction and long-term aggregation, thereby bridging the divide between localized sensor networks and distributed computational resources.

Data Security and Integrity in Cloud Transactions

The secure transmission and storage of data in cloud-based systems demand the integration of stringent cryptographic protocols and error detection mechanisms. The design of a secure cloud data integration framework involves the implementation of encryption layers—typically utilizing protocols such as TLS/SSL—to establish a protected channel for data exchange. Additionally, the integrity of the transmitted information is fortified by the incorporation of error-checking algorithms. For instance, a hash function $H(E(d))$ may be computed over the encoded data packet and appended as a digital signature to the payload. Upon arrival at the cloud endpoint, the received hash is compared against a locally computed value to verify data integrity. This dual approach of encryption and integrity verification provides a robust safeguard against unauthorized access and transmission errors, ensuring that the cloud repository accurately reflects the true state of the sensor network.

Performance Optimization in Cloud Data Integration

Optimizing performance in cloud data integration involves a delicate balance between computational efficiency and communication overhead. The operational latency associated with wireless data transmission, when coupled with the processing demands of the ESP32, necessitates the adoption of non-blocking and asynchronous programming models. Strategies such as minimizing the message size through data compression and employing efficient scheduling algorithms for transmission introduce significant performance gains. In formal terms, the encoding and transmission process is designed such that for a data structure of size n, the time complexity $T(E(d))$ conforms to

$$T(E(d)) \in \mathcal{O}(n).$$

This constraint ensures that as the system scales, the cloud integration process remains computationally feasible and resilient. The design also contemplates adaptive mechanisms that adjust transmission parameters based on real-time network performance metrics, thereby maintaining a consistent and high-throughput channel between the ESP32 and the cloud service.

ESP32 For IoT With Arduino Code Snippet

```
#include <WiFi.h>
#include <HTTPClient.h>

// WiFi credentials
const char* ssid     = "your_SSID";
const char* password = "your_PASSWORD";

// Cloud server endpoint and session token ()
const char* serverName = "https://api.example.com/data";
const char* authToken  = "TOKEN12345";

// Data transmission interval (in milliseconds)
const unsigned long interval = 10000; // 10 seconds
unsigned long previousMillis = 0;

//
↪  ----------------------------------------------------------------
// getSensorData()
// Simulates obtaining raw sensor data (d ).
// In a real scenario, replace this with actual sensor readings.
float getSensorData() {
  // Simulate sensor data as a float between 20.0 and 30.0
  float sensorValue = 20.0 + (random(0, 1000) / 1000.0) * 10.0;
  return sensorValue;
}

//
↪  ----------------------------------------------------------------
// encodeData()
// Implements the encoding function E(d) which serializes sensor
↪  input.
// Here, we convert the sensor value into a JSON formatted string.
String encodeData(float d) {
```

```
  String json = "{\"sensor_value\":";
  json += String(d, 2); // Format with two decimal places
  json += "}";
  return json;
}

//
↳  --------------------------------------------------------------------------
// hashData()
// Computes a simple checksum serving as H(E(d)) over the encoded
↳  string.
// This checksum aids in verifying data integrity.
uint8_t hashData(const String &data) {
  uint8_t sum = 0;
  for (int i = 0; i < data.length(); i++) {
    sum += data.charAt(i);
  }
  return sum; // Basic checksum mod 256
}

//
↳  --------------------------------------------------------------------------
// createRequest()
// Constructs the complete request payload R = f(E(d), )
// combining encoded data, authentication token, and checksum.
String createRequest(String encodedData, String token, uint8_t
↳  checksum) {
  String request = "{";
  request += "\"data\":" + encodedData + ", ";
  request += "\"token\":\"" + token + "\", ";
  request += "\"checksum\":" + String(checksum);
  request += "}";
  return request;
}

//
↳  --------------------------------------------------------------------------
// sendToCloud()
// Sends the prepared payload to a remote cloud service using HTTP
↳  POST.
// This function encapsulates T(E(d)) as the transmission and
// A(·) as the application layer handling in the abstraction:
//     C(d) = A( T( E(d) ) ).
void sendToCloud(String payload) {
  if (WiFi.status() == WL_CONNECTED) {
    HTTPClient http;
    http.begin(serverName);
    http.addHeader("Content-Type", "application/json");

    // Transmit payload via HTTP POST
    int httpResponseCode = http.POST(payload);
    if (httpResponseCode > 0) {
      String response = http.getString();
```

331

```
    Serial.println("HTTP Response Code: " +
    ↪   String(httpResponseCode));
    Serial.println("Cloud Response: " + response);
  } else {
    Serial.println("HTTP Request Failed. Error code: " +
    ↪   String(httpResponseCode));
  }
  http.end();
} else {
    Serial.println("WiFi Disconnected. Unable to send data.");
  }
}

void setup() {
  Serial.begin(115200);
  delay(1000);

  // Seed random number generator (optional but useful for
  ↪   simulation)
  randomSeed(analogRead(34));

  // Connect to WiFi network
  Serial.print("Connecting to WiFi");
  WiFi.begin(ssid, password);
  while (WiFi.status() != WL_CONNECTED) {
    delay(500);
    Serial.print(".");
  }
  Serial.println("\nWiFi Connected.");
}

void loop() {
  unsigned long currentMillis = millis();

  // Non-blocking method to send data at regular intervals
  if (currentMillis - previousMillis >= interval) {
    previousMillis = currentMillis;

    // Step 1: Acquire raw sensor data (d  )
    float sensorValue = getSensorData();

    // Step 2: Encode the sensor data E(d)
    String encodedData = encodeData(sensorValue);

    // Step 3: Generate a hash H(E(d)) for data integrity
    uint8_t checksum = hashData(encodedData);

    // Step 4: Construct the request payload R = f(E(d), )
    String payload = createRequest(encodedData, authToken,
    ↪   checksum);

    // Debug outputs to Serial Monitor
    Serial.println("Sensor Value    : " + String(sensorValue, 2));
```

```
    Serial.println("Encoded Data    : " + encodedData);
    Serial.println("Checksum        : " + String(checksum));
    Serial.println("Request Payload : " + payload);

    // Step 5: Send the data to the cloud.
    sendToCloud(payload);
  }
}
```

Chapter 53

Utilizing Encryption for Secure Data Transmission

Fundamental Concepts in Cryptographic Security

Encryption provides the mathematical mechanism by which plain data, denoted by P, is transformed into an unintelligible format, represented by the ciphertext C. This transformation is achieved through an encryption function E, operating with a key K, such that

$$C = E_K(P).$$

The inverse operation, decryption, is defined by a corresponding function D, which recovers the original plaintext via

$$P = D_K(C).$$

In secure communications among Internet of Things (IoT) devices, the rigorous application of these fundamental concepts is essential. Cryptographic security ensures both confidentiality and authentication, and its theoretical underpinnings lie in well-established hardness assumptions and probabilistic models that guarantee the infeasibility of unauthorized decryption.

Symmetric Encryption Techniques

Symmetric encryption involves the use of a single, shared key K for both the encryption and decryption processes. The mathematical model for such a scheme is succinctly expressed as

$$C = E_K(P) \quad \text{and} \quad P = D_K(C).$$

Algorithms in this category, which include block ciphers and stream ciphers, are particularly well-suited for environments where computational resources are constrained. In block cipher modes, plaintext is divided into fixed-size blocks that are systematically transformed, whereas stream ciphers operate on data as a continuous flow. The design of symmetric encryption algorithms emphasizes both operational efficiency and high levels of security, with the Advanced Encryption Standard (AES) being a paradigmatic example in numerous IoT applications.

Asymmetric Encryption Techniques

Asymmetric encryption employs a pair of mathematically linked keys: a public key K_{pub} and a private key K_{priv}. The encryption process using a public key is defined as

$$C = E_{K_{\text{pub}}}(P),$$

with decryption performed using the corresponding private key, following

$$P = D_{K_{\text{priv}}}(C).$$

This dual-key structure enables secure key distribution and facilitates tasks such as digital signatures and identity verification. Asymmetric methods are integral to establishing a secure channel for key exchange in IoT deployments, particularly during the initiation of secure sessions where the provisioning of a symmetric key is required for ongoing high-speed communication.

Hybrid Cryptographic Systems and Key Exchange Protocols

Hybrid encryption schemes combine the strengths of both symmetric and asymmetric methodologies. In this approach, an asymmetric encryption process is initially employed to securely exchange a session key K_s. The session key is then used in a symmetric encryption algorithm for the remainder of the communication session. This methodology can be formalized as a two-phase process: first, the secure establishment of K_s via a key exchange protocol and, second, the efficient encryption of data according to

$$C = E_{K_s}(P).$$

Such a design leverages the computational efficiency of symmetric schemes while preserving the robust security properties inherent in asymmetric protocols.

Mathematical Foundations and Algorithmic Complexity

The security of encryption systems is fundamentally underpinned by advanced mathematical constructs from number theory and algebra. For instance, the RSA algorithm is based on the challenge of factoring large composite numbers, typically represented as

$$N = p \cdot q,$$

where p and q are large, randomly chosen prime numbers. In contrast, elliptic curve cryptography (ECC) utilizes the algebraic structure of elliptic curves over finite fields to achieve robust security with comparatively smaller key sizes. The computational complexity of these algorithms is analyzed through time complexity classes such as $O(n)$ and $O(n^2)$, where n reflects the bit-length of the keys involved. The integration of efficient encryption algorithms with provable security guarantees remains a central concern, particularly when evaluating their resilience against contemporary attack vectors.

Resource Constraints and Adaptation in IoT Environments

IoT devices commonly operate under stringent resource limitations, including constrained computational power and limited energy reserves. In such scenarios, encryption algorithms must be carefully tailored to maintain security without imposing excessive processing overhead. Lightweight cryptographic algorithms are designed to fulfill these requirements, ensuring that the encryption function $E(K, P)$ can be executed with minimal resource consumption while still providing the necessary level of security. The adaptability of these algorithms is characterized by their ability to perform streamlined arithmetic and logical operations, thereby achieving a balance between computational efficiency and cryptographic strength.

Threat Models and Cryptographic Resilience

The design of secure data transmission protocols necessitates a thorough understanding of potential threat models, which may include man-in-the-middle attacks, replay attacks, and side-channel attacks. Cryptographic resilience is enhanced by incorporating mechanisms such as message authentication codes (MAC) and hash functions, denoted by a function H, to verify data integrity. These mechanisms are integrated into the encryption process such that the transmitted payload is accompanied by an integrity check, complementing the primary encryption procedure. The synthesis of encryption with additional layers of verification forms a comprehensive security framework that is essential for safeguarding data integrity during transmission across diverse IoT networks.

ESP32 For IoT With Arduino Code Snippet

```
#include <Arduino.h>
#include <AESLib.h>
#include "mbedtls/sha256.h"

// -----------------------------------------------------------
// This example demonstrates key cryptographic principles discussed
↪  in the chapter:
//    - Symmetric Encryption: C = E_K(P) and P = D_K(C)
//    - Hybrid Cryptographic Systems: simulation of session key
↪  (K_s) generation
//    - Integrity Verification: computing SHA256 hash (H)
// The AES encryption/decryption here uses a 128-bit key in CBC mode
↪  with an IV.
// -----------------------------------------------------------

// Define buffer size for ciphertext and decrypted text
#define BUFFER_SIZE 128
```

```
// Create an instance of the AES library
AESLib aesLib;

// Global variables for symmetric encryption
byte sessionKey[16];  // 128-bit session key (K_s)
byte aesIV[16] = {    // Initialization Vector for AES (CBC mode)
  0xA0, 0xA1, 0xA2, 0xA3,
  0xA4, 0xA5, 0xA6, 0xA7,
  0xA8, 0xA9, 0xAA, 0xAB,
  0xAC, 0xAD, 0xAE, 0xAF
};

// Function to simulate the secure exchange and generation of a
↪   session key.
// In a real hybrid system, an asymmetric algorithm would securely
↪   transmit K_s.
void generateSessionKey() {
  for (int i = 0; i < 16; i++) {
    sessionKey[i] = random(0, 256);  // Generate a random byte for
    ↪   each key position.
  }
}

// Helper function: Print a byte array in hexadecimal format.
void printBytes(const char *label, const byte *data, int len) {
  Serial.print(label);
  for (int i = 0; i < len; i++) {
    if (data[i] < 16) Serial.print("0");
    Serial.print(data[i], HEX);
    Serial.print(" ");
  }
  Serial.println();
}

// Helper function: Compute SHA256 hash of input data.
// This demonstrates the use of a cryptographic hash for data
↪   integrity checks.
void computeSHA256(const char *data, byte *hashOutput) {
  mbedtls_sha256_context ctx;
  mbedtls_sha256_init(&ctx);
  mbedtls_sha256_starts_ret(&ctx, 0);  // 0 selects SHA-256 (as
  ↪   opposed to SHA-224).
  mbedtls_sha256_update_ret(&ctx, (const unsigned char *)data,
  ↪   strlen(data));
  mbedtls_sha256_finish_ret(&ctx, hashOutput);
  mbedtls_sha256_free(&ctx);
}

void setup() {
  Serial.begin(115200);
  while (!Serial) { ; } // Wait for Serial port to be ready.

  Serial.println("ESP32 IoT With Arduino: Encryption Demo");
```

338

```
// Seed the random number generator using an unconnected analog
↪ pin.
randomSeed(analogRead(34));

// ---- Hybrid Cryptographic Step: Session Key Generation ----
generateSessionKey();
printBytes("Session Key (K_s): ", sessionKey, 16);

// ---- Plaintext Message (P) ----
const char *plaintext = "Hello, ESP32 IoT Secure World!";
Serial.print("Plaintext (P): ");
Serial.println(plaintext);

// ---- Integrity Verification ----
// Compute SHA256 hash of the plaintext. This hash can be used as
↪ a MAC.
byte hash[32];
computeSHA256(plaintext, hash);
printBytes("SHA256 Hash (H): ", hash, 32);

// ---- Symmetric Encryption: C = E_K(P) ----
// Prepare buffers to hold the ciphertext and the recovered
↪ plaintext.
byte cipherBuffer[BUFFER_SIZE];
byte decryptedBuffer[BUFFER_SIZE];

// Encrypt the plaintext using AES with the session key and IV.
// This represents the encryption operation: C = E_{K_s}(P).
int cipherLength = aesLib.encrypt((byte*)plaintext,
↪ strlen(plaintext),
                                  cipherBuffer, sessionKey,
                                  ↪ aesIV);
Serial.print("Ciphertext (C): ");
// Print each byte of the ciphertext in hexadecimal.
for (int i = 0; i < cipherLength; i++) {
  if (cipherBuffer[i] < 16) Serial.print("0");
  Serial.print(cipherBuffer[i], HEX);
  Serial.print(" ");
}
Serial.println();

// ---- Symmetric Decryption: P = D_K(C) ----
// Decrypt the ciphertext using the same session key and IV.
int decryptedLength = aesLib.decrypt(cipherBuffer, cipherLength,
                                     decryptedBuffer, sessionKey,
                                     ↪ aesIV);
decryptedBuffer[decryptedLength] = '\0'; // Null-terminate the
↪ decrypted string.
Serial.print("Decrypted Text: ");
Serial.println((char*)decryptedBuffer);

// The above code exemplifies:
```

```
//   1. Generation of a session key (hybrid encryption
↪    initiation).
//   2. AES encryption and decryption operations corresponding to:
//        C = E_{K}(P) and P = D_{K}(C)
//   3. Computation of a SHA256 hash for verifying data integrity.
}

void loop() {
  // No repeated operations necessary.
}
```

Chapter 54

Generating Pseudo-Random Numbers

Mathematical Foundations and Statistical Properties

Pseudo-random number generators (PRNGs) are deterministic algorithms designed to produce sequences of numbers that mimic the properties of true randomness. Such sequences typically form a recurrence defined by a function

$$X_{n+1} = f(X_n),$$

where X_0, the seed, is an initial value chosen from a finite set. The statistical properties of nominal randomness are quantified in terms of uniformity, independence, and lack of correlation. Criteria such as equidistribution over the unit interval and the absence of discernible patterns are essential for validating the efficacy of a PRNG. The period of a PRNG, defined as the integer T such that

$$X_{n+T} = X_n,$$

for all n, is of critical importance for applications that demand a high degree of variability over long sequences of numbers.

Deterministic Algorithms for Pseudo-Random Number Generation

A wide class of deterministic algorithms has been developed to generate pseudo-random numbers. One of the classical forms is the linear congruential generator (LCG), mathematically expressed as

$$X_{n+1} = (aX_n + c) \mod m,$$

where constants a, c, and m are selected to achieve a maximum period and to minimize statistical defects. The multiplicative congruential generator, a variant with $c = 0$, and more advanced techniques such as the Mersenne Twister are designed to meet different constraints of computational environments and target applications. The algorithmic structure of these generators ensures that, provided the parameters are optimally chosen, the resulting sequence exhibits properties approaching those of an ideal random sequence, albeit within the bounds of determinism.

Seed Initialization and Entropy Sources in Arduino Environments

The quality and unpredictability of pseudo-random sequences are highly sensitive to the method of seed initialization. In embedded systems, such as those driven by Arduino, the seed value X_0 is often derived from physical processes that exhibit stochastic behavior, such as analog noise or thermal fluctuations. These entropy sources, while not entirely unpredictable in an absolute sense, provide sufficient variability for many simulation and non-critical security applications. The challenge in resource-constrained environments lies in harnessing a source of entropy that is both minimally invasive in terms of computational overhead and sufficiently robust to mitigate the deterministic nature inherent in the algorithmic design of the PRNG.

Applications in Simulation, Security, and Variability

Pseudo-random numbers are employed across a broad spectrum of applications in computing. In simulation and modeling, these numbers serve as the backbone for Monte Carlo methods and other probabilistic computations, enabling the emulation of stochastic processes with high fidelity. In the domain of security, the generation of pseudo-random sequences is integral to key generation, nonce production, and cryptographic protocol design, although the deterministic limitations of some PRNGs necessitate the incorporation of additional measures to guard against predictive attacks. Furthermore, the inherent variability introduced by pseudo-random sequences contributes to algorithmic diversity in applications such as game development and procedural content generation. The careful selection of PRNG algorithms and their parameters is hence imperative to ensure that the generated sequences meet the specific demands of simulation fidelity, cryptographic strength, or application-specific randomness without incurring undue computational burden.

ESP32 For IoT With Arduino Code Snippet

```
#include <Arduino.h>

/*
  Pseudo-Random Number Generation using a Linear Congruential
  ↪  Generator (LCG)

  This implementation demonstrates key equations and algorithms
  ↪  discussed in the chapter.
  The core recurrence is defined as:
      X[n+1] = (a * X[n] + c) mod m
  where:
      - a is the multiplier (here: 1664525)
      - c is the increment     (here: 1013904223)
      - m is the modulus, implicitly 2~32 due to 32-bit unsigned
      ↪  arithmetic.

  In this code, an initial seed is acquired using analog noise from
  ↪  an unconnected analog pin (pin 36)
  combined with the microsecond timer to increase entropy. The
  ↪  resulting pseudo-random numbers are then
  normalized to the range [0, 1) by dividing by 2~32.
*/

// Constants for LCG parameters
const uint32_t LCG_A = 1664525;      // Multiplier coefficient
const uint32_t LCG_C = 1013904223;   // Increment coefficient
```

343

```cpp
// The modulus m is taken as 2^32. Using 32-bit unsigned integers,
//   overflow automatically applies modulo 2^32.

// Global variable to hold the current state of the generator (seed)
uint32_t rng_state = 0;

/*
  Function: nextLCG
  Purpose: Generate the next pseudo-random number using the LCG
  ↪   algorithm.
  Implements the recurrence:
      X[n+1] = (LCG_A * X[n] + LCG_C) mod 2^32
*/
uint32_t nextLCG() {
  rng_state = LCG_A * rng_state + LCG_C; // 32-bit overflow acts as
  ↪   modulus 2^32
  return rng_state;
}

void setup() {
  Serial.begin(115200);
  // Wait until the Serial Monitor is ready (useful for native USB
  ↪   devices)
  while (!Serial) { ; }

  // Seed Initialization:
  // Read an analog value from pin 36 to capture ambient noise.
  // Combine it with the current microsecond timer value via XOR to
  ↪   enhance entropy.
  int analogValue = analogRead(36);
  unsigned long seed = analogValue ^ micros();
  rng_state = seed;  // Set the initial seed for our LCG

  Serial.println("ESP32 Pseudo-Random Number Generation using LCG");
  Serial.print("Initial Seed: ");
  Serial.println(seed);

  // Optionally, also seed the Arduino built-in PRNG for other uses:
  randomSeed(seed);
}

void loop() {
  // Generate a pseudo-random number using our LCG function.
  uint32_t randNum = nextLCG();

  // Normalize the random number to obtain a floating-point value in
  ↪   [0, 1)
  // Normalization formula: normalized = randNum / 2^32
  float normalized = randNum / 4294967296.0;

  // Output the raw and normalized pseudo-random numbers over
  ↪   Serial.
  Serial.print("Random Number: ");
```

344

```
Serial.print(randNum);
Serial.print(" | Normalized: ");
Serial.println(normalized, 8); // Print with 8-digit precision

// A brief delay to throttle serial output for visualization
↪  purposes.
delay(500);
}
```

Chapter 55

Implementing Hash Functions and Checksums

Conceptual Foundations

Hash functions and checksums serve as fundamental mechanisms for ensuring data integrity during transmission and storage. A hash function can be formally defined as a mapping $H : \mathcal{M} \to \mathcal{D}$, where $\mathcal{M}$ represents the set of input messages of arbitrary length and $\mathcal{D}$ denotes the fixed-size output domain, commonly referred to as the digest. In contrast, a checksum typically represents a specialized form of hash function designed to summarize data using simple arithmetic operations, such as additive or modular reductions. Both constructs aim to capture essential characteristics of the original data and to provide mechanisms by which accidental modifications can be detected.

Mathematical Framework and Formal Properties

The theoretical basis for hash functions rests on principles from number theory and abstract algebra, wherein the mapping from an input space to a fixed-size output is analyzed in terms of collision resistance, uniformity, and the avalanche effect. In designing a simple hash function, one often employs modular arithmetic and linear operations; for instance, the mapping may be described in the form

$$H(x) = (\alpha x + \beta) \bmod \gamma,$$

where α, β, and γ are constants carefully selected to optimize the spread of output values and to minimize the rate of collisions. The properties of uniformity ensure that each possible digest value is equally likely under a random input, whereas the avalanche effect mandates that a small change in the input, such as a single bit inversion, produces a substantial alteration in the output. In the context of checksums, the formalism is often simplified. A checksum can be expressed as

$$C = \left(\sum_{i=1}^{n} m_i \right) \bmod k,$$

where $\{m_i\}_{i=1}^{n}$ represents the sequence of message components and k is a chosen modulus. The mathematical rigor behind these formulations underpins their efficacy in detecting errors introduced during transmission or storage.

Design Considerations for Simple Hash Functions

When implementing simple hash functions in resource-constrained environments, the balance between computational efficiency and error detection capability dominates the design criteria. The selection of parameters such as the multiplier α and the modulus γ is crucial, as inappropriate choices may lead to a clustering of output values or an increased probability of collisions. The design process involves a careful analysis of the input distribution and the intended application; for instance, if the objective is to detect small perturbations in data, the hash function must exhibit a high sensitivity to input modifications. Structural simplicity is often a guiding principle, leading to the adoption of linear or near-linear algorithms that are computationally lightweight while still delivering sufficient pseudo-random behavior. The concept of diffusion, ensuring that variations are propagated across the entire hash output, is equally important and is achieved through a combination of multiplicative factors and modular reductions.

Checksum Construction and Error Detection Mechanisms

Checksums are typically constructed using elementary arithmetic operations that provide rapid computation and minimal resource usage. The conceptual model for a checksum involves summing the individual data elements and applying a modulus operation to prevent overflow, thereby encapsulating the additive properties of the input. In many instances, a checksum is calculated as

$$C = \left(\sum_{i=1}^{n} m_i \right) \bmod k,$$

and the resultant value C is compared against a precomputed reference to ascertain the integrity of the data. The robustness of a checksum is often evaluated by its capacity to detect common error types, such as single-bit errors, transpositions, and burst errors. Although checksum algorithms are generally simpler than cryptographic hash functions, their comparative computational efficiency renders them a practical choice in systems where low latency and minimal power consumption are paramount. The emphasis here lies in guaranteeing that even a minor corruption of data is reflected in a mismatch between the computed and expected checksum values, thereby serving as an effective early warning for data integrity violations.

Computational Efficiency and Trade-Off Analysis

The implementation of hash functions and checksums entails a delicate trade-off between the complexity of the algorithm and its error detection performance. Lightweight algorithms predicated on modular arithmetic and linear operations are favored when computational resources are limited. An analysis of the computational efficiency often involves an examination of the number of arithmetic operations required per data unit processed and an assessment of the algorithm's susceptibility to collision events. The trade-off analysis also extends to considerations of memory footprint, scalability, and the degree of randomness achieved. In applications where only rudimentary error detection is sufficient, the simplicity of additive or modular-based checksum techniques may be preferred. Conversely, scenarios demanding a more rigorous assurance of data integrity necessitate the adoption of hash functions with higher levels of diffusion and collision resistance. The interplay between algorithmic simplicity and robust performance remains a critical area of investigation, guiding the selection and optimization of hash-based error checking mechanisms in modern data communication and storage systems.

ESP32 For IoT With Arduino Code Snippet

```
#include <Arduino.h>

// Constants for the simple hash function: H(x) = (ALPHA * x + BETA)
↪  mod GAMMA
const unsigned long ALPHA = 31;    // Multiplier for hash function
const unsigned long BETA  = 17;    // Additive constant for hash
↪  function
const unsigned long GAMMA = 101;   // Modulus (preferably a prime
↪  number to improve distribution)

// Constant for checksum computation: C = (sum of message bytes) mod
↪  CHECKSUM_MODULUS
const unsigned long CHECKSUM_MODULUS = 256;

// Function to compute a simple hash for a single numeric input
↪  using the equation:
// H(x) = (ALPHA * x + BETA) mod GAMMA
unsigned long computeHash(unsigned long x) {
  return (ALPHA * x + BETA) % GAMMA;
}

// Function to compute a hash for an array of data bytes.
// This function iterates over each byte in the input and applies
↪  the hash function iteratively.
// It demonstrates the concept of diffusion where each byte
↪  influences the final hash.
unsigned long computeHashForData(const uint8_t *data, size_t length)
↪  {
  unsigned long hash = 0;
  for (size_t i = 0; i < length; i++) {
    // Update hash based on current hash and the data byte, then
    ↪  apply modular reduction.
    hash = (ALPHA * (hash + data[i]) + BETA) % GAMMA;
  }
  return hash;
}
```

```
// Function to compute a checksum for an array of data bytes using
↪   the equation:
// C = (sum of message bytes) mod CHECKSUM_MODULUS
uint8_t computeChecksum(const uint8_t *data, size_t length) {
  unsigned long sum = 0;
  for (size_t i = 0; i < length; i++) {
    sum += data[i];
  }
  return sum % CHECKSUM_MODULUS;
}

void setup() {
  // Initialize serial communication for debugging output.
  Serial.begin(115200);
  while (!Serial) {
    ; // Wait for serial port to connect (useful for native USB port
    ↪   boards)
  }

  Serial.println("ESP32 IoT With Arduino - Hash Function and
  ↪   Checksum Demonstration");

  // Example message to demonstrate the hash and checksum functions.
  const char *message = "Hello ESP32 IoT";
  size_t msgLength = strlen(message);

  // Demonstrate computing a simple hash for a single numerical
  ↪   input (e.g., the message length).
  unsigned long simpleHash = computeHash(msgLength);
  Serial.print("Simple Hash (for message length ");
  Serial.print(msgLength);
  Serial.print("): ");
  Serial.println(simpleHash);

  // Compute hash for the entire message using the iterative hash
  ↪   function for data arrays.
  unsigned long dataHash = computeHashForData((const uint8_t
  ↪   *)message, msgLength);
  Serial.print("Data Hash (for message \"");
  Serial.print(message);
  Serial.print("\"): ");
  Serial.println(dataHash);

  // Compute checksum for the message.
  uint8_t checksum = computeChecksum((const uint8_t *)message,
  ↪   msgLength);
  Serial.print("Checksum (for message \"");
  Serial.print(message);
  Serial.print("\"): ");
  Serial.println(checksum);
```

```
// Display the important equations and formulas used in this
↪  demonstration.
Serial.println("\nFormulas:");
Serial.println("Hash Function: H(x) = (ALPHA * x + BETA) mod
↪  GAMMA");
Serial.println("Checksum:       C = (sum of message bytes) mod
↪  CHECKSUM_MODULUS");
}

void loop() {
// In this demonstration, all processing is done in the setup.
// In a real application, one might update the hash and checksum
↪  periodically.
}
```

Chapter 56

Real-Time Data Acquisition Strategies

Fundamental Principles of Continuous Data Sampling

Continuous data acquisition is predicated on the formal principles of temporal sampling and signal reconstruction. In real-time systems, the data collection process must adhere to the Nyquist criterion, which mandates that the sampling frequency f_s satisfies the inequality

$$f_s \geq 2f_{\max},$$

where $f_{\max}$ represents the highest frequency component within the input signal. This inequality guarantees that the original signal can be reconstructed with minimal aliasing. In addition, the mathematical treatment of continuous signals involves considerations of quantization error, stochastic noise profiles, and the probabilistic distribution of transient events. The system dynamics are often captured by a time-discrete representation, where time is partitioned into successive intervals of duration T_s, with $T_s = 1/f_s$. The fidelity of the acquired data depends critically on both the temporal resolution and the inherent noise characteristics of the sensors involved.

Hardware Considerations in the ESP32 Ecosystem

The ESP32 microcontroller offers a robust platform for real-time data acquisition through its integrated analog-to-digital converters (ADCs), versatile peripheral interfaces, and dual-core architecture. The ADC modules provide high-speed conversion of analog signals into corresponding digital values, a process that involves the capture of voltage levels at discrete time intervals. This conversion is subject to nonidealities, such as differential nonlinearity and thermal noise, which necessitate the application of calibration techniques and digital filtering algorithms in subsequent processing stages. Furthermore, the ESP32's hardware timers and interrupt controllers support precise scheduling, enabling the implementation of periodic sampling with minimal temporal jitter. The orchestration of these hardware components plays a central role in maintaining data integrity in applications where temporal precision is paramount.

Buffering Strategies and Data Stream Management

Efficient buffering is essential to reconcile the inherent disparities between the rate of data acquisition and the processing or transmission capabilities within the system. A typical strategy involves the implementation of circular buffers or first-in-first-out (FIFO) queues, which temporarily store data samples prior to further processing. Let B denote the buffer capacity and f_s the sampling rate; then the approximate data retention period D can be expressed as

$$D = \frac{B}{f_s}.$$

The design of these buffers must account for possible overflows, underflows, and synchronization issues between the acquisition and processing subsystems. Moreover, the architecture may incorporate direct memory access (DMA) channels, which enable data transfer between peripheral registers and main memory without burdening central processing unit (CPU) cycles. The selection of appropriate buffer sizes and data management policies is fundamental to ensuring that transient spikes in data acquisition do not result in the irreversible loss of critical measurement information.

Temporal Synchronization and Timing Analysis

The maintenance of strict temporal synchronization is a cornerstone of real-time data acquisition systems. The ESP32 platform leverages hardware timers and interrupt-driven scheduling to provide a deterministic sampling process. Each sampling event is triggered in accordance with a nominal sampling period T_s, while actual timing performance is influenced by latency and interrupt handling overhead. The effective sampling interval can be modeled as

$$T_{\text{effective}} = T_s + \Delta T,$$

where ΔT represents the cumulative timing error or jitter introduced by system latency. Analytical methods, often based on statistical evaluations of ΔT, are applied in order to quantify the precision of the sampling process. The use of synchronized clocks and prioritized interrupt servicing mitigates the impact of timing irregularities, thereby ensuring that the temporal structure of the acquired data remains consistent with the underlying physical phenomena.

Data Integrity and Continuity in Dynamic Environments

Ensuring data integrity in continuously varying and potentially noisy environments necessitates the implementation of robust acquisition strategies. The detection of transient anomalies, the reduction of background noise, and the mitigation of error propagation are addressed through a combination of real-time signal conditioning and digital filtering techniques. Mathematical models, such as moving average filters and exponential smoothing algorithms, are employed to extract relevant signal characteristics while suppressing random fluctuations. Additionally, the continuous monitoring of sensor outputs involves dynamic thresholding mechanisms, where established baseline statistics are used to detect deviations in the acquired data stream. This intrinsic assessment of data continuity is critical in environments where the signal-to-noise ratio may vary dynamically, thereby ensuring that the overall system responsiveness remains uncompromised by transient disturbances.

ESP32 For IoT With Arduino Code Snippet

```
#include <Arduino.h>

/*
  This code implements real-time data acquisition on the ESP32.
  It demonstrates the following key principles and formulas from the
  ↪  chapter:

  1. Nyquist Criterion:
       Sampling frequency (fs) must satisfy: fs >= 2 * f_max.
       (Here, we set fs to a constant value, ensuring our chosen f_max
       ↪  is met.)

  2. Sampling Interval:
       T_s = 1 / fs.
       (Calculated as samplingIntervalMicros in microseconds.)

  3. Buffer Retention Time:
       D = B / fs,
       where B is the buffer size.

  4. Effective Sampling Interval:
       T_effective = T_s + T,
       where T is the average jitter due to timing imperfections.

  5. Data Filtering:
       A simple moving average filter is applied to the circular
       ↪  buffer.

  Additionally, the code uses a hardware timer interrupt to perform
  ↪  periodic ADC sampling,
  emulating real-time acquisition with precise hardware support.
*/

// ADC input pin for ESP32 (use an appropriate ADC-capable pin)
const int ADC_PIN = 34;

// Sampling parameters
const int samplingRateHz = 1000; // Sampling rate in Hz (1 kHz)
const unsigned long samplingIntervalMicros = 1000000 /
↪  samplingRateHz;  // T_s = 1/fs (in microseconds)
```

```
// Circular buffer for ADC samples
const int bufferSize = 100;  // Buffer capacity (B)
volatile int sampleBuffer[bufferSize];
volatile int bufferIndex = 0;  // Current index in the circular
↪  buffer
volatile bool bufferReady = false;  // Flag to indicate that the
↪  buffer is full and ready for processing

// Variables for timing analysis
volatile unsigned long lastSampleTime = 0;    // Timestamp of the
↪  last sample (in microseconds)
volatile unsigned long totalJitter = 0;        // Accumulator for
↪  jitter (T)
volatile unsigned long jitterCount = 0;        // Number of jitter
↪  measurements

hw_timer_t *timer = NULL;  // Pointer to the hardware timer

// ISR: Triggered on each timer interrupt to perform ADC sampling
void IRAM_ATTR onTimer() {
  unsigned long currentMicros = micros();

  // Read ADC value from the defined ADC pin
  int adcValue = analogRead(ADC_PIN);

  // Store the ADC reading in the circular buffer
  sampleBuffer[bufferIndex] = adcValue;
  bufferIndex++;
  if (bufferIndex >= bufferSize) {
    bufferIndex = 0;
    bufferReady = true;
  }

  // Timing analysis: Calculate the actual interval between samples
  ↪  and compute jitter
  if (lastSampleTime > 0) {
    unsigned long delta = currentMicros - lastSampleTime;
    // Jitter: absolute difference between measured delta and
    ↪  nominal sampling interval
    unsigned long jitter = (delta > samplingIntervalMicros) ? (delta
    ↪  - samplingIntervalMicros) : (samplingIntervalMicros -
    ↪  delta);
    totalJitter += jitter;
    jitterCount++;
  }
  lastSampleTime = currentMicros;
}

// A simple moving average filter to smooth the ADC readings from
↪  the buffer
float movingAverage(const int *data, int size) {
  long sum = 0;
  for (int i = 0; i < size; i++) {
```

356

```
    sum += data[i];
  }
  return (float)sum / size;
}

void setup() {
  Serial.begin(115200);
  while (!Serial); // Wait for serial connection

  // Set ADC resolution (ESP32 default is 12 bits)
  analogReadResolution(12);

  // Initialize hardware timer:
  // Timer 0, with a prescaler value of 80 (for ~1MHz timer tick if
  ↪  APB clock is 80 MHz), counting up.
  timer = timerBegin(0, 80, true);
  timerAttachInterrupt(timer, &onTimer, true);
  // Configure the timer to trigger every samplingIntervalMicros
  ↪  microseconds (T_s)
  timerAlarmWrite(timer, samplingIntervalMicros, true);
  timerAlarmEnable(timer);

  Serial.println("ESP32 Real-Time Data Acquisition Started");
  Serial.println("Following key formulas are implemented:");
  Serial.println("  - Nyquist Criterion: fs >= 2 * f_max");
  Serial.println("  - Sampling Interval T_s = 1/fs");
  Serial.println("  - Buffer Retention Time D = B/fs");
  Serial.println("  - Effective Sampling Interval T_effective = T_s
  ↪  + T");
}

void loop() {
  // Process the buffer when it is filled with 'bufferSize' samples
  if (bufferReady) {
    // Safely copy the volatile circular buffer into a local array
    noInterrupts();
    int localBuffer[bufferSize];
    for (int i = 0; i < bufferSize; i++) {
      localBuffer[i] = sampleBuffer[i];
    }
    bufferReady = false; // Reset the flag for future acquisitions
    interrupts();

    // Apply a moving average filter to the acquired data
    float avgValue = movingAverage(localBuffer, bufferSize);

    // Calculate average jitter (T average)
    float avgJitter = (jitterCount > 0) ? ((float)totalJitter /
    ↪  jitterCount) : 0;

    // Compute the effective sampling interval:
    // T_effective = T_s + T_average
```

```
float effectiveIntervalMicros = samplingIntervalMicros +
↪  avgJitter;
// Calculate effective sampling frequency (in Hz)
float effectiveFs = 1000000.0 / effectiveIntervalMicros;

// Compute buffer retention time:
// D = Buffer Size (B) / fs
float retentionTimeSec = (float)bufferSize / samplingRateHz;

// Output the analysis results via Serial Monitor
Serial.println("----- Data Acquisition Analysis -----");
Serial.print("Moving Average ADC Value: ");
Serial.println(avgValue);
Serial.print("Nominal Sampling Interval T_s (us): ");
Serial.println(samplingIntervalMicros);
Serial.print("Average Jitter T (us): ");
Serial.println(avgJitter);
Serial.print("Effective Sampling Interval (us): ");
Serial.println(effectiveIntervalMicros);
Serial.print("Effective Sampling Frequency (Hz): ");
Serial.println(effectiveFs);
Serial.print("Buffer Retention Time D (s): ");
Serial.println(retentionTimeSec);
Serial.println("----------------------------------");

// Reset jitter accumulators for the subsequent measurement
↪  cycle
noInterrupts();
totalJitter = 0;
jitterCount = 0;
interrupts();
}

// Additional processing (e.g., digital filtering, anomaly
↪  detection) can be added here.
}
```

Chapter 57

Implementing Data Filtering Methods

Mathematical Foundations of Filtering Algorithms

The raw data captured by IoT sensor inputs is conventionally modeled as a discrete time sequence, where each measurement can be expressed as

$$x[k] = s[k] + n[k],$$

with $s[k]$ representing the intrinsic signal component and $n[k]$ denoting the additive noise. The process of filtering is mathematically formulated through convolution operations that enable the isolation of $s[k]$ from the noisy input. In the general case, a linear time-invariant filter is described by the convolution sum

$$y[k] = \sum_{i=0}^{M-1} h[i]\, x[k-i],$$

where $y[k]$ is the filtered output, $h[i]$ is the impulse response function, and M is the filter order. The optimal choice of $h[i]$ is dictated by the requirement to attenuate frequencies associated with noise while preserving the vital characteristics of the underlying signal. The frequency response

$$H(e^{j\omega}) = \sum_{i=0}^{M-1} h[i]\, e^{-j\omega i}$$

359

serves as a critical criterion in the design process, ensuring that the filter meets precise amplitude attenuation and phase linearity specifications.

Design Considerations for Linear and Nonlinear Filtering Schemes

In the implementation of filtering algorithms, design considerations involve a careful balance between computational complexity and the fidelity of signal reconstruction. Finite impulse response (FIR) filters, characterized by non-recursive structures, offer inherent stability and the possibility of achieving exact linear phase responses when the filter coefficients are symmetric. In contrast, infinite impulse response (IIR) filters incorporate recursive elements and can achieve more selective frequency attenuation with lower orders; however, their design mandates that the poles of the filter remain strictly within the unit circle in the complex z-plane to guarantee stability. The design process typically involves the derivation of filter coefficients using methods such as the windowing technique or frequency domain optimization. These approaches aim to tailor the amplitude response $|H(e^{j\omega})|$, ensuring that frequency components beyond a designated cutoff frequency f_c experience significant attenuation, thereby reducing the propagation of undesired noise artifacts.

Adaptive Filtering and Statistical Approaches

While static filter designs address fixed noise profiles, dynamic sensor environments often require adaptive filtering techniques that adjust to variations in noise statistics and signal dynamics. Adaptive algorithms, such as the least mean squares (LMS) and recursive least squares (RLS) methods, iteratively update filter coefficients to minimize a cost function based on the mean square error between the estimated and actual output. A representative update rule for an adaptive filter under the LMS paradigm is given by

$$h(k + 1) = h(k) + \mu\, e(k)\, x(k),$$

where μ is a step-size parameter, $e(k)$ is the error signal defined as the difference between the desired output and the current filtered signal, and $x(k)$ is the input vector. Such algorithms are particularly advantageous when the noise characteristics, denoted as the statistical distribution of $n[k]$, change over time. Statistical approaches further complement adaptive filtering by incorporating measures of dispersion and bias, enabling the suppression of outliers through methods rooted in robust statistical inference. These techniques ensure that the filtering process remains resilient in the face of non-stationary or impulsive noise, thereby maintaining the integrity of the extracted signal features.

Algorithmic Integration for Value Extraction from Sensor Inputs

Beyond the elimination of noise, the implementation of data filtering methods is fundamentally geared toward the extraction of valuable insights from sensor measurements. Following the application of a filtering algorithm, the resultant signal may be subjected to further analyses to detect features such as edges, peaks, or repetitive patterns. Techniques for secondary processing often include the computation of time derivatives, where the rate of change

$$\frac{dy[k]}{dk} \approx y[k] - y[k-1]$$

serves to highlight transient events and abrupt variations in the signal. In addition, methods such as moving average and median filtering can be employed in tandem to mitigate the influence of occasional outlier measurements, thereby enhancing the robustness of subsequent feature-extraction algorithms. The integration of filtering with statistical hypothesis testing allows for the identification of significant deviations from established baseline behaviors, facilitating the isolation of events or anomalies within the data stream. Such algorithmic synthesis – which leverages both linear and nonlinear filtering paradigms – lays the foundation for higher-level inference tasks, ensuring that the filtered sensor data retains its predictive and descriptive potential within the context of IoT applications.

ESP32 For IoT With Arduino Code Snippet

```
/*
  This code snippet demonstrates the key filtering equations
  ↪  outlined in this chapter.

  Sensor data is modeled as:
    x[k] = s[k] + n[k]

  A Finite Impulse Response (FIR) filter is implemented via the
  ↪  convolution sum:
    y[k] = [i=0 to M-1] h[i] * x[k-i]
  where h[i] are the filter coefficients.

  Additionally, an adaptive filtering algorithm is demonstrated
  ↪  using the
  Least Mean Squares (LMS) update rule:
    h(k+1) = h(k) +  * e(k) * x(k)
  where:
    -  is the step-size parameter;
    - e(k) = desired output - current filter output;
    - The desired output is here approximated by the FIR filtered
    ↪  signal.

  Finally, the time derivative of the filtered output is estimated
  ↪  as:
    dy[k]/dk  y[k] - y[k-1]
*/

const int sensorPin = 34; // ADC pin on ESP32 for sensor input
const int M = 5;          // Filter order

// FIR filter coefficients for a simple moving average
float hFIR[M] = {0.2, 0.2, 0.2, 0.2, 0.2};

// LMS adaptive filter coefficients initialized to zero
float hLMS[M] = {0.0, 0.0, 0.0, 0.0, 0.0};

// Circular buffer to store the most recent sensor readings
float sensorBuffer[M] = {0.0, 0.0, 0.0, 0.0, 0.0};

const float mu = 0.01; // LMS step-size parameter

// Variables to store the previous filtered values for derivative
// ↪  calculation
float previousFilteredFIR = 0.0;
float previousFilteredLMS = 0.0;

void updateSensorBuffer(float newValue) {
```

```
  // Shift the buffer values: sensorBuffer[0] holds the newest
  ↪ sample
  for (int i = M - 1; i > 0; i--) {
    sensorBuffer[i] = sensorBuffer[i - 1];
  }
  sensorBuffer[0] = newValue;
}

float computeFIRFilter() {
  // Compute the FIR output using convolution:
  // y[k] = h[0]*x[k] + h[1]*x[k-1] + ... + h[M-1]*x[k-M+1]
  float output = 0.0;
  for (int i = 0; i < M; i++) {
    output += hFIR[i] * sensorBuffer[i];
  }
  return output;
}

float computeLMSFilter() {
  // Compute the adaptive filter output:
  float output = 0.0;
  for (int i = 0; i < M; i++) {
    output += hLMS[i] * sensorBuffer[i];
  }
  return output;
}

void updateLMSCoefficients(float error) {
  // Update each coefficient according to the LMS algorithm:
  // h(k+1) = h(k) +  * e(k) * x(k)
  for (int i = 0; i < M; i++) {
    hLMS[i] += mu * error * sensorBuffer[i];
  }
}

void setup() {
  Serial.begin(115200);

  // Initialize the sensor buffer with initial readings
  // to avoid garbage values during the first iterations.
  for (int i = 0; i < M; i++) {
    sensorBuffer[i] = analogRead(sensorPin);
    delay(10);
  }
  Serial.println("ESP32 IoT Data Filtering Demonstration
  ↪ Initialized");
}

void loop() {
  // Read the raw sensor value (simulate x[k] = s[k] + n[k])
  int rawValue = analogRead(sensorPin);
  float sensorValue = (float)rawValue; // Scale as necessary based
  ↪ on sensor specifications
```

363

```
// Update the circular sensor buffer with the new sample
updateSensorBuffer(sensorValue);

// FIR Filtering: Compute filtered output using convolution sum
float filteredFIR = computeFIRFilter();
// Estimate the time derivative: dy[k]/dk ~ y[k] - y[k-1]
float derivativeFIR = filteredFIR - previousFilteredFIR;

// Adaptive Filtering using LMS:
// Compute the LMS filtered output and measure the error relative
↪  to the FIR output
float filteredLMS = computeLMSFilter();
float error = filteredFIR - filteredLMS;
updateLMSCoefficients(error);

// Estimate the derivative for the adaptive filter output
float derivativeLMS = filteredLMS - previousFilteredLMS;

// Update previous values for the next time-step calculation
previousFilteredFIR = filteredFIR;
previousFilteredLMS = filteredLMS;

// Output the raw, filtered, derivative, and error data via Serial
↪  monitor
Serial.print("Raw: ");
Serial.print(sensorValue);
Serial.print(" | FIR: ");
Serial.print(filteredFIR);
Serial.print(" (Deriv: ");
Serial.print(derivativeFIR);
Serial.print(") | LMS: ");
Serial.print(filteredLMS);
Serial.print(" (Deriv: ");
Serial.print(derivativeLMS);
Serial.print(") | Error: ");
Serial.println(error);

delay(100); // Adjust the delay as needed for your sampling rate
}
```

364

Chapter 58

Noise Reduction and Smoothing Algorithms

Mathematical Foundations of Smoothing Filters

Sensor data acquired in practical systems is typically corrupted by high-frequency noise, which complicates the extraction of the underlying true signal. A core approach to mitigating this degradation is the use of smoothing filters, mathematically represented by convolution operations. For example, a simple moving average filter may be defined by

$$y[k] = \frac{1}{N} \sum_{i=0}^{N-1} x[k-i],$$

where $x[k]$ denotes the raw sensor measurement at discrete time step k, N is the window length, and $y[k]$ is the filtered output. This operator effectively convolves the input sequence with a rectangular window, resulting in a low-pass filtering effect that attenuates high-frequency fluctuations.

An alternative formulation uses exponential smoothing, where the recursive definition

$$y[k] = \alpha x[k] + (1 - \alpha)y[k-1]$$

incorporates a smoothing factor α that controls the relative weight given to the most recent input versus the historical output. The mathematical properties of these filters can be further examined in the frequency domain. The convolution in time translates to multiplication in frequency, with the frequency response given by

$$H(e^{j\omega}) = \sum_{i=0}^{N-1} h[i]\, e^{-j\omega i},$$

where $h[i]$ are the coefficients of the filter. Such an analysis provides insight into how the choice of N or α shapes the attenuation of undesired noise components.

Smoothing Techniques for Sensor Data Stabilization

The application of smoothing techniques in sensor data stabilization exploits the assumption that noise predominantly occupies higher spectral regions relative to the underlying signal. One widely used method involves convolving the sensor data with a symmetric kernel. A prominent example is the Gaussian filter, defined by the kernel

$$g[i] = \frac{1}{\sqrt{2\pi\sigma^2}} \exp\left(-\frac{i^2}{2\sigma^2}\right),$$

where σ is a parameter that determines the spread, or standard deviation, of the kernel. The filtered output is then computed as

$$y[k] = \sum_{i=-M}^{M} g[i]\, x[k-i],$$

with $2M+1$ representing the span of the window over which the convolution is performed. The Gaussian kernel, owing to its decay properties and smooth characteristics, is effective in reducing noise while preserving essential features of the signal.

In addition to linear methods, non-linear smoothing techniques such as median filtering provide robustness against impulsive disturbances. While median filters do not conform to linear convolution frameworks, their operational principle—replacing a data point by the median value among its neighbors—ensures minimal distortion of sharp transitions, thereby maintaining relevant signal details in the presence of outliers.

Algorithmic Strategies for Noise Reduction

The design of noise reduction algorithms is driven by the need to minimize error between the true signal and its estimate obtained from noisy measurements. This objective is often formalized by a cost function such as

$$J(\theta) = \mathbb{E}\{(s[k] - y[k])^2\},$$

where $s[k]$ denotes the latent true signal, $y[k]$ is the filtered estimate, and the expectation operator reflects the statistical nature of the noise. Minimizing $J(\theta)$ is instrumental in configuring the parameters of the smoothing algorithm for optimal performance.

In the context of fixed noise profiles, linear filters—including finite impulse response (FIR) filters—are employed due to their inherent stability and ease of analysis. Conversely, non-stationary or time-varying noise environments motivate the use of adaptive filters. These algorithms update their coefficients iteratively based on local error metrics, thereby tuning their frequency response in accordance with changing conditions. The analysis of adaptive strategies involves studying convergence properties and stability, typically requiring that update parameters satisfy certain bounds derived from the underlying noise statistics.

Design Trade-offs and Parameter Selection

The efficacy of a smoothing or noise reduction algorithm depends critically on the appropriate choice of design parameters. In a moving average filter, for instance, increasing the window size N enhances noise attenuation by reducing the influence of high-frequency fluctuations; however, this comes at the expense of temporal resolution. The effective cutoff frequency f_c of the filter is inversely related to the window size, establishing a trade-off between smoothness and responsiveness.

For recursive filters such as those based on exponential smoothing, the parameter α governs the balance between the immediate response to new data and the retention of historical trends. Choice of a small α yields a highly smoothed output with slow adaptation to rapid changes, whereas a large α allows the filter to follow dynamic signal variations more closely, albeit with diminished noise suppression.

Adaptive filtering methods further introduce parameters such as the step-size μ, constrained by stability conditions that ensure convergence. The parameter μ must be selected judiciously to balance rapid adaptation with the risk of divergence, particularly under varying noise conditions. Quantitative performance metrics like the mean square error (MSE) and the signal-to-noise ratio (SNR) are employed to systematically evaluate and fine-tune these parameters, providing a rigorous framework for the comparative analysis of different noise reduction strategies.

ESP32 For IoT With Arduino Code Snippet

```
#include <Arduino.h>
#include <math.h>

// Define constants for filter window sizes
#define MOVING_AVG_SIZE      5
#define GAUSS_FILTER_SIZE    5
#define MEDIAN_SIZE          5
#define ADAPTIVE_FILTER_SIZE 3

#ifndef PI
  #define PI 3.14159265
#endif

// Global parameters for filters
const float alpha = 0.2;                  // Smoothing factor for
↪   exponential filter
const unsigned long sampleInterval = 100; // Sampling period in
↪   milliseconds

// ------------------- Moving Average Filter -------------------
float movAvgBuffer[MOVING_AVG_SIZE] = {0};
int movAvgIndex = 0;
bool movAvgBufferFilled = false;

float movingAverage(float newVal) {
  movAvgBuffer[movAvgIndex] = newVal;
  movAvgIndex = (movAvgIndex + 1) % MOVING_AVG_SIZE;
  if (movAvgIndex == 0) {
    movAvgBufferFilled = true;
  }
  int count = movAvgBufferFilled ? MOVING_AVG_SIZE : movAvgIndex;
```

```
  float sum = 0;
  for (int i = 0; i < count; i++) {
    sum += movAvgBuffer[i];
  }
  return sum / count;
}

// -------------------- Exponential Smoothing Filter
↪   --------------------
float expSmoothValue = 0;
bool firstExp = true;

float exponentialSmoothing(float newVal) {
  if (firstExp) {
    expSmoothValue = newVal;
    firstExp = false;
  } else {
    expSmoothValue = alpha * newVal + (1 - alpha) * expSmoothValue;
  }
  return expSmoothValue;
}

// -------------------- Gaussian Filter --------------------
float gaussBuffer[GAUSS_FILTER_SIZE] = {0};
int gaussIndex = 0;
bool gaussBufferFilled = false;
float gaussKernel[GAUSS_FILTER_SIZE];
const float sigma = 1.0;

float gaussianFilter(float newVal) {
  // Update circular buffer with new value
  gaussBuffer[gaussIndex] = newVal;
  gaussIndex = (gaussIndex + 1) % GAUSS_FILTER_SIZE;
  if (gaussIndex == 0) {
    gaussBufferFilled = true;
  }
  int count = gaussBufferFilled ? GAUSS_FILTER_SIZE : gaussIndex;
  // For a proper Gaussian convolution, wait until the buffer is
  ↪   full
  if (count < GAUSS_FILTER_SIZE) {
    return movingAverage(newVal);
  }
  // Reorder the buffer into time sequence (oldest to newest)
  float ordered[GAUSS_FILTER_SIZE];
  int start = gaussBufferFilled ? gaussIndex : 0;
  for (int i = 0; i < GAUSS_FILTER_SIZE; i++) {
    ordered[i] = gaussBuffer[(start + i) % GAUSS_FILTER_SIZE];
  }
  // Convolve with the precomputed Gaussian kernel
  float sum = 0;
  float weightSum = 0;
  for (int i = 0; i < GAUSS_FILTER_SIZE; i++) {
    sum += ordered[i] * gaussKernel[i];
```

369

```
    weightSum += gaussKernel[i];
  }
  return (weightSum != 0) ? (sum / weightSum) : newVal;
}

// ------------------- Median Filter -------------------
float medianBuffer[MEDIAN_SIZE] = {0};
int medianIndex = 0;
bool medianBufferFilled = false;

// Helper: simple bubble sort to compute median
float median(float arr[], int n) {
  float temp[n];
  for (int i = 0; i < n; i++) {
    temp[i] = arr[i];
  }
  for (int i = 0; i < n - 1; i++) {
    for (int j = i + 1; j < n; j++) {
      if (temp[j] < temp[i]) {
        float swap = temp[i];
        temp[i] = temp[j];
        temp[j] = swap;
      }
    }
  }
  return temp[n / 2];
}

float medianFilter(float newVal) {
  medianBuffer[medianIndex] = newVal;
  medianIndex = (medianIndex + 1) % MEDIAN_SIZE;
  if (medianIndex == 0) {
    medianBufferFilled = true;
  }
  int count = medianBufferFilled ? MEDIAN_SIZE : medianIndex;
  return median(medianBuffer, count);
}

// ------------------- Adaptive Filter (LMS Algorithm)
↪ -------------------
float adaptiveWeights[ADAPTIVE_FILTER_SIZE] = {0.0};
float adaptiveBuffer[ADAPTIVE_FILTER_SIZE] = {0.0};
int adaptiveIndex = 0;
bool adaptiveBufferFilled = false;
const float mu = 0.01; // Step-size for weight adaptation

float adaptiveFilter(float newVal, float trueVal) {
  // Update circular buffer for adaptive filter input
  adaptiveBuffer[adaptiveIndex] = newVal;
  adaptiveIndex = (adaptiveIndex + 1) % ADAPTIVE_FILTER_SIZE;
  if (adaptiveIndex == 0) {
    adaptiveBufferFilled = true;
  }
}
```

```
  int count = adaptiveBufferFilled ? ADAPTIVE_FILTER_SIZE :
  ↪  adaptiveIndex;
  // Wait until the buffer is full to perform adaptation
  if (count < ADAPTIVE_FILTER_SIZE) {
    return movingAverage(newVal);
  }
  // Reorder the buffer into chronological order
  float ordered[ADAPTIVE_FILTER_SIZE];
  int start = adaptiveBufferFilled ? adaptiveIndex : 0;
  for (int i = 0; i < ADAPTIVE_FILTER_SIZE; i++) {
    ordered[i] = adaptiveBuffer[(start + i) % ADAPTIVE_FILTER_SIZE];
  }
  // Compute filtered output as inner product between weights and
  ↪  inputs
  float y = 0;
  for (int i = 0; i < ADAPTIVE_FILTER_SIZE; i++) {
    y += adaptiveWeights[i] * ordered[i];
  }
  // Calculate error with respect to the known true signal
  float error = trueVal - y;
  // Update filter coefficients using the Least Mean Squares (LMS)
  ↪  rule
  for (int i = 0; i < ADAPTIVE_FILTER_SIZE; i++) {
    adaptiveWeights[i] += 2 * mu * error * ordered[i];
  }
  return y;
}


// -------------------- Simulation Parameters --------------------
const float amplitude = 1.0; // Amplitude of the true (noise-free)
↪  signal
const float freq = 0.5;      // Frequency in Hz

// -------------------- Arduino Setup --------------------
void setup() {
  Serial.begin(115200);
  while (!Serial) {
    ; // Wait for Serial port to be ready
  }
  // Precompute the Gaussian kernel for the fixed window
  int M = (GAUSS_FILTER_SIZE - 1) / 2;
  float sum = 0;
  for (int i = 0; i < GAUSS_FILTER_SIZE; i++) {
    int offset = i - M;
    gaussKernel[i] = exp(- (offset * offset) / (2 * sigma * sigma))
    ↪  / (sqrt(2 * PI) * sigma);
    sum += gaussKernel[i];
  }
  // Normalize the kernel so that it sums to one
  for (int i = 0; i < GAUSS_FILTER_SIZE; i++) {
    gaussKernel[i] /= sum;
  }
  Serial.println("ESP32 IoT Smoothing Filters Demonstration");
```

371

```
}

// -------------------- Main Loop --------------------
void loop() {
  static unsigned long lastSampleTime = 0;
  unsigned long currentTime = millis();

  if (currentTime - lastSampleTime >= sampleInterval) {
    lastSampleTime = currentTime;
    float t = currentTime / 1000.0; // Time in seconds
    // Simulate a true sensor signal (e.g., a sine wave)
    float trueSignal = amplitude * sin(2 * PI * freq * t);
    // Add random noise to simulate a realistic sensor measurement
    float noise = ((float)random(-50, 50)) / 50.0;
    float sensorValue = trueSignal + noise;

    // Apply the different noise reduction / smoothing algorithms
    float movAvg      = movingAverage(sensorValue);
    float expSmooth   = exponentialSmoothing(sensorValue);
    float gaussOut    = gaussianFilter(sensorValue);
    float medOut      = medianFilter(sensorValue);
    float adaptiveOut = adaptiveFilter(sensorValue, trueSignal);

    // Print the raw and filtered values to the Serial Monitor
    Serial.print("Time: ");
    Serial.print(t, 2);
    Serial.print(" s, True: ");
    Serial.print(trueSignal, 3);
    Serial.print(", Sensor: ");
    Serial.print(sensorValue, 3);
    Serial.print(", MA: ");
    Serial.print(movAvg, 3);
    Serial.print(", Exp: ");
    Serial.print(expSmooth, 3);
    Serial.print(", Gauss: ");
    Serial.print(gaussOut, 3);
    Serial.print(", Med: ");
    Serial.print(medOut, 3);
    Serial.print(", Adaptive: ");
    Serial.println(adaptiveOut, 3);
  }
}
```

Chapter 59

Sensor Data Calibration Techniques

Mathematical Framework for Calibration

Sensor data often embody a combination of the underlying true signal and an array of systematic and random error components. A common abstraction models the raw sensor measurement, denoted by x_{raw}, as

$$x_{raw} = \alpha s + \beta + \eta,$$

where s represents the true physical quantity, α is a multiplicative factor embodying gain errors, β is an additive bias, and η accounts for stochastic noise. The objective of calibration is to determine appropriate values for α and β, thereby defining a mapping that yields the calibrated output

$$x_{cal} = \frac{x_{raw} - \beta}{\alpha}.$$

When a set of calibration points $\{(s_i, x_{raw,i})\}_{i=1}^{N}$ is available, estimation techniques such as least squares minimization are employed to obtain optimal parameters. In such instances, the cost function

$$J(\alpha, \beta) = \sum_{i=1}^{N} \left(s_i - \frac{x_{raw,i} - \beta}{\alpha} \right)^2$$

is minimized with respect to α and β. In scenarios where the noise component η follows a Gaussian distribution, maximum likelihood estimation further underpins the derivation of these parameters, framing calibration as a well-posed optimization problem.

Static Calibration Methodologies

Static calibration paradigms assume a time-invariant sensor error profile, wherein the sensor operates under controlled and stable conditions. In these scenarios, extensive experimental data are acquired using known reference standards. One frequently encountered approach involves fitting a linear model to the collected data. However, nonlinearity in sensor responses may necessitate the use of higher-order polynomial models. Such a polynomial calibration model is typically expressed as

$$x_{cal} = \sum_{i=0}^{n} c_i \, x_{raw}^i,$$

where c_i are the calibration coefficients determined via regression analysis and n denotes the chosen degree of the polynomial. The calibration process must carefully balance model complexity; higher-order models may lead to overfitting, while overly simplistic models might fail to capture significant nonlinearities. Robust outlier detection techniques are often integrated into the static calibration process to ensure that the estimated parameters reliably depict the sensor behavior over its intended operational range.

Dynamic Calibration Strategies

In many practical applications, sensor characteristics are subject to temporal variations arising from environmental influences, component aging, or transient operational conditions. Dynamic calibration strategies are designed to address such nonstationary behavior through continual adjustment of the calibration parameters. A common approach involves the use of adaptive algorithms that update the gain and bias estimates recursively. For example, given a sensor measurement at discrete time index k, the parameter updates can be represented by

$$\alpha[k+1] = \alpha[k] + \mu_\alpha \, e[k] \, x_{raw}[k],$$

$$\beta[k+1] = \beta[k] + \mu_\beta \, e[k],$$

where $e[k] = s[k] - x_{cal}[k]$ is the instantaneous calibration error and μ_α, μ_β are small, positive adaptation rates chosen to ensure algorithmic stability. The use of such iterative schemes allows the calibration process to accommodate gradual drift and abrupt changes in sensor output. Techniques analogous to those found in adaptive signal processing, including exponential forgetting and sliding window estimation, are often employed to refine the responsiveness and robustness of the parameter adjustment mechanism.

Parameter Estimation and Error Analysis

Precise estimation of calibration parameters is central to ensuring the accuracy and reliability of sensor measurements. The efficacy of a calibration procedure is quantified through statistical error metrics, with the root mean square error (RMSE) serving as a prototypical example:

$$RMSE = \sqrt{\frac{1}{N} \sum_{i=1}^{N} (s_i - x_{cal,i})^2}.$$

A low RMSE value indicates that the calibrated output closely approximates the true signal. Sensitivity analysis is performed by introducing small perturbations to the calibration parameters and observing the impact on the output. This analysis elucidates the robustness of the calibration method and highlights the potential propagation of uncertainty in measurement. Furthermore, examining the residuals between the calibrated sensor outputs and the reference measurements is crucial for detecting unmodeled nonlinearities or systemic biases. By ensuring that the gradient of the cost function approaches zero, optimal calibration parameter values are attained, reinforcing the reliability of subsequent sensor-based evaluations.

ESP32 For IoT With Arduino Code Snippet

```
/*
    ESP32 IoT Sensor Calibration Example
```

```
-----------------------------------------------------------
This code demonstrates several calibration techniques for sensor
↪   data
on the ESP32 using the Arduino framework, as discussed in the
"Sensor Data Calibration Techniques" chapter.

Implemented Models and Algorithms:
1. Sensor Measurement Model:
     x_raw = alpha_real * s + beta_real + noise
     where:
         s          = true physical value,
         alpha_real = multiplicative (gain) error,
         beta_real  = additive (bias) error.

2. Calibration Mapping:
     x_cal = (x_raw - beta) / alpha
     (Determines calibrated output based on estimated parameters.)

3. Static Calibration using Linear Regression:
     From calibration data points { (s_i, x_raw_i) },
     estimate parameters by minimizing:
         J(alpha,beta) = Sigma [ s_i - (x_raw_i - beta)/alpha ]^2.
     Regression yields:
         alpha = (n*(s_i*x_raw_i) - s_i*x_raw_i) / (n*(s_i^2) -
         ↪   (s_i)^2)
         beta  = (x_raw_i - alpha*s_i) / n

4. Dynamic Calibration Update:
     Parameter updates for each new reading:
         error = s - x_cal
         alpha = alpha + mu_alpha * error * x_raw
         beta  = beta  + mu_beta * error

5. Polynomial Calibration Option:
     x_cal = c0 + c1*x_raw + c2*x_raw^2   (for nonlinear sensor
     ↪   responses)

6. Parameter Estimation and Error Analysis:
     RMSE = sqrt( [ s_i - x_cal_i ]^2 / n)

This complete code snippet includes:
   - Simulation of sensor raw measurements with noise.
   - A static calibration function using a set of calibration
   ↪   points.
   - A dynamic calibration algorithm updating parameters in real
   ↪   time.
   - An optional polynomial calibration function.
   - RMSE computation for error analysis.
*/

#include <Arduino.h>
#include <math.h>
```

```
// ----------------------------------------------------------
// Simulation parameters (unknown to the calibration algorithm)
// ----------------------------------------------------------
float alpha_real = 1.05;     // Actual multiplicative gain error
float beta_real = -2.0;      // Actual additive bias error
float noiseAmplitude = 0.5;  // Noise amplitude

// True sensor value (simulated constant physical quantity)
float trueValue = 100.0;

// ----------------------------------------------------------
// Global calibration parameters (initial estimates)
// ----------------------------------------------------------
float alpha = 1.0;   // Estimated gain factor (will be updated)
float beta = 0.0;    // Estimated bias (will be updated)

// Adaptation rates for dynamic calibration update
float mu_alpha = 0.0001;
float mu_beta = 0.0001;

// ----------------------------------------------------------
// Static Calibration Data (using known calibration points)
// ----------------------------------------------------------
#define NUM_CAL_POINTS 5
float s_calibrations[NUM_CAL_POINTS] = {80.0, 90.0, 100.0, 110.0,
↪   120.0}; // Reference true values
float raw_calibrations[NUM_CAL_POINTS];   // Measured raw values
↪   corresponding to s_calibrations

// ----------------------------------------------------------
// Function: simulateRawSensorReading
// Simulates a raw sensor reading based on a given true value "s"
// using the sensor model: x_raw = alpha_real * s + beta_real +
↪   noise.
// ----------------------------------------------------------
float simulateRawSensorReading(float s) {
  float noise = ((float)random(-100, 101) / 100.0) * noiseAmplitude;
  return alpha_real * s + beta_real + noise;
}

// ----------------------------------------------------------
// Function: getRawSensorReading
// Obtains the raw sensor reading for the current simulation
↪   trueValue.
// ----------------------------------------------------------
float getRawSensorReading() {
  return simulateRawSensorReading(trueValue);
}

// ----------------------------------------------------------
// Function: calibrate
// Applies the linear calibration mapping to a raw sensor reading:
//        x_cal = (x_raw - beta) / alpha
```

```
// ------------------------------------------------------------
float calibrate(float raw) {
  return (raw - beta) / alpha;
}


// ------------------------------------------------------------
// Function: polynomialCalibrate
// Implements a polynomial calibration model:
//       x_cal = c0 + c1*x_raw + c2*x_raw^2
// Useful when sensor response shows nonlinearity.
// ------------------------------------------------------------
const int polyDegree = 2;
float polyCoeffs[polyDegree + 1] = {0.0, 1.0, 0.0}; // Default
↪  coefficients (linear behavior)

float polynomialCalibrate(float raw) {
  float calibrated = 0.0;
  for (int i = 0; i <= polyDegree; i++) {
    calibrated += polyCoeffs[i] * pow(raw, i);
  }
  return calibrated;
}


// ------------------------------------------------------------
// Function: performStaticCalibration
// Performs a static calibration using linear regression on
↪  calibration data.
// It computes the optimal "alpha" and "beta" such that:
//       raw = alpha * s + beta
// ------------------------------------------------------------
void performStaticCalibration() {
  // Acquire raw calibration data for each known sensor value
  for (int i = 0; i < NUM_CAL_POINTS; i++) {
    raw_calibrations[i] =
    ↪  simulateRawSensorReading(s_calibrations[i]);
  }

  // Compute sums required for regression
  float sumS = 0.0, sumRaw = 0.0, sumSRaw = 0.0, sumS2 = 0.0;
  for (int i = 0; i < NUM_CAL_POINTS; i++) {
    sumS    += s_calibrations[i];
    sumRaw  += raw_calibrations[i];
    sumSRaw += s_calibrations[i] * raw_calibrations[i];
    sumS2   += s_calibrations[i] * s_calibrations[i];
  }

  float n = NUM_CAL_POINTS;
  // Calculate calibration parameters using linear regression
  ↪  formulas:
  //   alpha = (n*(s_i * raw_i) - s_i * raw_i) / (n*(s_i^2) -
  ↪  (s_i)^2)
  //   beta  = (raw_i - alpha*s_i) / n
  alpha = (n * sumSRaw - sumS * sumRaw) / (n * sumS2 - sumS * sumS);
```

378

```
  beta  = (sumRaw - alpha * sumS) / n;

  Serial.println("Static Calibration Completed:");
  Serial.print("Estimated Alpha: ");
  Serial.println(alpha, 4);
  Serial.print("Estimated Beta: ");
  Serial.println(beta, 4);
}

// ----------------------------------------------------------
// Function: computeRMSE
// Computes the Root Mean Square Error (RMSE) for the static
↪   calibration.
// RMSE = sqrt( [ s_i - ((raw_i - beta) / alpha) ]^2 / n)
// ----------------------------------------------------------
float computeRMSE() {
  float sumSquaredError = 0.0;
  for (int i = 0; i < NUM_CAL_POINTS; i++) {
    float calibrated = (raw_calibrations[i] - beta) / alpha;
    float error = s_calibrations[i] - calibrated;
    sumSquaredError += error * error;
  }
  return sqrt(sumSquaredError / NUM_CAL_POINTS);
}

// ----------------------------------------------------------
// Arduino Setup Function
// Initializes Serial communication, seeds the random generator,
// and performs static calibration.
// ----------------------------------------------------------
void setup() {
  Serial.begin(115200);
  randomSeed(analogRead(0));  // Seed based on analog noise

  // Perform static calibration once using known calibration
  ↪   standards
  performStaticCalibration();

  // Compute and print RMSE for the static calibration
  float rmse = computeRMSE();
  Serial.print("Static Calibration RMSE: ");
  Serial.println(rmse, 4);
}

// ----------------------------------------------------------
// Arduino Loop Function
// Continuously reads raw sensor data, applies calibration mapping,
// performs dynamic calibration updates, and outputs data.
// ----------------------------------------------------------
void loop() {
  // 1. Acquire raw sensor reading for current trueValue simulation
  float rawVal = getRawSensorReading();
```

```cpp
// 2. Perform linear calibration using the current parameters
float calibratedVal = calibrate(rawVal);

// 3. Optionally, compute calibrated value using a polynomial
//    model
float polyCalibratedVal = polynomialCalibrate(rawVal);

// 4. Compute instantaneous error for dynamic calibration:
//     error = true value - calibrated sensor value
float error = trueValue - calibratedVal;

// 5. Dynamic parameter update (adaptive calibration):
//     alpha[k+1] = alpha[k] + mu_alpha * error * rawVal
//     beta[k+1]  = beta[k]  + mu_beta  * error
alpha += mu_alpha * error * rawVal;
beta  += mu_beta  * error;

// 6. Output sensor readings, calibrated values, error, and
//    updated parameters
Serial.print("Raw: ");
Serial.print(rawVal, 4);
Serial.print(" | Calibrated: ");
Serial.print(calibratedVal, 4);
Serial.print(" | PolyCalibrated: ");
Serial.print(polyCalibratedVal, 4);
Serial.print(" | Error: ");
Serial.print(error, 4);
Serial.print(" | Alpha: ");
Serial.print(alpha, 4);
Serial.print(" | Beta: ");
Serial.println(beta, 4);

delay(1000);  // Wait for 1 second before next measurement
}
```

Chapter 60

Asynchronous Operations and Non-blocking Code

Theoretical Foundations of Asynchronous Execution

Within the realm of embedded and IoT systems, asynchronous execution is formulated as a paradigm in which system operations are structured to proceed concurrently without imposing blocking delays during input/output or computational tasks. The model is constructed upon the premise that tasks with indeterminate duration—such as peripheral interactions, sensor readouts, or network communication—must be serviced without halting the progression of the primary control flow. In formal terms, if a particular operation is represented by a function f that is invoked at time t_0, asynchronous architectures decouple the initiation of f from its completion, thereby ensuring that subsequent tasks may progress without incurring latency. In analogous mathematical descriptions, an asynchronous function can be conceptualized as the mapping $t_0 \rightarrow \{f(t_0), \}$, where signifies the interim state in which the result is pending.

The established abstract models of concurrency often rely on constructs such as event loops, futures, and promises to encapsulate asynchronous behavior. These constructs provide a formal mechanism to handle the potential indeterminacy inherent in operations that interact with external devices or remote servers. The correctness criteria for such systems may be encapsulated in the requirement that all pending operations eventually satisfy the property of eventual consistency, such that for any asynchronous process A, there exists a time $t_f > t_0$ at which the result $A(t_f)$ is reproducible within the bounds of an acceptable error margin.

Architectural Patterns for Non-blocking System Design

Architectural designs for non-blocking code are predicated on the necessity to maintain system responsiveness even under the influence of high-latency operations. A salient principle is the decoupling of task initiation from task completion, where the system dispatches operations to dedicated execution contexts and continues to process subsequent tasks. A common pattern within these architectures is the event-driven model, whereby an event loop continuously polls for events and dispatches corresponding handlers upon detection. Although the event loop itself is susceptible to delays if an individual handler does not yield promptly, robust design methodologies mandate the design of handlers that execute in quantifiably bounded time intervals.

The architectural strategy extends to the incorporation of non-blocking paradigms in resource management. For instance, the implementation of asynchronous I/O operations may lean on techniques in which the system issues requests that are later fulfilled by hardware interrupts or internal scheduler notifications. In such cases, hardware signals are converted into software events that are enqueued and dispatched based on priority or temporal constraints. Moreover, the theoretical model underlying these approaches can be elucidated through queuing theory, where the system state is represented by a queue Q such that incoming events are appended to Q, and the cumulative service rate S is designed to exceed the arrival rate λ, thereby ensuring that the expected waiting time W satisfies the inequality $W < \epsilon$ for a system-defined threshold ϵ.

Mechanisms for Asynchronous Task Management and Scheduling

Central to the management of asynchronous operations is the formulation of scheduling algorithms that judiciously allocate processor time among concurrently executing tasks. In this context, scheduling is achieved by employing techniques that monitor the readiness state of tasks and invoke them subject to a preordained set of constraints. These constraints may be defined in terms of real-time deadlines, task priorities, or temporal jitter limits. The scheduling mechanism is inherently non-blocking in that tasks are selected based on their readiness rather than their arrival order; this circumvents the limitations imposed by sequential task processing.

The underlying scheduler must accurately manage the transition between active and waiting states, which is often achieved by maintaining a task control block (TCB) for each asynchronous task. Each TCB contains metadata, including the task's state, priority, and callback function. The scheduler operates on the invariant that the execution of any individual callback function must converge in a time period that does not disrupt the overall throughput of the system. This invariant can be formally expressed by the relation $T_{\text{callback}} < T_{\text{max}}$, where T_{callback} is the time required for a task to complete its callback, and T_{max} is a system-specific upper bound on acceptable latency.

Resource Management and Concurrency Control

Non-blocking designs necessitate robust strategies for managing shared resources among concurrently executing tasks. The synchronization mechanisms employed in this environment aim to mitigate contention without resorting to blocking methods that could undermine system responsiveness. Instead of traditional mutual exclusion locks that naturally induce pause conditions, non-blocking synchronization constructs such as atomic operations and lock-free data structures are employed. These techniques enable multiple tasks to engage in an interleaved execution sequence without incurring the overhead of context switching induced by lock contention.

The formal analysis of such synchronization mechanisms often involves the derivation of invariants that guarantee progress. For example, an atomic update on a shared variable V may be delineated as an operation $V \leftarrow V \oplus \Delta$, where $\oplus$ denotes an operation that satisfies the property of atomicity. Concurrency control in this framework is predicated on the notion that the partial order induced by the execution sequence of operations must preserve the consistency of V under concurrent modifications. The absence of blocking is thus ensured by designing every such operation to be impervious to external interruption, thereby preventing deadlock and ensuring liveliness in the presence of asynchronous task execution.

Design Strategies for Maintaining System Responsiveness

The intricacies of IoT applications necessitate design strategies that prioritize system responsiveness amid a proliferation of asynchronous tasks. One pervasive strategy is to isolate long-duration operations into discrete tasks that operate independently from the central event loop. By compartmentalizing these operations, the delay associated with their execution does not impede the core processing loop, which is responsible for reactive event handling. In formal terms, if an operation O is decomposed into $O = O_1 \cup O_2 \cup \cdots \cup O_m$, then the scheduling algorithm can interleave the execution instances of each O_i with minimal latency, thereby ensuring that no individual operation monopolizes system resources.

Another pertinent approach involves the exploitation of hardware-assisted concurrency. Modern IoT devices, including microcontrollers equipped with dual cores or specialized processing units, provide the substrate for concurrent execution streams that can be dynamically allocated to background tasks. In such systems, asynchronous operations may be distributed across multiple processing units such that the aggregate computational overhead remains within the prescribed bounds of real-time performance. The theoretical framework supporting this distributed execution paradigm is deeply intertwined with the concepts of parallelism and inter-process communication, wherein the design goals are to minimize inter-task interference and to ensure that asynchronous operations adhere to deterministic timing constraints.

The combination of these strategies culminates in system designs that manifest exceptional responsiveness and reliability, strongly adhering to the principles of non-blocking execution. Each design decision is underpinned by rigorous theoretical models and empirical performance analyses, which collectively contribute to the formulation of best practices in the domain of asynchronous operations for IoT applications.

ESP32 For IoT With Arduino Code Snippet

```
// Comprehensive ESP32 for IoT with Arduino Code Example
// This example demonstrates asynchronous operations and
↪    non-blocking code
// using FreeRTOS tasks on the ESP32. Core concepts include:
// - Asynchronous sensor data acquisition without blocking the main
↪    event loop.
// - Non-blocking scheduling using vTaskDelayUntil.
// - Enforcement of callback execution limits (T_callback < T_max).
// - Atomic updates and inter-task communication via a FreeRTOS
↪    queue.
// - Event-driven design principles juxtaposed against traditional
↪    blocking paradigms.
//
// Theoretical models referenced:
//    - Asynchronous mapping: t0 -> { f(t0),  }
//    - Scheduling invariant: T_callback < T_max
//    - Atomic update: V ← V
//
// This code integrates these concepts into a practical ESP32 IoT
↪    application.

#include <Arduino.h>

// Configuration parameters
#define SENSOR_INTERVAL 1000     // Sensor reading interval in
↪    milliseconds
#define T_MAX 50                 // Maximum allowed callback
↪    execution time in milliseconds

// Global FreeRTOS queue for sensor data communication between tasks
QueueHandle_t sensorQueue;

// Sensor Task:
//    - Reads sensor data asynchronously from an analog pin.
//    - Simulates a non-blocking callback (ensuring T_callback <
↪    T_max).
//    - Dispatches sensor values via a queue to a separate network
↪    task.
void sensorTask(void *parameter) {
```

```
TickType_t lastWakeTime = xTaskGetTickCount();    // Reference for
↪   periodic task scheduling
while (true) {
  // Simulate asynchronous sensor reading:
  // Read from an analog pin (e.g., GPIO34); adjust hardware
  ↪   wiring as needed.
  int simulatedSensorValue = analogRead(34);
  // Alternatively, generate a pseudo-random sensor value:
  // int simulatedSensorValue = random(0, 1024);

  // Atomic update simulation:
  // In a real scenario, one might update a shared variable as: V
  ↪   = V  .
  // Here, we simply use a critical section to protect operations.
  portENTER_CRITICAL();
  // (Atomic update can be inserted here if needed)
  portEXIT_CRITICAL();

  // Send the sensor value to the network task non-blockingly.
  if (sensorQueue != NULL) {
    xQueueSend(sensorQueue, &simulatedSensorValue, 0);
  }

  // Simulate callback processing and ensure the duration is below
  ↪   T_MAX:
  unsigned long callbackStart = millis();
  // Non-blocking operations should complete quickly; here, we
  ↪   simulate with a short delay.
  delay(5);    // Simulated processing time (milliseconds)
  unsigned long callbackEnd = millis();

  if ((callbackEnd - callbackStart) > T_MAX) {
    Serial.println("Warning: Callback exceeded maximum execution
    ↪   time!");
  }

  // Maintain periodic sensor readings using a non-blocking delay
  vTaskDelayUntil(&lastWakeTime, pdMS_TO_TICKS(SENSOR_INTERVAL));
  }
}

// Network Task:
//   - Receives sensor data from the sensor task via a queue.
//   - Constructs an HTTP payload to emulate non-blocking network
↪   communication.
//   - Demonstrates an event-driven approach to handle asynchronous
↪   events.
void networkTask(void *parameter) {
  int receivedData;
  while (true) {
    // Attempt to receive sensor data from the queue with a timeout
    ↪   (non-blocking call)
```

386

```
    if (xQueueReceive(sensorQueue, &receivedData,
    ↪  pdMS_TO_TICKS(200)) == pdPASS) {
      // Build HTTP request payload with the sensor data:
      // This emulates the construction and parsing of HTTP requests
      ↪  as outlined in the theoretical section.
      char httpPayload[64];
      snprintf(httpPayload, sizeof(httpPayload), "sensorValue=%d",
      ↪  receivedData);

      // Simulate sending the HTTP request by printing to Serial.
      Serial.print("Sending HTTP request: ");
      Serial.println(httpPayload);
    }

    // Additional non-blocking network maintenance tasks or event
    ↪  handling can be placed here.
    vTaskDelay(pdMS_TO_TICKS(100));  // Yield CPU time to other
    ↪  tasks.
  }
}

void setup() {
  // Initialize Serial communication for monitoring and debugging.
  Serial.begin(115200);
  delay(1000);
  Serial.println("ESP32 Asynchronous Non-blocking Code Example
  ↪  Starting...");

  // Set the analog read resolution (10-bit resolution by default on
  ↪  ESP32).
  analogReadResolution(10);

  // Create a FreeRTOS queue for sensor data; capacity of 5 integer
  ↪  values.
  sensorQueue = xQueueCreate(5, sizeof(int));
  if (sensorQueue == NULL) {
    Serial.println("Error: Failed to create sensorQueue!");
    while (true);  // Halt execution if the queue creation fails.
  }

  // Create the sensor task; pin this task to core 1.
  xTaskCreatePinnedToCore(
    sensorTask,      // Task function
    "SensorTask",    // Name of the task
    2048,            // Stack size in words
    NULL,            // Task input parameter
    1,               // Task priority
    NULL,            // Task handle
    1                // Core to run the task on
  );

  // Create the network task; pin this task to core 0.
  xTaskCreatePinnedToCore(
```

387

```
    networkTask,        // Task function
    "NetworkTask",      // Task name
    2048,               // Stack size in words
    NULL,               // Task input parameter
    1,                  // Task priority
    NULL,               // Task handle
    0                   // Core to run the task on
  );
}

void loop() {
  // The main loop remains lightweight, performing non-blocking
  ↪  periodic checks.
  // Here, we print the system uptime every 5 seconds.
  static unsigned long lastPrint = 0;
  if (millis() - lastPrint > 5000) {
    lastPrint = millis();
    Serial.print("System Uptime: ");
    Serial.print(millis() / 1000);
    Serial.println(" seconds");
  }
  // Note: The loop does not block, ensuring system responsiveness
  ↪  in accordance with asynchronous design.
}
```

Chapter 61

Efficient Memory Allocation Strategies

Dynamic Allocation Semantics and Theoretical Models

Memory allocation in resource-constrained environments is formally modeled as a mapping from a set of memory requests to contiguous regions of a finite memory space. Let M denote the total available memory and $A : R \to \mathcal{P}(M)$ represent an allocation function, where R is the set of memory requests and $\mathcal{P}(M)$ is the power set of memory addresses. In this context, dynamic allocation refers to the runtime determination of memory regions, decomposing the overall memory space into allocated and free segments. The allocation process is inherently governed by an invariant condition, namely that the cumulative sum of allocated memory segments must not exceed M. This paradigm requires that each allocation request $r \in R$ is paired with a deallocation operation, thereby enforcing the invariant

$$\sum_{r \in R_{\text{active}}} \text{size}(r) \leq M,$$

where R_{active} is the set of active (not yet deallocated) requests at any time.

The operational semantics of dynamic allocation involve a decision procedure that selects an appropriate free block from a managed list of memory segments. The decision is influenced by factors such as the requested block size and the current state of memory fragmentation. A rigorous understanding of these semantics provides the foundation for developing strategies that optimize both time and spatial performance.

Fragmentation and Its Impact on Performance

Fragmentation represents the inefficiency that arises when memory is allocated and deallocated in a non-uniform pattern, resulting in isolated free segments that cannot be effectively reused. Two principal forms of fragmentation are identified: internal fragmentation, which occurs when allocated blocks contain unused memory, and external fragmentation, which arises when free memory is split into smaller non-contiguous blocks.

Let F denote the total free memory and n the number of free blocks. External fragmentation can be quantified by the relation

$$\text{Fragmentation} = 1 - \frac{\max\{f_1, f_2, \ldots, f_n\}}{F},$$

where the f_i represent the sizes of individual free blocks. A high fragmentation value indicates a substantial portion of memory available only in small fragments that are inadequate for large allocation requests. On resource-limited devices such as the ESP32, even moderate levels of external fragmentation can induce significant performance degradation by increasing the time required for allocation and limiting effective memory utilization.

Allocation Strategies and Best Practices for the ESP32 Environment

Due to the constrained nature of memory in the ESP32, best practices in dynamic allocation are critical for maintaining performance and preventing system instability. One effective strategy is the minimization of allocation frequency by precomputing static memory regions whenever the application architecture permits. When dynamic allocation is necessary, it is beneficial to consolidate requests into pools of fixed-size blocks. This approach reduces fragmentation by ensuring that each allocation targets a predetermined block size, and the corresponding deallocation returns the block to a well-defined free pool.

Furthermore, the allocation strategy may incorporate a scanning mechanism that prioritizes the selection of the smallest free block capable of satisfying a request. Formally, given a request of size s, the allocator seeks a free block b such that

$$b = \min\{f_i \mid f_i \geq s\},$$

greatly reducing the waste incurred by internal fragmentation. Additionally, a continuous monitoring mechanism of the allocated versus free memory ratio can provide insights into the emergent pattern of allocation, enabling the dynamic adjustment of allocation heuristics in accordance with the current operational conditions.

Deallocation and Memory Reclamation Techniques

Deallocation in the ESP32 context necessitates prompt and reliable reclamation of memory to prevent leakage and reduce fragmentation. The deallocation procedure is designed to reintegrate freed memory into the pool of available blocks while attempting to coalesce contiguous free segments. Let b_{j-1} and b_{j+1} be the immediately adjacent blocks relative to a deallocated block b_j. The coalescing operation is governed by the condition

$$b_{j-1} \cup b_j \cup b_{j+1} \quad \text{if} \quad \text{adjacent}(b_{j-1}, b_j) \wedge \text{adjacent}(b_j, b_{j+1}),$$

thereby yielding a larger free block that improves the allocator's ability to satisfy future requests.

Memory reclamation policies must ensure that the deallocation routine operates within a bounded time constraint, denoted T_{dealloc}, such that

$$T_{\text{dealloc}} < T_{\text{max}},$$

where T_{max} is a system-specific threshold that guarantees overall system responsiveness. This deterministic behavior is essential in avoiding performance pitfalls that can manifest in real-time applications and preserving the integrity of inter-process communication channels on the ESP32.

Empirical Guidelines and Optimization Considerations

Empirical evaluations reveal that the performance of a dynamic memory allocator in a resource-limited environment is heavily contingent on the allocation patterns encountered over time. The dynamic interplay between allocation size, request frequency, and deallocation timing dictates that a holistic approach is necessary to optimize memory usage. Optimization techniques include minimalistic allocation regimes that avoid excessive fragmentation, periodic defragmentation procedures, and tailored allocation strategies that account for typical workload characteristics.

Consider the allocation cost function

$$C(s) = \alpha \cdot \text{time}(s) + \beta \cdot \text{fragmentation}(s),$$

where α and β are weighting parameters that capture the relative importance of execution time and fragmentation, respectively, and time(s) denotes the time overhead associated with an allocation of size s. Optimizing the total cost over a sequence of allocations $\{s_i\}$ involves selecting allocation and deallocation strategies that minimize

$$\sum_i C(s_i),$$

thereby ensuring that the performance constraints of the ESP32 are met while efficiently managing a limited memory resource.

Through rigorous measurement and dynamic adjustment of the memory allocation framework, the system can maintain a state of high efficiency despite the inherent limitations imposed by hardware constraints. Each best practice, from block pooling to coalescing of free segments, contributes to a cumulative effect that safeguards against memory exhaustion and maintains a predictable performance profile within the stringent boundaries defined by the system architecture.

ESP32 For IoT With Arduino Code Snippet

```
#include <Arduino.h>

// Total available memory (M) in our simulated environment
```

```cpp
const int TOTAL_MEMORY = 256;

// Maximum number of memory blocks we can track
const int MAX_BLOCKS = 10;

// Structure representing a memory block.
// Each block is modeled by its starting address, size, and
↪    allocation status.
// This simulation helps illustrate the invariant:
//    _{r R_active} size(r)   M
struct MemoryBlock {
  int start;      // Starting address of the block
  int size;       // Size (in bytes) of the block
  bool allocated; // true if the block is allocated; false if free
};

// Global array to store memory blocks and a counter for the number
↪    of blocks.
MemoryBlock memoryBlocks[MAX_BLOCKS];
int numBlocks = 0;

// Function prototypes
void initMemory();
int allocateBlock(int requestSize);
void deallocateBlock(int address);
void printMemoryStatus();
int totalFreeMemory();
int maxFreeBlock();
double computeFragmentation();
double allocationCost(int requestSize, unsigned long opTime);

void setup() {
  Serial.begin(115200);
  while (!Serial); // Wait for Serial to connect
  Serial.println("ESP32 Memory Allocation Simulation");

  // Initialize memory with one free block covering the entire
  ↪    region.
  initMemory();
  printMemoryStatus();

  // --- Simulation of Allocation Operations ---
  Serial.println("\nAllocating 50 bytes...");
  int addr1 = allocateBlock(50);
  printMemoryStatus();

  Serial.println("\nAllocating 30 bytes...");
  int addr2 = allocateBlock(30);
  printMemoryStatus();

  Serial.println("\nAllocating 70 bytes...");
  int addr3 = allocateBlock(70);
  printMemoryStatus();
```

```cpp
  // Compute fragmentation using the equation:
  //   Fragmentation = 1 - (max{f_i} / F)
  double frag = computeFragmentation();
  Serial.print("Fragmentation factor: ");
  Serial.println(frag, 4);

  // --- Simulation of Deallocation and Coalescing ---
  Serial.println("\nDeallocating block at address:");
  Serial.println(addr2);
  deallocateBlock(addr2);
  printMemoryStatus();

  frag = computeFragmentation();
  Serial.print("Fragmentation factor after deallocation: ");
  Serial.println(frag, 4);

  // --- Simulate Allocation Cost Function ---
  // The cost function is defined as:
  //   C(s) =  · time(s) +  · fragmentation(s)
  // where  and  are weighting parameters.
  const double alpha = 0.5;
  const double beta = 0.5;
  unsigned long startTime = millis();
  int addr4 = allocateBlock(40);
  unsigned long opTime = millis() - startTime;
  double cost = allocationCost(40, opTime);
  Serial.print("Allocation cost for 40 bytes: ");
  Serial.println(cost, 4);
  printMemoryStatus();
}

void loop() {
  // Simulation complete - No repeated operations.
}

// Initialize the simulated memory by setting a single free block
// ↪   that spans TOTAL_MEMORY.
void initMemory() {
  numBlocks = 1;
  memoryBlocks[0].start = 0;
  memoryBlocks[0].size = TOTAL_MEMORY;
  memoryBlocks[0].allocated = false;
}

// Allocation function that implements the following decision
// ↪   algorithm:
// Given a request size 's', select the smallest free block 'b' such
// ↪   that:
//    b = min { f_i | f_i >= s }
// This minimizes internal fragmentation.
int allocateBlock(int requestSize) {
  int bestBlockIndex = -1;
```

```
int bestSize = TOTAL_MEMORY + 1; // Initialize to larger than any
↪  possible block size

// Search through all blocks for the best fit free block.
for (int i = 0; i < numBlocks; i++) {
  if (!memoryBlocks[i].allocated && memoryBlocks[i].size >=
  ↪  requestSize) {
    if (memoryBlocks[i].size < bestSize) {
      bestSize = memoryBlocks[i].size;
      bestBlockIndex = i;
    }
  }
}

// If no free block can satisfy the request, report allocation
↪  failure.
if (bestBlockIndex == -1) {
  Serial.println("Allocation failed: Not enough free memory.");
  return -1;
}

int allocAddress = memoryBlocks[bestBlockIndex].start;

// If the block is an exact fit, mark it as allocated.
if (memoryBlocks[bestBlockIndex].size == requestSize) {
  memoryBlocks[bestBlockIndex].allocated = true;
} else {
  // Split the free block:
  // Create an allocated block of size requestSize and a new free
  ↪  block for the remainder.
  MemoryBlock allocatedBlock;
  allocatedBlock.start = memoryBlocks[bestBlockIndex].start;
  allocatedBlock.size = requestSize;
  allocatedBlock.allocated = true;

  MemoryBlock freeBlock;
  freeBlock.start = allocatedBlock.start + requestSize;
  freeBlock.size = memoryBlocks[bestBlockIndex].size -
  ↪  requestSize;
  freeBlock.allocated = false;

  // Replace the original block with the allocated block.
  memoryBlocks[bestBlockIndex] = allocatedBlock;

  // Insert the free block immediately after to maintain order.
  if (numBlocks < MAX_BLOCKS) {
    for (int j = numBlocks; j > bestBlockIndex + 1; j--) {
      memoryBlocks[j] = memoryBlocks[j - 1];
    }
    memoryBlocks[bestBlockIndex + 1] = freeBlock;
    numBlocks++;
  } else {
```

```
    Serial.println("Error: Maximum block count reached, cannot
    ↪  split block.");
  }
}

Serial.print("Allocated block of size ");
Serial.print(requestSize);
Serial.print(" at address ");
Serial.println(allocAddress);
return allocAddress;
}

// Deallocation function that marks a block as free and attempts to
↪  coalesce adjacent free blocks.
// This corresponds to the operation:
//    b_{j-1}  b_j  b_{j+1} if adjacent(b_{j-1}, b_j)  adjacent(b_j,
↪  b_{j+1})
void deallocateBlock(int address) {
  int index = -1;
  for (int i = 0; i < numBlocks; i++) {
    if (memoryBlocks[i].start == address &&
    ↪  memoryBlocks[i].allocated) {
      index = i;
      break;
    }
  }
  if (index == -1) {
    Serial.println("Deallocation error: Block not found or already
    ↪  free.");
    return;
  }
  memoryBlocks[index].allocated = false;
  Serial.print("Deallocated block starting at address ");
  Serial.println(address);

  // Coalesce with previous free block if adjacent
  if (index > 0 && !memoryBlocks[index - 1].allocated) {
    memoryBlocks[index - 1].size += memoryBlocks[index].size;
    for (int j = index; j < numBlocks - 1; j++) {
      memoryBlocks[j] = memoryBlocks[j + 1];
    }
    numBlocks--;
    index--; // Update index to the merged block
  }

  // Coalesce with next free block if adjacent
  if (index < numBlocks - 1 && !memoryBlocks[index + 1].allocated) {
    memoryBlocks[index].size += memoryBlocks[index + 1].size;
    for (int j = index + 1; j < numBlocks - 1; j++) {
      memoryBlocks[j] = memoryBlocks[j + 1];
    }
    numBlocks--;
  }
```

396

```
}

// Utility function to print the current status of memory blocks.
void printMemoryStatus() {
  Serial.println("Current Memory Blocks:");
  for (int i = 0; i < numBlocks; i++) {
    Serial.print("Block ");
    Serial.print(i);
    Serial.print(": Start = ");
    Serial.print(memoryBlocks[i].start);
    Serial.print(", Size = ");
    Serial.print(memoryBlocks[i].size);
    Serial.print(", ");
    Serial.println(memoryBlocks[i].allocated ? "Allocated" :
    ↪   "Free");
  }
}

// Calculate the total free memory available by summing sizes of all
↪  free blocks.
int totalFreeMemory() {
  int total = 0;
  for (int i = 0; i < numBlocks; i++) {
    if (!memoryBlocks[i].allocated) {
      total += memoryBlocks[i].size;
    }
  }
  return total;
}

// Find the maximum free block size available.
int maxFreeBlock() {
  int maxSize = 0;
  for (int i = 0; i < numBlocks; i++) {
    if (!memoryBlocks[i].allocated && memoryBlocks[i].size >
    ↪   maxSize) {
      maxSize = memoryBlocks[i].size;
    }
  }
  return maxSize;
}

// Compute the fragmentation factor using the formula:
//    Fragmentation = 1 - (max free block / total free memory)
double computeFragmentation() {
  int totalFree = totalFreeMemory();
  if (totalFree == 0) {
    return 0.0;
  }
  int maxBlock = maxFreeBlock();
  double fragmentation = 1.0 - ((double)maxBlock / totalFree);
  return fragmentation;
}
```

```
// Compute an allocation cost using the cost function:
//    C(s) =   · time(s) +   · fragmentation(s)
// This provides an insight into the interplay between allocation
↪  overhead and memory fragmentation.
double allocationCost(int requestSize, unsigned long opTime) {
  const double alpha = 0.5;
  const double beta = 0.5;
  double frag = computeFragmentation();
  double cost = alpha * opTime + beta * frag;
  return cost;
}
```

Chapter 62

Implementing Modular Code Architecture

Fundamental Concepts of Modularity in Embedded Systems

Modular code architecture in the context of Arduino projects is founded upon principles that seek to partition a complex system into a collection of independent, cohesive units. Each module, denoted as M_i, is conceived as an encapsulated entity that addresses a specific subset of the overall functionality. The aggregate structure can be mathematically characterized by the relation

$$\bigcup_{i=1}^{n} M_i = M,$$

with the additional invariant that for any distinct modules M_i and M_j,

$$M_i \cap M_j = .$$

This formulation ensures that the implementation boundaries are clearly delineated and that internal complexities are confined within individual modules. In resource-constrained environments, such as those prevalent in IoT devices, the emphasis on modularization also contributes to predictable memory allocation patterns and streamlined management of system resources.

Encapsulation and Abstraction Mechanisms

A critical aspect of modular design is the rigorous application of encapsulation and abstraction. In a well-structured code architecture, each module exposes only a defined interface, thereby concealing its underlying implementation details. The concept of an interface can be formalized as a set $I(M_i)$ that specifies the legal operations, while the internal state of the module remains abstracted. Formally, if F represents the functionality provided by M_i, then

$$I(M_i) \subseteq F,$$

such that the external interactions are confined to $I(M_i)$ and any inherent complexity remains hidden. This separation of concerns is instrumental in reducing coupling among the modules, allowing each component to evolve independently without adverse ripple effects through the system. The layered abstraction not only simplifies debugging and testing but also facilitates the reuse of modules across multiple projects.

Structuring Reusable Modules and Libraries

The creation of reusable modules necessitates a careful consideration of the design patterns and architectural conventions that foster maintainability. A modular Arduino project is typically decomposed into several logical components: drivers interfacing with hardware, middleware managing communication protocols, and application logic that orchestrates system behavior. Each of these components is systematically encapsulated within libraries that are organized according to their purpose and scope. The design may be guided by the principle of loose coupling and high cohesion, ensuring that each module performs a distinct function while cooperating seamlessly with other modules. The delineation of responsibilities is often captured in a dependency graph, where vertices represent individual modules and directed edges indicate the dependency relations. Such a graph can be expressed as

$$G = (V, E),$$

with care taken to minimize cyclic dependencies, thus ensuring that the structure remains acyclic and amenable to independent compilation and testing.

Inter-module Communication and Dependency Management

The interaction between modules is orchestrated through well-defined interfaces and a controlled exchange of data. In an ideal modular architecture, inter-module communication is achieved using abstract data types and application programming interfaces (APIs) that govern the exchange of information. The design of these interfaces typically adheres to the principle of minimality; namely, each interface should expose only the necessary functions to enable interaction without imposing undue dependencies. If C_{ij} denotes the communication channel between modules M_i and M_j, then the integrity of the exchange is maintained provided that

$$\forall x \in I(M_i), \quad x \notin \mathrm{impl}(M_i),$$

where $\mathrm{impl}(M_i)$ represents the internal implementation of M_i. Furthermore, dependency management is streamlined by the adoption of abstraction layers that decouple core functionality from peripheral concerns. Such layers allow for the substitution and updating of modules with minimal impact on the broader system, thereby enhancing the maintainability and extensibility of Arduino projects. The systematic application of these techniques results in an architecture that is not only robust and scalable but also optimized for the nuanced constraints of embedded IoT environments.

ESP32 For IoT With Arduino Code Snippet

```
#include <Arduino.h>
#include <WiFi.h>

//
↪  -----------------------------------------------------------------
// Modular Code Architecture: Theoretical Invariants and
↪  Relationships
//
↪  -----------------------------------------------------------------
// Let M = (M_i) for i = 1,...,n where each module M_i performs a
↪  unique function.
// Invariant: For any distinct modules M_i and M_j, M_i  M_j =  (no
↪  overlapping responsibilities).
// Each module exposes an interface I(M_i) such that I(M_i)  F (F
↪  represents the complete functionality).
```

```cpp
// A dependency graph representation: G = (V, E), with vertices V as
//  individual modules and edges E as dependency relations.
// Example Dependencies: ApplicationModule --> SensorModule,
//  ApplicationModule --> CommunicationModule.
//
//  ----------------------------------------------------------------------

// Abstract Module Interface to enforce encapsulation and
//  abstraction.
class Module {
  public:
    virtual void init() = 0;
    virtual void update() = 0;
};

// SensorModule: Handles sensor data acquisition.
// Implements the module M1, a disjoint component of the system M.
class SensorModule : public Module {
  public:
    int sensorValue;

    void init() {
      sensorValue = 0;
      Serial.println("SensorModule Initialized");
    }

    void update() {
      // Reading an analog sensor on ESP32 analog pin 34.
      sensorValue = analogRead(34);
      Serial.print("SensorModule - Sensor value: ");
      Serial.println(sensorValue);
    }
};

// CommunicationModule: Manages Wi-Fi connectivity.
// Implements module M2 with a clearly defined interface for network
//  operations.
class CommunicationModule : public Module {
  public:
    const char* ssid = "yourSSID";
    const char* password = "yourPASSWORD";

    void init() {
      Serial.println("CommunicationModule: Initializing Wi-Fi...");
      WiFi.begin(ssid, password);
      while (WiFi.status() != WL_CONNECTED) {
        delay(500);
        Serial.print(".");
      }
      Serial.println("\nCommunicationModule: Wi-Fi connected");
    }

    void update() {
```

```cpp
    // Check connection status and simulate transmission
    ↪  verification.
    if (WiFi.status() == WL_CONNECTED) {
      Serial.println("CommunicationModule: Connection stable");
    } else {
      Serial.println("CommunicationModule: Connection lost");
    }
  }
};

// ApplicationModule: Processes sensor data and coordinates with
↪  communication.
// This module (M3) exemplifies dependency injection by relying on
↪  SensorModule and CommunicationModule.
class ApplicationModule : public Module {
  public:
    SensorModule* sensor;
    CommunicationModule* comm;

    // Constructor demonstrating loose coupling via dependency
    ↪  injection.
    ApplicationModule(SensorModule* s, CommunicationModule* c) :
    ↪  sensor(s), comm(c) {}

    void init() {
      Serial.println("ApplicationModule Initialized");
    }

    void update() {
      // Process the sensor data and trigger alerts if the value
      ↪  exceeds a threshold.
      int value = sensor->sensorValue;
      if (value > 1000) { // Arbitrary threshold for demonstration.
        Serial.println("ApplicationModule: Alert! Sensor value
        ↪  exceeded threshold.");
        // Constructing a data packet for transmission.
        String dataPacket = "Sensor Value: " + String(value);
        Serial.println("ApplicationModule: Sending data packet -> "
        ↪  + dataPacket);
        // In real applications, this packet could be sent using
        ↪  HTTP or MQTT protocols.
      }
    }
};

// DependencyGraph: A simple representation to illustrate module
↪  dependencies.
// Here, we simply print the vertices and edges as per the
↪  dependency graph G = (V, E).
struct DependencyGraph {
  void printGraph() {
    Serial.println("Dependency Graph G = (V, E):");
```

403

```
    Serial.println("Vertices: SensorModule, CommunicationModule,
    ↪  ApplicationModule");
    Serial.println("Edges: ApplicationModule -> SensorModule");
    Serial.println("       ApplicationModule ->
    ↪  CommunicationModule");
  }
};

// Global instances ensure disjoint module implementations (M_i  M_j
↪  = ).
SensorModule sensorModule;
CommunicationModule commModule;
ApplicationModule appModule(&sensorModule, &commModule);
DependencyGraph depGraph;

void setup() {
  Serial.begin(115200);
  delay(1000);
  Serial.println("Initializing Modular Architecture for ESP32 IoT
  ↪  with Arduino...");

  // Initialize all modules demonstrating the union property:
  // M = SensorModule  CommunicationModule  ApplicationModule
  sensorModule.init();
  commModule.init();
  appModule.init();

  // Display the dependency graph to ensure proper module
  ↪  interactions.
  depGraph.printGraph();
}

void loop() {
  // Periodically update each module to simulate modular task
  ↪  scheduling.
  sensorModule.update();
  commModule.update();
  appModule.update();

  // Delay for periodic execution (simulation of non-blocking
  ↪  periodic tasks).
  delay(2000);
}
```

Chapter 63

Code Optimization and Performance Tuning

Foundations of Performance Evaluation in Embedded Architectures

In resource-constrained environments, precise quantification of execution metrics forms the backbone of effective performance evaluation. Execution time, denoted as T_{comp}, can be modeled by the summation

$$T_{comp} = \sum_{i=1}^{n} t_i,$$

where each t_i represents the fine-grained execution duration of a specific operation or module. This formulation provides a framework for decomposing the overall performance into constituent parts. Measurement variability inherent to such systems calls for statistical analyses, with techniques such as mean computation and variance estimation, to attain reliable insights into computational overhead. The systematic use of clock cycle counters and event timers enables the construction of robust performance models, which are fundamental to identifying latent bottlenecks.

Algorithmic Refinement and Computational Complexity

Optimization in embedded applications frequently pivots on algorithmic efficiency. The performance of a given algorithm is characterized by its computational complexity, often expressed in the asymptotic notation $C(n) = \mathcal{O}(f(n))$, where n is a representative measure of input size. Efforts to compress the operational complexity from $\mathcal{O}(n)$ or $\mathcal{O}(n^2)$ to more efficient classes such as $\mathcal{O}(\log n)$ or $\mathcal{O}(1)$ yield substantial benefits in real-time scenarios. Refinement of algorithms involves both theoretical analysis and empirical validation. Techniques such as loop unrolling, precomputation of invariant expressions, and elimination of redundant operations contribute to reducing the instruction count executed per cycle. The interplay between algorithmic design choices and their manifest computational costs necessitates a rigorous approach where mathematical modeling guides the selection of optimal strategies.

Optimizing Memory Utilization and Data Access Patterns

Memory constraints dictate that efficient data management is indispensable in optimizing code performance. The architecture of the ESP32 imposes strict limits on available memory, making it imperative to employ memory access patterns that capitalize on data locality. The effective memory access time can be represented as

$$T_{mem} = p \cdot t_{cache} + (1 - p) \cdot t_{main},$$

where p is the probability of a cache hit, t_{cache} is the latency of accessing the cache, and t_{main} reflects the access time for main memory. This formalism underscores the importance of structuring data to maximize p, thereby reducing the average latency. Techniques such as data alignment, cache-friendly data structure design, and minimization of memory fragmentation are pivotal in achieving optimal resource usage. A deliberate arrangement of memory layout coupled with the judicious management of dynamic allocations further contributes to sustained performance in constrained systems.

Low Latency Strategies in Real-Time Processing

Minimization of latency is of paramount importance in real-time processing environments. The aggregate latency L may be decomposed into a sum of distinct components:

$$L = L_{proc} + L_{comm} + L_{overhead},$$

where L_{proc} quantifies processing delays, L_{comm} encapsulates communication-induced latency, and $L_{overhead}$ accounts for the extraneous delays associated with task scheduling, synchronization, and context switching. Reducing L mandates not only streamlined computational routines, but also the implementation of non-blocking methodologies and concurrent processing paradigms. Techniques such as interrupt-driven processing, event-based scheduling, and asynchronous operation design are intrinsic to achieving minimal latency. The rigorous management of execution pipelines ensures that transient delays do not propagate through the system, thereby maintaining a consistent performance profile under varying operational loads.

Systematic Approaches to Performance Tuning

Advancements in performance tuning are predicated on an iterative process of analysis, refinement, and validation. This cycle is formally encapsulated by the minimization of a composite performance metric

$$P = \alpha \cdot C + \beta \cdot M + \gamma \cdot L,$$

where C represents the computational complexity, M quantifies memory usage, L reflects the latency components, and α, β, and γ are weighting coefficients defined by the specific application requirements. Each tuning iteration leverages comprehensive profiling techniques, utilizing hardware counters and software instrumentation to identify inefficiencies. Subsequent modifications are informed by rigorous quantitative analysis, ensuring that the refined architectures achieve measurable improvements. The systematic nature of this approach fosters a disciplined methodology that aligns theoretical optimizations with empirical performance targets, thereby enhancing overall system robustness and scalability.

ESP32 For IoT With Arduino Code Snippet

```
#include <Arduino.h>

// Weighting coefficients for composite performance metric
#define ALPHA 0.5  // Weight for computational complexity
#define BETA  0.3  // Weight for memory usage
#define GAMMA 0.2  // Weight for latency

// Function to measure the execution time of a given operation (in
↪  microseconds)
// Equation: T_comp = \sum_{i=1}^{n} t_i
unsigned long measureOperationTime(void (*operation)()) {
  unsigned long startTime = micros();
  operation();
  unsigned long endTime = micros();
  return endTime - startTime;
}

// Dummy operation to simulate computational work (e.g. loop
↪  operations)
// This function represents a part of the overall computational
↪  workload.
void dummyOperation1() {
  volatile unsigned long sum = 0;
  for (int i = 0; i < 1000; i++) {
    sum += i;
  }
}

// Dummy operation to simulate memory access and data processing
// Represents another constituent part contributing to T_comp.
void dummyOperation2() {
  int data[100];
  for (int i = 0; i < 100; i++) {
    data[i] = i * 2;
  }
}

// Dummy function to simulate non-blocking communication delay
// This approximates L_comm in the latency decomposition:
// L = L_proc + L_comm + L_overhead
void dummyCommunication() {
  // Simulate communication delay (e.g., sending/receiving data)
  delayMicroseconds(50);
}

void setup() {
  Serial.begin(115200);
  // Wait for serial monitor to initialize
```

```
delay(1000);

Serial.println("ESP32 For IoT With Arduino: Performance
  ↪ Evaluation");

// Measure execution times for individual operations
unsigned long t_op1 = measureOperationTime(dummyOperation1);
unsigned long t_op2 = measureOperationTime(dummyOperation2);
unsigned long t_comm = measureOperationTime(dummyCommunication);

// Compute total computational time (T_comp)
// T_comp = t_op1 + t_op2
unsigned long T_comp = t_op1 + t_op2;

// Calculate effective memory access time using:
// T_mem = p * t_cache + (1 - p) * t_main
// Assume cache hit probability p = 0.8, t_cache = 5 µs, t_main =
  ↪ 50 µs
float p = 0.8;
float t_cache = 5.0;
float t_main = 50.0;
float T_mem = p * t_cache + (1 - p) * t_main;

// Decompose latency into processing, communication, and overhead
  ↪ components:
// L = L_proc + L_comm + L_overhead
unsigned long L_proc = T_comp;        // Processing delay from
  ↪ computations
unsigned long L_comm = t_comm;          // Communication delay
unsigned long L_overhead = 10;          // Fixed overhead for
  ↪ scheduling/synchronization (µs)
unsigned long L = L_proc + L_comm + L_overhead;

// For algorithmic refinement, assign a placeholder computational
  ↪ complexity (C)
// and memory usage (M). In a real scenario, these would be
  ↪ derived from analytical models.
unsigned long C = 2000;  // Example: Number of operations
  ↪ performed
unsigned long M = 1500;  // Example: Memory usage in bytes

// Compute the composite performance metric:
// P =  * C +  * M +  * L
float performanceMetric = ALPHA * C + BETA * M + GAMMA * L;

// Output the measured and computed performance parameters
Serial.println("-------------------------------");
Serial.print("Operation 1 Time (µs): ");
Serial.println(t_op1);
Serial.print("Operation 2 Time (µs): ");
Serial.println(t_op2);
Serial.print("Total Computation Time T_comp (µs): ");
Serial.println(T_comp);
```

```cpp
  Serial.print("Estimated Memory Access Time T_mem (µs): ");
  Serial.println(T_mem);
  Serial.print("Communication Delay (µs): ");
  Serial.println(t_comm);
  Serial.print("Total Latency L (µs): ");
  Serial.println(L);
  Serial.print("Composite Performance Metric P: ");
  Serial.println(performanceMetric);
  Serial.println("-----------------------------");
}

void loop() {
  // In a production system, you might continuously re-run
  ↪   performance evaluations.
  // For this demonstration, re-run the setup sequence every 5
  ↪   seconds.
  delay(5000);
  setup();
}
```

Chapter 64

Best Practices for Debugging and Testing

Systematic Debugging Methodologies

In complex embedded systems, debugging constitutes a critical phase wherein intricate software behaviors and hardware interactions are meticulously dissected. An effective methodology entails the iterative isolation of fault domains, wherein the execution of distinct software modules is analyzed individually. The decomposition of overall system execution into constituent segments facilitates the identification of anomalies, particularly in the context of asynchronous events and concurrent processes inherent in ESP32 deployments. Quantitative metrics, such as the differential execution time $\Delta t_i = t_i - t_{i-1}$ between successive operations, prove instrumental in pinpointing bottlenecks and aberrant behavior. Through rigorous temporal correlation and causal inference, systematic debugging endeavors yield a granular insight into the operational dynamics of Arduino code, thereby ensuring that latent defects are exposed and addressed prior to deployment.

Instrumentation and Diagnostic Measures

The deployment of comprehensive instrumentation enables the precise capture of runtime parameters essential for effective diagnosis. Diagnostic measures incorporate both hardware and software instrumentation techniques, including the incorporation of time-stamped event logging and the deployment of high-resolution cycle counters. Metrics such as the cycle time T_{cycle} and the overall execution latency T_{exec} serve as fundamental indicators of system performance. By instrumenting critical code paths, it becomes feasible to construct detailed execution profiles. These profiles facilitate the subsequent identification of irregularities in memory accesses, control flow interruptions, and similar suboptimal conditions that undermine system reliability. The methodological integration of diagnostic data into performance models engenders a data-driven approach to debugging, wherein statistical analyses and heuristic evaluations are applied to extensive runtime datasets.

Automated Testing and Verification Frameworks

Automated testing frameworks constitute an indispensable component in the endeavor to systematically validate Arduino code under diverse operational scenarios. The implementation of unit tests, integration tests, and system-level validations ensures that functionality is preserved across incremental revisions. Automated verification strategies leverage predefined test cases and simulated inputs to rigorously evaluate both nominal and edge-case behaviors. The isolation of individual software components within controlled test environments permits the reproducible observation of test outcomes, while the verification of inter-module interactions provides assurance that composite functionalities adhere to specified performance constraints. Furthermore, the formulation of error propagation models, expressed mathematically as $E(t) = \sum_{i=1}^{n} e_i(t)$ with each $e_i(t)$ representing the error contribution of an individual module, underscores a systematic approach to quantifying and mitigating cumulative system failures.

Static and Dynamic Analysis Approaches

Static analysis methods offer a pre-execution evaluation of source code, wherein the examination of syntax, control structures, and data dependencies precedes runtime validation. Advanced static analysis tools parse the abstract syntax tree to reveal inconsistencies, potential memory leaks, and deviations from established coding conventions. In parallel, dynamic analysis techniques scrutinize the system during execution, allowing for real-time monitoring of variable states, memory allocations, and system interrupts. The integration of these methodologies provides a dual-layered assurance of code quality, wherein static examination preempts many classes of run-time errors, and dynamic scrutiny captures irregularities that manifest only under specific operational conditions. The combined deployment of static and dynamic analysis forms a formidable barrier against a wide spectrum of software anomalies.

Robustness Evaluation in Constrained Environments

Robustness evaluation in resource-limited contexts necessitates the implementation of deliberate testing paradigms that stress both computational and memory subsystems. Under high-load conditions, the aggregate latency observed in the system, denoted as $L = L_{proc} + L_{I/O} + L_{sys}$, is decomposed into processing delays, I/O latencies, and systemic overheads. The controlled introduction of faults and stress conditions serves to evaluate the resilience of the ESP32 platform when executing Arduino code. Specific robustness tests aim to simulate worst-case memory fragmentation, synchronous and asynchronous communication delays, and interrupt service routine preemptions. Quantitative assessments derived from these tests, in conjunction with statistical variance analyses, furnish an empirical basis for evaluating the operational integrity of the deployed system. Such comprehensive evaluation strategies ensure that the final system configuration adheres rigorously to the predefined thresholds of performance and stability.

ESP32 For IoT With Arduino Code Snippet

```
#include <Arduino.h>
#include <WiFi.h>

// ------------------------------------------------------------
// This code snippet demonstrates how to integrate several key
↪    diagnostic and
// debugging metrics in ESP32 IoT applications using Arduino. The
↪    following
```

```cpp
// equations and algorithms are incorporated:
//
// 1. Differential Execution Time:
//    t_i = t_i - t_{i-1}
//    (Calculated using micros() between loop iterations)
//
// 2. Cycle Time and Total Execution Time:
//    T_cycle is simulated as the delta time for each loop, and
↪  T_exec is the
//    cumulative execution time.
//
// 3. Latency Decomposition:
//    L = L_proc + L_I/O + L_sys
//    (Simulated processing, I/O, and system delays)
//
// 4. Error Propagation Model:
//    E(t) = e_i(t) for i = 1 to n
//    (Summation of simulated error contributions from multiple
↪  modules)
//
// Automated testing routines are included to flag if the aggregated
↪  error
// levels exceed a predefined threshold.
// -------------------------------------------------------------

// WiFi credentials and error threshold for testing
const char* ssid = "Your_SSID";
const char* password = "Your_PASSWORD";
const int errorThreshold = 10;   // Threshold for acceptable error
↪  sum

// Timing variables for debugging measurements
unsigned long lastTime = 0;          // Previous timestamp in
↪  microseconds
unsigned long currentTime = 0;       // Current timestamp in
↪  microseconds
unsigned long deltaTime = 0;         // t_i = t_i - t_{i-1}
unsigned long cycleTime = 0;         // T_cycle (simulated as
↪  deltaTime)
unsigned long totalExecTime = 0;     // T_exec (cumulative cycle
↪  time)

// Variables for latency decomposition
unsigned long procDelay = 0;   // L_proc: Processing delay in µs
unsigned long ioDelay = 0;     // L_I/O: I/O delay in µs
unsigned long sysDelay = 0;    // L_sys: System overhead delay in µs
unsigned long totalLatency = 0; // L = L_proc + L_I/O + L_sys

// Variables for error propagation across modules
const int nModules = 3;         // Number of modules contributing
↪  errors
int moduleErrors[nModules];     // Simulated error values for each
↪  module
```

414

```
int errorSum = 0;                    // E(t) = e_i(t)

// -------------------------------------------------------------
// Function: simulateDelays
// Simulates measurement of processing, I/O, and system delays. In a
↪ real
// application, these would be measured through instrumentation.
// -------------------------------------------------------------
void simulateDelays() {
  procDelay = random(100, 200);  // Simulated processing delay (μs)
  ioDelay  = random(50, 100);    // Simulated I/O delay (μs)
  sysDelay = random(10, 50);     // Simulated system overhead (μs)
  totalLatency = procDelay + ioDelay + sysDelay;
}


// -------------------------------------------------------------
// Function: simulateModuleErrors
// Simulates error contributions from multiple software modules.
// -------------------------------------------------------------
void simulateModuleErrors() {
  errorSum = 0;
  for (int i = 0; i < nModules; i++) {
    moduleErrors[i] = random(0, 5);  // Random error value between 0
    ↪ and 4
    errorSum += moduleErrors[i];
  }
}


// -------------------------------------------------------------
// Function: automatedTesting
// Performs an automated test to verify that the aggregated module
↪ errors
// remain within an acceptable threshold.
// -------------------------------------------------------------
void automatedTesting() {
  if(errorSum > errorThreshold) {
    Serial.println("ERROR: Aggregated module errors exceed
    ↪ acceptable threshold!");
    // Additional handling (e.g., watchdog reset) can be inserted
    ↪ here.
  } else {
    Serial.println("Automated Test: Module error levels within
    ↪ acceptable range.");
  }
}

// -------------------------------------------------------------
// Function: setupWiFi
// Connects the ESP32 to a specified WiFi network for IoT
↪ communication.
// -------------------------------------------------------------
void setupWiFi() {
  Serial.print("Connecting to WiFi");
```

```
  WiFi.begin(ssid, password);
  while(WiFi.status() != WL_CONNECTED) {
    delay(500);
    Serial.print(".");
  }
  Serial.println();
  Serial.println("WiFi connected.");
}

// ------------------------------------------------------------
// Function: setup
// Initializes Serial communication, WiFi connection, and timing
↪   variables.
// ------------------------------------------------------------
void setup() {
  Serial.begin(115200);
  // Initialize random generator for simulation purposes
  randomSeed(analogRead(0));
  setupWiFi();
  lastTime = micros(); // Initialize the last timestamp for t
  ↪   calculation
}

// ------------------------------------------------------------
// Function: loop
// Implements the main execution loop with integrated debugging,
↪   instrumentation,
// and automated testing routines. It calculates timing
↪   differentials, latency
// components, and error propagation metrics, and prints them via
↪   Serial.
// ------------------------------------------------------------
void loop() {
  // Update timing measurements
  currentTime = micros();
  deltaTime = currentTime - lastTime; // t_i = t_i - t_{i-1}
  lastTime = currentTime;

  cycleTime = deltaTime;           // Simulated cycle time (T_cycle)
  totalExecTime += deltaTime;      // Accumulate total execution time
  ↪   (T_exec)

  // Simulate delays and errors for diagnostic purposes
  simulateDelays();
  simulateModuleErrors();

  // Output debugging and instrumentation metrics to Serial Monitor
  Serial.println("=== Debug and Instrumentation Metrics ===");

  Serial.print("Delta Time (t): ");
  Serial.print(deltaTime);
  Serial.println(" µs");
```

```
Serial.print("Cycle Time (T_cycle): ");
Serial.print(cycleTime);
Serial.println(" µs");

Serial.print("Total Execution Time (T_exec): ");
Serial.print(totalExecTime);
Serial.println(" µs");

Serial.print("Processing Delay (L_proc): ");
Serial.print(procDelay);
Serial.println(" µs");

Serial.print("I/O Delay (L_I/O): ");
Serial.print(ioDelay);
Serial.println(" µs");

Serial.print("System Delay (L_sys): ");
Serial.print(sysDelay);
Serial.println(" µs");

Serial.print("Total Latency (L): ");
Serial.print(totalLatency);
Serial.println(" µs");

Serial.print("Error Sum (E(t)): ");
Serial.println(errorSum);

// Execute automated testing to verify error levels
automatedTesting();

Serial.println(); // Blank line for readability in Serial output

delay(1000); // Pause for 1 second before next iteration
}
```

Chapter 65

Utilizing Watchdog Timers for Application Stability

Fundamental Principles of Watchdog Timers

Watchdog timers serve as an autonomous monitoring mechanism designed to detect and mitigate system anomalies in embedded environments. In this paradigm, a dedicated hardware or software counter is configured with a predetermined timeout parameter, denoted by T_{wd}. Should the watchdog timer not be refreshed—or "kicked"—within the allocated interval, it triggers an automatic system reset to restore normal operation. This architectural safeguard is predicated on the assumption that regular execution of critical routines is indicative of proper system functionality, whereas the absence of such activity suggests the presence of transient faults or irrevocable lock-ups. The inherent reliability offered by a watchdog timer is therefore closely linked to the accurate determination of its timeout threshold and the synchronization with task execution sequences.

Architecture and Integration on the ESP32 Platform

The ESP32 microcontroller incorporates integrated modules specifically tailored for watchdog functionality, thereby facilitating streamlined integration into real-time operating environments. Embedded within the architectural framework are multiple timer subsystems, each capable of independently monitoring various execution contexts. In this configuration, effective synchronization is achieved through periodic resets of the watchdog timer, which are interleaved with the principal control loops and ancillary processing tasks. Special attention is devoted to the initialization routines and register configurations that define the operational characteristics of the watchdog subsystem. Meticulous calibration is essential to ensure that the watchdog timer neither preempts valid processing sequences nor fails to initiate a corrective reset during unforeseen operational stalls.

Timing Analysis and Mathematical Modeling

Quantitative analysis of watchdog timer performance is predicated on the precise measurement of execution intervals and the establishment of reliable timing constraints. The operational threshold of the watchdog can be mathematically expressed as

$$T_{\text{timeout}} = T_{\text{cycle}} + T_{\text{margin}},$$

where T_{cycle} represents the maximum expected duration of a complete operational cycle, and T_{margin} is an additional temporal allowance designed to accommodate minor variabilities in processing time. Furthermore, the differential interval between successive resets is characterized by

$$\Delta t = t_i - t_{i-1},$$

with the condition $\Delta t < T_{\text{timeout}}$ serving as a necessary constraint to avoid spurious system resets. The analytical evaluation of these parameters facilitates the derivation of optimal watchdog settings, thereby ensuring that the system remains resilient under a diverse range of runtime conditions. This mathematical formulation provides a deterministic basis for assessing the trade-offs between responsiveness and stability in the context of watchdog timer deployment.

Fault Recovery Mechanisms and Stability Assurance

The primary function of a watchdog timer is to instigate a systematic recovery from states indicative of system failure. Upon detection of irregularities—such as a missed reset within the expected interval—the watchdog timer autonomously initiates a reset sequence that reverts the system to a predefined state. This enforced reinitialization is critical in precluding the propagation of catastrophic system errors and in mitigating the persistence of latent faults. The recovery process is typically structured as a multi-stage protocol, beginning with an immediate reset of system resources followed by the reestablishment of essential operational parameters. The efficacy of such fault recovery mechanisms is tightly coupled with the deterministic behavior of the watchdog timer and its seamless integration with the overall system reset strategy. The controlled reinitialization thus ensures that the system maintains operational stability, even after encountering transient or persistent failures.

Empirical Considerations and Best Practices in Deployment

Robust integration of watchdog timers within ESP32-based applications demands a comprehensive approach that encompasses both theoretical analysis and empirical validation. The selection of an appropriate timeout T_{wd} necessitates careful consideration of the inherent latency contributions from peripheral interactions, interrupt service routines, and computational load variability. Empirical evaluations often involve the methodical injection of synthetic fault conditions into controlled test environments, followed by rigorous monitoring of system response metrics. Such investigations yield critical insights into the optimal configuration parameters, thereby informing best practices that ensure minimal incidence of both false positives and overlooked system stalls. Moreover, the integration of supplementary monitoring subsystems can enhance the granularity of fault detection, further reinforcing the resilience and stability of the deployed application.

ESP32 For IoT With Arduino Code Snippet

```
#include <Arduino.h>
#include <esp_task_wdt.h>

// Define timing parameters based on the mathematical model:
// T_timeout = T_cycle + T_margin
const unsigned long T_cycle  = 1000;     // Maximum expected
↪   processing time per cycle (in ms)
const unsigned long T_margin = 200;      // Additional allowance to
↪   account for variability (in ms)
const unsigned long T_timeout = T_cycle + T_margin;  // Computed
↪   timeout threshold (in ms)

unsigned long lastCycleTime;

void setup() {
  Serial.begin(115200);
  // Seed the random number generator for simulation of processing
  ↪   delays.
  randomSeed(analogRead(0));
  while (!Serial) {
    ; // Wait for the serial port to initialize
  }
  Serial.println("Starting ESP32 Watchdog Timer Demonstration...");

  // Initialize the hardware watchdog timer.
  // Note: The watchdog timeout here is set in seconds. Make sure
  ↪   this value is greater than T_timeout.
  // For demonstration, we configure a 3-second watchdog timeout.
  esp_task_wdt_init(3, true);  // 'true' enables the panic handler
  ↪   (which restarts the system)
  esp_task_wdt_add(NULL);      // Add the current task (loop task)
  ↪   to the watchdog monitoring

  // Initialize the baseline timestamp for cycle measurement.
  lastCycleTime = millis();
}

void loop() {
  // Capture the current time and calculate the elapsed time (t)
  ↪   since the last cycle.
  unsigned long currentMillis = millis();
  unsigned long delta_t = currentMillis - lastCycleTime;
```

```
// Display the measured cycle time and the computed threshold.
Serial.print("Cycle time (t): ");
Serial.print(delta_t);
Serial.print(" ms, Threshold (T_timeout): ");
Serial.print(T_timeout);
Serial.println(" ms");

// Evaluate if the elapsed time has exceeded the computed watchdog
↪   threshold.
// This corresponds to the condition: t < T_timeout must be
↪   maintained.
if (delta_t >= T_timeout) {
  Serial.println("Watchdog Alert: Cycle time exceeded threshold,
  ↪   initiating system reset!");
  delay(100);  // Optional: Delay for log printing before reset
  ESP.restart();  // Trigger a software reset to recover from
  ↪   potential faults
}

// Simulate variable processing loads.
// The delay here is randomized between 500 ms and 1200 ms to
↪   represent normal operation
// and conditions where processing takes longer than expected.
int simulatedProcessingDelay = random(500, 1200);
delay(simulatedProcessingDelay);

// Refresh ("kick") the hardware watchdog timer to prevent an
↪   unintended system reset.
esp_task_wdt_reset();

// Update the timestamp marking the beginning of the next
↪   operational cycle.
lastCycleTime = millis();
}
```

Chapter 66

Building Modular and Maintainable ESP32 Code

Modularity and Code Organization

The decomposition of an embedded application into discrete, logically independent modules constitutes a foundational principle in the pursuit of maintainable software architectures. In the context of ESP32-based IoT applications developed with Arduino, modularity entails the precise separation of hardware interfacing routines, communication protocol handlers, and higher-level application logic. Such decomposition is not merely an exercise in aesthetic code organization; rather, it underpins the capability to isolate functional domains so that modifications in one module impose minimal coupling on the overall system. This reduction in inter-module dependency is instrumental in achieving a robust codebase where each component may be updated, tested, and debugged in isolation. When the system is characterized by a set of n modules, the design objective is to reduce the effective interdependence measured by the coupling metric to a value asymptotically lower than $O(n^2)$, thereby facilitating scalable integration and iterative development.

Design Patterns in Embedded Development

The deliberate application of established design patterns plays an essential role in structuring code that is simultaneously elegant, resilient, and maintainable. In embedded environments, where resource constraints impose stringent performance requirements, the adoption of patterns such as the Observer, State, and Singleton enables the formalization of interaction protocols among autonomous modules. For instance, the implementation of an event-driven State pattern allows the ESP32 to navigate through discrete operational modes, ensuring that transient events and asynchronous occurrences are managed in a controlled fashion. Concurrently, the Singleton pattern can be judiciously applied to manage shared resources that demand a singular point of access across disparate modules. The abstraction of these patterns from their implementation details not only enhances readability but also provides a conceptual framework that supports the systematic evolution of the application without incurring uncontrolled complexity.

Separation of Concerns and Layered Architectures

A refined architectural stratification is achieved through the rigorous application of the separation of concerns principle. This design ethos mandates that individual modules conform to a singular, well-defined responsibility, thereby reducing the likelihood of inadvertent side effects and simplifying the confluence of independent processing streams. In a prototypical ESP32 IoT system, the layered architecture commonly comprises a hardware abstraction layer (HAL), which encapsulates the specifics of peripheral interfacing; a middleware layer, responsible for managing communication protocols and system services; and an application layer, which orchestrates the core logic of the device's operation. By delineating these layers, the overall control flow is rendered transparent, and each stratum is afforded the opportunity to be optimized or refactored without fundamentally altering the system-wide data exchanges. Such a configuration not only streamlines debugging and verification efforts but also promotes the integration of future enhancements in a modular and scalable manner.

Refactoring and Code Readability

The iterative process of refactoring constitutes an indispensable mechanism for maintaining the clarity and efficacy of a substantial codebase deployed on the ESP32. Systematic code reviews, guided by quantitative metrics such as cyclomatic complexity (expressed mathematically as $C = E - N + 2P$, where E, N, and P denote the number of edges, nodes, and connected components respectively), provide objective measures that signal the need for structural improvements. The mitigation of code smells—manifested as redundant routines, extensive conditional logic, or overly coupled modules—is essential to sustain long-term maintainability. By reengineering sections of the code that exhibit high complexity or ambiguous dependency graphs, developers preserve the semantic clarity of the application logic while facilitating future adaptations. This disciplined approach to refactoring is particularly valuable in environments where limited computational resources mandate a precise balance between performance optimization and structural organization.

Scalability in Resource-Constrained Environments

Ensuring the scalability of Arduino-based ESP32 applications necessitates a comprehensive evaluation of both the algorithmic efficiency and the resource allocation strategies employed within each module. Scalability, in this context, pertains to the capacity of the system to accommodate additional functional requirements and manage increased processing demands without incurring detrimental effects on performance. The analytical modeling of resource usage—encompassing metrics such as memory allocation efficiency, computational overhead, and communication latency—facilitates a systematic approach wherein each module is tailored to operate within the stringent constraints characteristic of IoT devices. Architectures that are designed with scalability in mind incorporate dynamic memory management techniques and adopt asynchronous processing paradigms so that the overall system behavior remains predictable under variable load conditions. The deliberate calibration of these parameters enables the deployment of code that is not only efficient in its present operation but also resilient in the face of evolving application demands.

ESP32 For IoT With Arduino Code Snippet

```
// Comprehensive Example of Modular and Maintainable ESP32 Code
// This code integrates fundamental equations and design patterns
↪    mentioned in the chapter.
// Notably, it abstracts hardware control, networking, state
↪    management, and event-driven processing.
// It also references the cyclomatic complexity metric in comments:
↪    C = E - N + 2P,
// which is kept low by decomposing the system into modular
↪    components.

#include <Arduino.h>
#include <WiFi.h>
#include <freertos/FreeRTOS.h>
#include <freertos/task.h>

// Define LED pin for demonstration purposes
#define LED_PIN 2

// Enumeration for device state machine
enum DeviceState {
  STATE_INIT,
  STATE_RUN,
  STATE_ERROR
};

// Observer interface for sensor events (implements Observer design
↪    pattern)
class SensorObserver {
public:
  virtual void onSensorEvent(int data) = 0;
};

// Hardware Abstraction Layer (HAL)
// This module encapsulates low-level operations, such as sensor
↪    readings and LED control.
class HardwareAbstractionLayer {
public:
  void init() {
    // Initialize LED pin
    pinMode(LED_PIN, OUTPUT);
  }

  int readSensor() {
    // Simulate sensor data acquisition using an analog input.
    // For ESP32, GPIO34 is often used as an ADC input.
    int sensorValue = analogRead(34);
    return sensorValue;
  }
```

```
  void toggleLED() {
    // Toggle the LED state
    digitalWrite(LED_PIN, !digitalRead(LED_PIN));
  }
};

// Communication Manager (Singleton pattern)
// Manages Wi-Fi connectivity ensuring a single point of network
↪  access.
class CommunicationManager {
private:
  static CommunicationManager* instance;
  const char* ssid = "yourSSID";
  const char* password = "yourPASSWORD";

  // Private constructor to prevent multiple instantiations
  CommunicationManager() { }

public:
  // Provides unique instance of CommunicationManager.
  static CommunicationManager* getInstance() {
    if (instance == nullptr) {
      instance = new CommunicationManager();
    }
    return instance;
  }

  void connectWiFi() {
    WiFi.begin(ssid, password);
    Serial.print("Connecting to WiFi");
    // Loop until connected to Wi-Fi
    while (WiFi.status() != WL_CONNECTED) {
      delay(500);
      Serial.print(".");
    }
    Serial.println(" Connected!");
  }
};

CommunicationManager* CommunicationManager::instance = nullptr;

// Application Logic Module
// Combines state machine control, sensor event observation, and
↪  integration with HAL and CommunicationManager.
// This represents the high-level logic, keeping separation of
↪  concerns clear.
// The cyclomatic complexity of process() is minimized by clear
↪  segmentation into cases.
class ApplicationLogic : public SensorObserver {
private:
  HardwareAbstractionLayer hal;
  CommunicationManager* comm;
```

427

```cpp
  DeviceState currentState;
  unsigned long lastSensorRead;

public:
  ApplicationLogic() : currentState(STATE_INIT), lastSensorRead(0) {
    // Obtain the singleton instance of the CommunicationManager.
    comm = CommunicationManager::getInstance();
  }

  void init() {
    Serial.begin(115200);
    hal.init();
    comm->connectWiFi();
    currentState = STATE_RUN;
  }

  // Main processing function incorporating a state machine.
  void process() {
    switch (currentState) {
      case STATE_RUN:
        // Periodically read the sensor once per second.
        if (millis() - lastSensorRead > 1000) {
          int sensorVal = hal.readSensor();
          lastSensorRead = millis();
          onSensorEvent(sensorVal);  // Handle sensor event using
          ↪   Observer callback.
          hal.toggleLED();           // Visual feedback via LED
          ↪   toggling.
        }
        break;
      case STATE_ERROR:
        // Error handling: log and reinitialize system.
        Serial.println("Error state encountered. Reinitializing
        ↪   system...");
        init();
        break;
      default:
        break;
    }
  }

  // Observer design pattern implementation: handles sensor events.
  void onSensorEvent(int data) override {
    Serial.print("Sensor data: ");
    Serial.println(data);
    // Example algorithm: if sensor data exceeds a threshold,
    ↪   trigger an event action.
    if (data > 3000) {
      Serial.println("Threshold exceeded, event triggered.");
      // Additional event handling logic, such as logging or
      ↪   notifying other modules, can be added here.
    }
  }
```

```
};

// Global instance of ApplicationLogic
ApplicationLogic appLogic;

// FreeRTOS Task for periodic processing.
// Demonstrates asynchronous, non-blocking operation through task
↪  scheduling.
void taskProcess(void* pvParameters) {
  for (;;) {
    appLogic.process();
    // Use vTaskDelay to schedule the next execution without
    ↪  blocking the processor.
    vTaskDelay(100 / portTICK_PERIOD_MS);
  }
}

void setup() {
  appLogic.init();
  // Create the FreeRTOS task to handle periodic application
  ↪  processing.
  xTaskCreate(taskProcess, "TaskProcess", 2048, NULL, 1, NULL);
}

void loop() {
  // The main loop remains empty as FreeRTOS tasks manage
  ↪  application execution.
}
```

www.ingramcontent.com/pod-product-compliance
Lightning Source LLC
Chambersburg PA
CBHW070931050326
40689CB00014B/3158